Restless Souls

Restless Souls

Rebels, Refugees, Medics And Misfits On The Thai-Burma Border

Phil Thornton

ASIA BOOKS

Published and Distributed by
Asia Books Co. Ltd.,
5 Sukhumvit Road Soi 61,
PO Box 40,
Bangkok 10110,
Thailand.
Tel: (66) 0-2715-9000 ext. 3202–4
Fax: (66) 0-2714-2799
E-mail: information@asiabooks.com
Website: www.asiabooks.com

Typeset by COMSET Limited Partnership.

Printed in Thailand.

ISBN 974-8303-91-8

To the Karen people
and
Kanchana

You shall no longer take things at second or third hand . . . nor look through the eyes of the dead . . . nor feed . . . on the spectre in books. . . . You shall not look through my eyes either, nor take things from me. . . . You shall listen to all sides and filter them for yourself. . . .

Walt Whitman

Contents

CONTENTS

Acknowledgements

Although this book appears under my name, it owes a debt to the many people who helped me achieve what I set out to do. My thanks to Anna Le Masurier and Sarah Rooney for their support, to John Hulme, Jack 'Bohemian' Picone, Fiona Baxter, Jim Pollard, Mauricio de Souza, Liam Phelan, Dani Cooper, Sarah Thornton, Cassia Williams, Andrew Ferguson, Ginny Stein, Saw Hla Henry, Saw Tay Tay, Blacktown, Miles Jury, Connie Levett, Jane Abbey, Orlando and Anna de Guzman, Soe Aung, Des Ball, Saw Simon, Ben Shipley, Brian McCartan, Jason Miller, Paul Keenan, Janejinda Pawadee, David Mathinson, Dr. Win Myint Than, Gina Frampton, Alison Tate, Annettte Blackwell, Dan and Jane Dwyer, David and Kathy Downham, the staff at Mae Tao Clinic, the CFMEU, the KHRG, the KNU, Karen soldiers and officers, and to the many Karen friends who gave so much and asked for so little

Special thanks to Richard Baker for his incisive editorial comments, Chris Roarty, Mark Soo, and to David Johnson for saying yes.

Introduction

This book is the result of five years living on the Thai-Burma border trying to make sense of the conflict between the Burmese military dictatorship and the people of Burma. In it I attempt to go beyond official reports, statistics, and quotes from non-government organizations (NGOs), aid agencies, and academic literature.

This book specifically looks at the armed resistance of the Karen minority, who have been fighting the world's longest civil war—57 years (at the time of publication)—and struggles with the constraints of modern journalism where the focus is on the big picture and complex stories are ignored. Some publishers warned me the story is too unknown and too remote for their readers.

They are right: Burma is remote, and an awful long way from what kills us. Most of us won't die from land-mines, malaria, dengue fever, malnourishment, or TB. It will be old age, car accidents, or lifestyle abuse that get us in the end. We won't be stopped at checkpoints, jailed, raped, beaten, shot at, or have our homes and crops burnt.

I ignored this well-intentioned advice and instead went looking for the ordinary people suffering at the centre of the conflict: the mothers and fathers, children, soldiers, villains and heroes of the civil war—and let them tell their stories.

I was horrified by the brutality of what land-mines do, the firsthand accounts of rape, torture, and killings. I talked with villagers used as human land-mine sweepers. I was shocked at the barbarism caused by over half a century of war.

As a journalist, I've spent time in city morgues and seen death in its many guises, but here on the border I was a witness to death that scared and shocked me. The sheer waste of human life and potential is devastating and soul destroying. At Mae La refugee camp, I spoke with an elderly Karen community leader and shaman, Sein Tin Aye, who told me Burma is in the putrid grip of a military regime reincarnated as "evil spirits" and that the horror is to be expected.

"These Burmese generals are hungry ghosts. They can't be satisfied or appeased. They're poisoned and contagious. They're trapped in their own evil. They may become weaker, but they will be here for some time yet."

The Karen, in spite of converting to Christianity and Buddhism, still retain some animist beliefs. In 1876, Colonel Alexander McMahon (deputy commissioner for British Burma) wrote in his book, *The Karens Of The Golden Chersonese*, about vampires known as *therets* and *thamus* and *tak-kas*—"spectres of wicked men, of tyrants, of unjust rulers"—who steal and torment people's souls. He could have been describing the present Burmese regime.

If the old shaman is right about the hungry ghosts and soul stealers being loose in Burma, their bloody footprints are easy to follow. What is puzzling is how these thugs manage to keep control of the country. Their economic bungling is mind boggling, yet they are still in power. An Orwellian line of text seen on a giant billboard in Burma sums up the dictators' intent: "Crush all internal and external destructive elements as the common enemy."

Diseases such as malaria, leprosy, elephantitis, tuberculosis, and polio that most other countries have eradicated, are common in Burma. Young children are traded as commodities, and women are sold into prostitution—a potential death sentence as the spread of HIV/AIDS is largely ignored and left uncontrolled by the regime.

But in spite of these threats to their survival, the Karen have resisted and retained their dignity. Mothers and fathers, forced to hide in jungles, get on with the everyday tasks of living and loving. They worry about feeding and educating their children. They learn to adjust to shelling, land-mines, hunger, and disease, and somehow find the will to cope and nurture. In jungle schools, spellbound children learn from teachers about their cultural heritage.

Even in exile in refugee camps in Thailand, the Karen leaders have kept in place the apparatus of government and a sense of community. They have organizations to look after the needs of women, youth, health, agriculture, law and order, defence, religion, education, and have working structures to defend and maintain the morale and welfare of their people. Most importantly, they give their people hope.

I acknowledge and take into account that *all* politicians including the Karen's push party lines, and that office bearers will often try to control information in their own interests.

I spent a lot of time on both sides of the border, and thanks have to be given to the numerous people who gave their time and risked their lives to make my journeys possible. In spite of knowing the risks, the Karen people always looked for a way to help.

Hundreds of thousands of Burmese cross borders hoping to escape. But crossing is no guarantee they are safe. Workers are killed, poisoned, or severely beaten for asking for wages. Others, like Ah Mee, escape Burma only to die unnecessary deaths.

Ah Mee was happy she had found a job cleaning and gardening for my landlady in Mae Sot. The pay wasn't great but she was 22 and, in general, a happy soul. It's easy to slip into well-worn clichés when talking about the dead, but Ah Mee was always full of life. That's the tragedy. A series of what seemed like unconnected incidents contributed to her death. My wife, Kanchana, and I were on our way back from Europe, spending a couple of days in Bangkok to see movies, buy books, and shop for items not available in Mae Sot. At the same time, our Canadian friends, Dr. David and his wife Cathy, who lived at the guesthouse where I was staying, decided to move into a house of their own. And Ma Naw, an older woman who worked with Ah Mee, had gone back to Burma to visit her family. Any one one of us would have been able to help her.

Ah Mee was on her own except for the company of the young factory worker who had got her pregnant. When she told him, he bolted. Alone, she decided to abort. Taking her meagre savings, she found a back-alley abortionist. She paid to have a dirty metal rod pushed and twisted inside her. Days later she became sick, her blood poisoned.

With no one to turn to, Ah Mee carried her pain until she collapsed. She was taken to hospital, but died. The tragedy was compounded knowing that she had a legal work permit, a reasonable life in Thailand, and was saving money to send home to her Karen family in Burma. Her death was a waste that should never have happened, but it did. And many more will, unless our world takes responsibility and forces the Burmese regime to release their political prisoners and hand over the country to its people.

1 Bar Whispers

As a journalist you hear many rumours from many sources, but there was something in the Mae Sot bar whisper about a secret camp across the Burmese border—run by a big, white American— that was exciting. The photographer I heard it from said that the American was training Karen soldiers fighting against the Burmese army. This whisper would eventually lead me into the complex story of the Karen struggle for independence waged against the second biggest army in Southeast Asia.

I must confess that before the whisper faded I had wrapped it in images of Conrad's *Heart of Darkness*, Herr's *Dispatches*, and Greene's *The Quiet American*. This had all the elements of a good read—a possibly crazed Vietnam veteran, armed rebels, and jungle hide-outs.

I had initially come to the Thai border town of Mae Sot in early 2000, at the request of Burmese democracy activists (based in Australia), to write about human rights abuses by the SPDC (State Peace and Development Council—the name the Burmese junta gives itself). I didn't know it at the time, but I was to stay five years. Like many journalists, I had a vague knowledge of the conflict within Burma. I knew of the 1988 student uprising, when hundreds of thousands of students, workers, monks, and teachers took to the streets to protest for political change. The dictators set the army loose and thousands were gunned down, their bodies bulldozed onto trucks. I was also aware of the jailing of the charismatic Nobel Prize winner and National League for Democracy (NLD) leader, Aung San Suu Kyi, but little else. My knowledge about the Karen people was zero.

Mae Sot lies three miles from the Moei River that separates Thailand from Burma. It is a bustling border town that owes much of its wealth to smuggling. Burmese gems, teak, antiquities, drugs, and people are all available for a price. The town itself appears unremarkable, but beneath its surface a dark heart beats. There are two main streets, two sets of traffic lights, and a number of sturdy old wooden Chinese houses wedged between rows of concrete shopfronts. A narrow market splits off the main street, dissecting small rows of shops selling fabric, pots and pans, groceries, electrical goods, and medical supplies. Untidy piles of merchandise tumble onto footpaths, forcing shoppers into traffic. A clutter of smaller roads and lanes criss-cross either side of the main streets. It is chaotic and more Burmese than Thai. Traders hawk pots of steaming curries, caged birds, insects, slabs of pork fat, buffalo meat, and bowls of wriggling fish and eels. Hilltribe families, off-duty soldiers, Burmese traders, factory workers, hustlers, spies, people traffickers, drug dealers, rebel soldiers, cops, rickshaw drivers, 'mercenaries,' volunteer teachers, and beggars ebb and flow in a human tide from one end of the market to the other.

One of the first things you notice about Mae Sot is the noise coming from every direction. Televisions are a constant background blare. Workshop machinery clatters in tight spaces. Fleets of pick-up trucks bellow advertising or political slogans from loudspeakers. The volume is cranked to insane levels. Restaurants, cafés, and shops play tinny music; temple speakers urge worshippers to get out of bed, and community broadcasts—from street-corner speakers—make announcements on everything from public health issues to the weather to lottery results.

Mae Sot hustles and bustles during daylight, but with the afternoon shadows comes trouble, and it doesn't matter which side of the shade you're on. Just before the sun drops over the horizon, trucks overloaded with consumer goods from Thailand make their way through the town to illegal border crossings to product-deprived Burma. Coming in the opposite direction are Burma's raw materials that have driven kings, pirates, gangsters, and governments to murder and war: rubies, pearls, jade, emeralds, sapphires, teak, opium, heroin, and sex slaves. Trafficking people through Mae Sot is profitable, and they're a valued commodity. Agents trawl the district looking for domestics, factory workers, and labourers. Refugee camps are fertile recruiting grounds.

Mae Sot is attractive to foreigners drawn to the town for work, visa renewal, or a walk on the wild side. Locals joke that most of the Westerners in Mae Sot are missionaries, medics, misfits, or 'mercenaries' attracted by the conflict, humanitarian crisis, or the edginess of the town itself.

A mid-morning walk through town is proof of the diversity of the people who make up Mae Sot. Thai, Burmese, Indian, Nepalese, and Chinese traders haggle on Prasatwithi Road. Dusty Hmong farmers push trolleys down supermarket aisles bulk shopping for coffee, milk, washing powder, toothpaste, soap, and tinned fish. Then there are the assorted Westerners.

By late afternoon, farmers and traders give way to industrious food vendors who take over space outside closed shops at the northern end of the town to set up a small night market. The night is also for smuggling, sex, and violence. Before the sun rises, Burmese itinerant workers have paid their border fees and hurried across the bridge to find underpaid work to feed their families. The cycle is continuous.

Mae Sot is also the unofficial headquarters for Burmese opposition groups and activists. Many aid agencies and NGOs have a strong visible presence in the town. It is also the closest contact point with Karen freedom fighters concealed in the surrounding mountains.

Reporting Burma's situation is difficult. There are no superpowers directly involved in the conflict, and sixty years of isolation from the rest of the world have kept it invisible. The forty or so acronymed opposition groups turn sentences into an unreadable alphabet soup. The constant, but never changing political position and daily killings make it an 'everyday event' for news editors, therefore not worth reporting. The Karen have been involved in full-scale battles with the Burmese army, but outside the Thai media their war barely rates a mention on international news.

In Western news rooms, some lives or deaths are worth more than others. A dead, white American rates a front-page lead, while 500 dead Indians, Asians, or Africans get buried in the 'news briefs' on page ten. But to be fair to those journalists who do care, tight deadlines, competition from other world events, lack of funds, and the difficulty of getting in and out of Burma make it a nightmare for them to verify accounts of atrocities or find witnesses.

In 1990, responding to international condemnation following the 1988 massacres, Rangoon allowed elections to be held. In spite of military intimidation, the NLD won a decisive victory—392 seats, eighty percent of the vote. The people had spoken, but the generals' response was to jail the NLD leaders, its elected representatives, and its members and supporters.

Burma remains a pariah state. It plays games using Aung San Suu Kyi to maintain a charade that it is willing to embrace democracy. For over fifteen years the regime has held never-ending 'talks' that usually conclude in her house arrest. Then she is released, re-arrested, and released again to hoodwink the international community and media that something is happening.

I was still trying to understand why the Karen did not regard their struggle as the same as that of the ordinary Burmese opposition. The Karen are one of the largest ethnic groups in Burma—an estimated seven percent of the population—while the Burmans, with around seventy percent, are the largest. The Karen disagree with these figures, saying that many of their people live in the central Irrawaddy Delta region and are not included.

There are various theories, but little evidence, of where the Karen originated. The Karen National Union (KNU) claims they came from China in 739 BC, migrating through Tibet from Mongolia. Karen elders say their people followed three rivers: the Irrawaddy to Rangoon and the Delta region; the Salween to Burma's eastern border with Thailand; and the Mekong, where they settled in Thailand, Laos, and Cambodia.

The Karen way of life has puzzled outsiders for centuries. The Reverend Harry Marshall in his 1922 anthropological study, *The Karen People Of Burma*, found that "politically and socially the village was the centre of their common life." The old were revered and their advice and wise counsel followed. Village heads tended the land like everyone else. The Karen had no caste system, nor even a privileged social class. Land belonged to the community. Karen literature has been handed down from from old to young. Proverbs and sayings, known as the *Hta*, reinforce humility as a virtue; greed, pride, cruelty, and personal ambition are avoided.

The Karen never wanted to fight the Burmans, but after centuries of discrimination and servitude they fought with the British in World War II and were promised autonomy for their efforts. That promise was never kept and the Karen have been battling for their freedom ever since. The odds against them are overwhelming: 20,000 poorly-armed rebels up against nearly 500,000 well-equipped government troops. They fight in the hope that their people can return to their homeland, Kawthoolei (translated directly as 'green land' but to the Karen 'land free of evil'). They fight for justice, equality, and the preservation of their culture, and they resist Burmese attempts at forced assimilation. Regardless of the superior strength of the Burmese army, the Karen remain a thorn in the side of the dictators.

Karen nationalism is not new. It dates back to the late 1800s, when the Karen National Association was formed during British colonial rule.

During World War II, Burman nationalists collaborated with the Japanese to push the British out of Burma. The Burmese Independent Army (BIA) took terrible revenge on the Karen for their support of the British. One KNU elder told me that BIA soldiers rounded up Karen and "started killing them by the hundreds each night" until the Japanese stopped them.

The Karen proved to be one of Britain's most loyal allies. Many tens of thousands of them were killed. Much to the shame and anger of British officers who fought with the Karen, that loyalty, paid for in Karen blood, was never to be honoured by the British government.

In 1947, following months of frustrated lobbying for autonomy and broken promises by the British, a charismatic English-educated Karen barrister, Saw Ba U Gyi, was chosen to lead the newly formed Karen National Union, that united the different Karen factions under one political office. Saw Ba U Gyi was no stranger to politics: he had held a position in the pre-independence Burmese cabinet under the British.

Following independence, the Karen's future was uncertain. By mid-1948, the newly-formed Burmese nation split into warring factions, and fighting started between the KNU and Burmese army.

By 1950, the KNU had spelled out their political principles in four short statements:

1. For us surrender is out of the question.
2. The recognition of the Karen State must be complete.
3. We shall retain our arms.
4. We shall decide our own political destiny.

Today, the Karen still believe that the only way to achieve their aims is by political dialogue, international pressure, and keeping their weapons to defend themselves.

Saw Ba U Gyi's reign was short-lived. He was ambushed and killed by Burmese soldiers in 1950. His bullet-riddled body was taken to Moulmein and dumped at sea, robbing the Karen of a formal burial ceremony and martyr's grave for their first leader.

In recent times the most influential Karen leaders have been General Bo Mya and Padho Mahn Sha. Bo Mya has a tough, well-earned reputation as the Karen National Liberation Army's (KNLA) hardman. Friends and foes describe him as ultra nationalistic, a devout Christian, conservative, and a great battlefield warrior. Mahn Sha, the KNU general secretary, by comparison, is invisible, but no less effective. He spent 37 years fighting the Burmese from the jungle and, some say, his nemesis, Bo Mya. Even though Mahn Sha is in his late sixties he is considered one of the new wave of Karen leaders. He is a Buddhist with a socialist background and has won plaudits for maintaining alliances with Burmese opposition and democratic groups.

Rangoon keeps the population in a political blackout. Many Burmese know little of the ethnic conflicts. All they have to rely on is manipulated information that causes them to fear savage ethnic hordes led by brutal warlords. Information is power. So it was no surprise when many Western activists and aid workers I met in Mae Sot took much condescending pleasure in continually driving me, the new boy, into cultural and academic dead-ends as I tried to fathom the issues and complexities. Reading scholarly texts did not necessarily make it any easier to understand the situation. Therefore, the whisper in Kung's Bar about the American 'mercenary' was a blessing. It was an exciting distraction from trying to report what the majority of the international media had collectively decided was a non-story.

However, before I could confirm the rumour, I had to find the American and his camp. Over many cold beers I urged the photographer to tell me all he knew. Before the bar closed, I had a rough location and a chance of finding the soldier.

The nights were still and as hot as the days. It was early April, 2000, close to the height of the hot season and Songkran, the Lunar New Year water festival celebrated in Thailand, Laos, Cambodia, and Burma. Temperatures were forty degrees and above.

In my five-dollar-a-night guesthouse room, I put together a small daypack: mosquito cream, antibiotics, torch, camera and 35-mm film, light trousers, and a knot of plastic bags to keep everything dry if it rained or if I had to wade or swim rivers. I laid out a pair of shorts, long-sleeved shirt, and rubber sandals. Faux military adventure clothing doesn't work in jungles—it's best kept for national parks and four-wheel-drive trips. Boots are too heavy, and they stay wet once they get wet. In spite of advertising spiel, man-made fibres make you sweat and keep you hot. In another plastic bag I took a fold of money—small bills and a couple of high-denomination Thai banknotes.

Sleep came in fits as, time and time again, I was snapped awake with questions I couldn't answer. What do I do if the American is hostile? How much money do I take with me? How long should I stay? What if they steal the hired car? What do I do if the Burmese attack the camp? How do I get back to Thailand? What story do I give the Burmese or Thai military if I'm arrested?

In their own way these nagging concerns energized me. I was awake early and ready to go before 6:00 a.m. I went to Mae Sot Market and bought bottles of water, tins of sardines, packets of instant noodles, fresh leafy vegetables, diced pineapple, sachets of three-in-one coffee, pomelo, and green bananas. At a stall I ordered breakfast: *kanom kai hong,* small balls of sugar-coated fried dough filled with mung bean, and a café *bolan.* The Thai-style coffee, done well, packs a caffeine punch equivalent to an espresso, the thick brew floating on a creamy bed of sweet condensed milk. Not knowing what was in store for me, the otherwise familiar scents of palm sugar caramelizing in a hot wok, incense smoke, and garlands of jasmine made the morning special.

After the trip to the market I picked up a worn-out rental car whose owner initially insisted on coming as my driver but eventually relented. I drove north of Mae Sot, away from the border, through dried rice fields and numerous checkpoints where armed police and soldiers looked for drug runners, illegal migrants, and the opportunity to increase their meagre wages with a bit of tea money. As a white man and, most likely, a simple tourist, I was waved through with smiles and no awkward questions from the young soldiers.

The road eventually shifted back towards the border and the Moei River. Following the photographer's rough directions, I turned off at a track that sloped down to the river's edge, where bamboo and other foliage screened the water. I bumped the rattling and dusty car onto the edge of an embankment that dropped thirty feet to the river below. Perched here was a bamboo lean-to with a sleeping platform but no side walls. As the handbrake didn't work, I had to rely on the gears and the small piece of flat ground to hold the car in place.

I parked facing the lean-to, where a young man sat in the shade. He looked up and then went back to fiddling one-handed with a two-way radio held between his feet. From the torn sleeves of his green military shirt protruded one good arm and hand. His other arm stopped just above his wrist, where a dirt-stained bandage was twisted around a stump. As I approached him, scrawny chickens scattered through the dried leaves. I smiled and said hello to the young man. He responded with a bored nod and then went back to the radio.

I moved closer to the platform. "Big American man? Trains Karen soldiers? Can you radio him? Where is he? Can you help me? Can I talk to him?"

He shrugged and concentrated on removing the batteries from the radio.

Hoping it would loosen him up, I got some fruit and water from the car. He dived in and sucked on chunks of warm pineapple between silent mouthfuls of pomelo until it was all finished. Still I got no response from him. I asked to share his shade. He shrugged and I moved under the small roof. After an hour of one-way conversation and feeble attempts at humour, I began to give up. Then the heat and the silence were broken by the chugging of a longtail boat coming towards us.

I moved to the edge of the embankment, but the man scowled and waved me back. The boat stopped below and a column of men marched up from the river. They wore an assortment of ragged T-shirts and sarongs. Black-ink tattoos trailed up their legs, arms, and shoulders. Some smoked green-leafed cheroots.

The column moved past the lean-to into the thick jungle behind. Nothing was said as they passed. Shortly after, they returned bent double under sacks of rice and other goods. When the boat was loaded with provisions and men, it re-started its loud engine and moved off. Soon the engine faded, leaving us in dismal silence. Just as I was deciding to either try radio man again or give up and leave, a small, lithe man in full green uniform stepped out of the trees and said, "You wish to visit our camp and speak with the major, our American friend?"

In quick response I nodded and moved forward to shake hands.

He said his name was Maw and indicated that I follow him as he moved down the bank to where another smaller boat was waiting. I got my gear and stumbled after him.

The boat had once been painted green but was now dulled and cracked from years in the elements. I squatted uncomfortably in the middle of it as ankle-deep water sloshed back and forth and the bare-legged boatman dragged it off the sandy bed. Once aboard, he tugged the motor into life. The engine caught, belching black smoke. We moved north through the green shallow water away from Thailand, passing silent fishermen. The red, white, and blue stripes of the Thai flag were visible for a moment above the trees.

We entered a deep channel. Maw unwrapped an M-16 from an old rice sack and checked its clip. As we edged closer to the Burmese side, Maw smiled and said, "Welcome to the Karen State. Unfortunately, we can no longer guarantee your safety." Then he dissolved into laughter.

2 Rebels And Devils

After forty minutes of hugging the Burmese shore, the boatman eased back on the throttle and used the current to move to the bank. I was now violating my Thai visa requirements and whatever passport controls the Burmese had. I considered what I would say if we were stopped or arrested by either side, and concluded that being escorted by rebel soldiers was not a plus.

Grey rock loomed out of the thick bamboo, and it looked as if there was nowhere a boat could possibly land, but as we bumped against the bank a narrow path revealed itself, then twisted out of sight behind the trees and rocks. I wobbled off the boat, followed by Maw, and waited for him to lead the way.

Even though the path looked well-trodden, I focused on Maw's steps. I knew that the Karen State was a nightmare of unmapped mines and booby traps. The number of people killed or maimed by them in Burma is now more than in Cambodia. The Thai army has reported that more than two-thirds of the 2,000-kilometre border has been mined. By now I was walking so close to Maw, we were almost an item.

As if reading my thoughts, Maw said, "There are no mines here, but keep to the path unless you're told not to. It's best you always follow someone."

The sand was hot. There were no sounds except the river lapping against the boat and my tight breath. It was a hard walk up the embankment, and I grabbed at bushes to help me along. As we approached the top, the path took a twist through the rock formation. Fresh-cut saplings and scorched grass were signs that the path had recently been cleared. It widened onto a small plateau that allowed a brief respite before the last ten metres to the top.

Whether it was intentional or not, my first sight of the American was dramatic. To look up at the top of the embankment, you had to force your neck back on your shoulders. But then the need to maintain balance compelled you to look down. When I next looked up he was blocking the small patch of blue sky, standing between two trees and looking directly down on us. He was tall and dressed in camouflage. His tanned arms were folded across his massive chest. He had the shoulders of a weight lifter, narrow waist, and long legs. A black beret covered his cropped hair. High on his hip, a pistol sat in a holster. I endured the uncomfortable feeling of being scrutinized as I laboured up the last few metres.

I approached him feeling drained. He held out his hand, smiled, and said, "Welcome to cobra country . . . king cobra country."

I shook his hand, gave my name, and expressed the hope that he wouldn't mind me gatecrashing his camp.

"No problem at all, you're welcome." He slapped his arm across my shoulder and walked me to a bamboo hut shaded by leafy banana trees, where a hammock was strung between two poles. A rough tabletop was nailed onto a tree stump, and seats had been fashioned from thick logs.

"Welcome to my jungle hotel," he added. "It's not much, but it's a lot better than what my boys have got." He pointed to some simple bamboo platforms perched on the edge of the embankment, where his rag-tag group of men loitered around. The smell of scorched earth clung to the camp. Large, smoke-blackened pots were steaming on red coals.

He unstrapped his holster and rolled out one of the seats for me. He clapped both hands together and a young boy in green vest, worn flip-flops, and baggy blue soccer shorts appeared. The boy's legs were covered in scars and fresh-picked insect bites. He looked no older than thirteen. Putting his arms around the boy, the major spoke to him in Karen, laughed loud while pushing and shooing him to go. Turning back to me, his face beamed as he spoke. "They're something, aren't they? I love them. These are my kids. I love them all."

I suspected the major was in need of an audience, and it wasn't long before he was on a roll.

"We started with 47 men and, after nine weeks of intensive training, we're down to 29. It's tough. Some can't handle the discipline and leave; others find the pressure of defusing land-mines too much, or the physical requirements too demanding. The standard's high. It has to be. I tell them they're going to die, and they will. The work we do is the most dangerous—assassinating Burmese officers or destroying drug factories behind enemy lines. To do this, you have to be able to deal with your own devils. You might have to wait three days or a week for a target to appear. You can't move. If you want to shit, you shit in your pants."

The boy returned with charcoal-smudged plastic cups of instant coffee sweetened with condensed milk.

"Drink up and enjoy, it's the last of the milk," said the major.

The coffee was surprisingly good. The major cracked lumps off a solid block of jaggery (palm sugar) and offered me a piece to suck.

He said that this camp was top secret and that I was lucky to be let in. He then berated me about journalists who had visited his old camp last year. "These turkey shites came promising us weapons if we let them photograph and interview my men. They fucked us over. And they had the cheek to send us useless knives that fuckin' broke on impact."

I felt I was on a roller-coaster. Getting to the camp had been tense, and my imagination was in overdrive. Adrenalin was rushing. It was hard to know how real the major was. But the camp, the KNLA soldiers, and the guns and ammunition definitely were. And I was a long way from being legally in Burma.

Loud gunshots smacked the air and I recoiled awkwardly at the sounds. The major stood up, grabbed his handgun, finished his coffee with a quick slurp, and indicated that I follow him.

We took a charred path away from the river towards the hills at the back of the camp. A large area roughly thirty metres by forty had been hacked and burnt clear of vegetation. A group of soldiers were sighting their automatic rifles at hand-drawn cardboard targets fastened to bamboo poles at the far edge of the clearing.

The major was all competition. "My Vietnam record means nothing to these kids. Half weren't even born, and most have never heard of the Vietnam War. So if I can't get it up, they ain't going to listen to this old man."

The men stopped shooting and looked up at the major, who flipped his ammunition clip and checked his sight. He handed me one of the bullets he had taken from the gun. The tip had been hollowed out and crossed. "It's a dumdum. If they come for me, I sure as hell want to blow the fuckers away."

I shrank at the thought of the damage this small projectile could do as it tore its way through a body at 2,000 feet per second.

He ordered one of the men to shoot at a target. The rifle cracked and the major grinned at my involuntary flinch. He took an AK-47 from one of his men and offered it to me. I refused, saying I'd stick with my pen.

The soldier climbed to his bare feet and strolled to check the target. The major signalled for him to bring the cardboard back to him. A rough, charcoal-drawn head had been torn at its edge by a bullet hole. The major was pleased. He told the man to replace the target and urged the others to bet against him beating the previous shot. He swaggered his shoulders, crouched, and took aim holding his pistol away from his body. Again, I let myself down by ducking as his gun fired.

The major laughed and eagerly awaited the return of the target. His shot had just bettered the first man's effort, but it was enough to keep him on a high. He slapped backs, palms, and heads. He'd done enough to keep his story intact.

"When I first came here, the Karen couldn't care less," he said. "I had to prove to them I knew what I was doing. These guys have been fighting for more than fifty years against an enormous army. My record meant shite to them."

Unbuttoning his sweat-stained shirt, he revealed a thumb-sized scar just below his left collarbone. "That happened in a hotel back in Mae Sot. Three of their people [Burmese Military Intelligence] came through the door. I was hit before I had time to do anything. I got out, but I never go anywhere without this baby now," he said, stroking his Walther pistol.

I filed this piece of information away to check out when I got back to Mae Sot.

We moved back to the major's hut and I asked permission to look around the camp and talk to his men. He looked hard at me before answering. "No photographs of me, and I'm serious about that. Over the years, we've had our share of journalists. They come here looking for a quick story, make promises of aid and equipment, and deliver nothing. They want action, blood, and our guts. Then they go away, print photos, and give location details that get these kids killed."

Unaware at the time of the well-trodden path of freelance journalists coming to the region, I tried to reassure him I wasn't here for a media 'quickie' and a few exotic photographs of rebel soldiers with guns.

"It's up to the men if they want to talk to you. I'll get Jannie to help you. He speaks English."

The setting sun left the camp in golden light and shadows. A young man arrived wearing a green army vest. He was good looking, no older than seventeen, softly spoken, and very mild-mannered. The major introduced him, telling me that next year Jannie would be attending a leadership course in Chiang Mai.

Training was over for the day, and the soldiers relaxed by preparing dinner, saying prayers, or washing in the river. Weapons hung from huts and trees or lay against posts. Out of sight and safe from the protein-starved soldiers, a couple of large green lizards scampered safely up a tree. Beyond the scrubby shoot-ing range, hidden guards and booby traps protected the narrow pass in the Dawna Range that was the only land entry into the camp. Shallow foxholes dotted the perimeter and, according to the major, if the Burmese attacked, the unit only needed fifteen minutes to evacuate.

"The mines, claymores, and the rearguard will hold them up. We don't take anything except our weapons and ammunition. They can have the rest," he said, nodding at the bamboo huts.

Jannie guided me around the camp and was quick to answer my questions. His father was a KNLA officer and his mother worked with the Karen Women's Organization (KWO). He had two elder brothers and one younger sister. His big eyes, lazy smile, and combat fatigues all enhanced his good looks. I assumed his respect toward me was partly due to his own good nature and partly down to the major's warm welcome. He introduced me to the soldiers as we went.

Sitting on a small platform overlooking the river, two shirtless men, Sawa and Pahtoo, picked and squashed large red ants from a pile of white ant eggs. The eggs, the size of rice grains, burst easily in the mouth, their juice tangy on my tongue. Hanging from the men's hut were their M-16s with grenade attachment, belts of grenades, and an AK-47. Sawa, the younger of the two, said that his reason for joining the KNLA started when the SPDC destroyed his village and took his father away to carry their supplies.

"When he tired, they killed him. I was thirteen when it happened. It made me hate them."

Sawa explained that Burmese soldiers called such forced labourers and porters '*thayae*' or 'ghosts.' It's a fitting name, as many never return to their villages. Porters are nothing more than disposable slaves to the military. With no all-weather roads in the Karen State, the Burmese army needs thousands of villagers to build its camps and carry supplies to operational units. When they need slaves, orders are sent to village headmen. Children and women are also used. At night, porters are kept under armed guard. Those suspected of planning to escape are shot on the spot. For villagers like Sawa's father, portering is a death sentence. They carry heavy loads with little or no food or rest. Forty-kilogram panniers held with bamboo straps or rough webbing cause strap burns that turn septic. Porters are beaten if they rest. Those who are ill or injured are left where they fall. They also risk death from getting caught in ambushes, and the Burmese use them as shields and human land-mine clearers.

Pahtoo, 31, had been a soldier for fourteen years, and it showed. His body was bullet scarred and tattooed with KNLA slogans. His village was shelled and torched. His eyes became hard black nuggets of hate as he talked.

"I lived on our farm with my family. The Burmese came to the village and burned it down. My mother couldn't run with us because she was nursing our new baby. They were burned to death. I was only three at the time. I get sick of fighting, but we must protect our people. I've seen many terrible things. I saw what the SPDC did at Sleeping Dog Hill. They used Karen girls as porters and at night raped them. My cousin was raped at gunpoint by them."

Sleeping Dog Hill fell to the Burmese in March 1992 after two months of intense fighting. It was the beginning of the end of the Karen's hold on fixed territory.

Pahtoo told me how Burmese soldiers use trickery to entrap young Karen women. "When our girls go through army checkpoints, soldiers search them and, while looking in their bags, drop in bullets. At the next checkpoint, other soldiers find the bullets and arrest them. They keep the girls and rape them. All the soldiers take turns. When they're released, many girls kill themselves from the shame."

Pahtoo said it would be hard to go back to being a villager after what he's seen and done. But he hoped the world would not forget their struggle, especially Karen refugees who have gone overseas.

"Tell Karen [overseas] people we need their help. We have soldiers but little money for weapons or uniforms."

Jannie said that Pahtoo was lucky to be alive considering the number of missions he had been on. He added that many of the major's elite squad had not survived the ravages of regular bouts of malaria or the constant battles.

The Karen have a justified case for defending their people against a brutal aggressor, and I understood their cause, but I still found it hard to reconcile the casual ease and serious intent to kill of the young men around me. Yet I knew my thinking would probably be different if my mother, father, brother, sister, or grandparents had been tortured, raped, beaten, or shot dead, with no likelihood of the attackers being brought to justice. These young men were willing to die at a moment's notice.

For the major, it was different. He was living a dysfunctional dream. To him, a 'normal' family life could not replace the adrenalin rushes he had experienced by killing and avoiding being killed. The major missed his war, which was why he was now in the jungle aged sixty, sleeping on a bamboo mat, catching malaria and dengue fever, and dodging more bullets—for no pay.

He wasn't the only one wanting to play war games on the Burmese killing fields. Many foreigners have offered their services to the Karen, including US Vietnam veterans, Australians and New Zealanders, South Africans, Israelis, Japanese, and assorted Europeans. Some have paid with their lives and are buried in the conflict area. At one time, they were mercenaries, but nowadays the Karen are strapped for cash.

Soldiers of fortune usually go where the money is. French mercenaries have been reported as being paid around 6,000 dollars a month to protect, from the KNLA, the 1-billion-dollar Burmese pipeline running from the Yadana gas field in the Gulf of Martaban, across Burma to Thailand. The 400-kilometre pipeline was built by Unocal Total using forced labour. To distance themselves from the inevitable international condemnation and to avoid anti-investment legislation, the French and American oil barons created a series of sub-contractors to work through. But no matter how much sleight of hand was involved, it doesn't get away from the allegations that, for oil and profit, Burmese soldiers killed and made hundreds of villagers homeless. The KNU accused oil investors who support the Burmese regime of being "killers."

Leaving Sawa and Pahtoo to sort their ants' eggs, Jannie led me towards a bundle of faded clothing slumped in a corner of the next hut. As we approached, the bundle moved and a man tilted his face towards us. Jannie introduced me to Lamon. He sat up and looked at us with his one remaining eye. A blue knitted beanie was slanted over his blind eye in an effort to hide his facial disfigurement. For his troubled mind, there was no relief: he had nurtured his hatred of the Burmese army for half his life.

Lamon said he was fifteen when they came to his village and demanded porters. He turned and stared into the distance, his one eye locked and unable to let go of the hurt. "They took ten of us. They made us dig up mines. If we refused, they said we'd be shot."

Lamon spent three days prodding the ground with a stick and removing the explosive devices by hand. Some needed just a kilo of pressure to detonate.

"I dug out about thirty before one exploded."

The mine ripped both Lamon's hands off, blew out his left eye, and dropped his soul somewhere dark.

"I was scared, but now I'm not afraid to die," he said as he rubbed his calloused stubs and picked up his treasured AK-47. "I have killed many Burmese soldiers. Since they took my hands and eye, I want to take their lives."

Listening to our conversation, another soldier, Wa, interrupted to say the major's unit had let him avenge his father's death many times over. His body was muscled by years of guerrilla warfare. Tattooed Karen symbols and slogans bragged of his loyalty. He said, as the body count among his friends continued to grow, so did his need to take revenge.

"Ambushes make it easy. From our positions we can kill them without getting hurt." Pointing to his M-16, Wa said, "This can do a lot of damage. I prefer ambushes . . . we have fewer casualties. But still, many friends have died."

In spite of his desire for revenge, Wa, like many of the other Karen soldiers I spoke with in the camp, said he hoped the war would end and he could return to a quiet village life.

"To kill is not easy. To destroy God's creation is not good. I want to go home to my village and live a good life. These men are like family to me, but I want my own family. I miss my father. I never saw him again after he was taken. All the killing I have done has not made him come back. This is the sadness of my life."

I followed Jannie along a path that lead to a clearing beneath a limestone cliff. Here, two long-haired, bare-chested men rested on their knees. A metal chain ran from their necks to their wrists, encircled their waists, and went through their trousers to shackles on their ankles. The chains were fastened around the trunk of a tree. Jannie looked anxious, clearly realizing that I shouldn't have seen the two men. He said we should leave. I nodded towards the men and asked Jannie if they were Karen. Before he could reply, the major lumbered up. "No! They're spies. We interrogated them and they've confessed. These bastards are officers. They've raped and ordered Karen people to be killed. They'll get what they deserve."

I looked at the men. They didn't look tough. They looked defeated. I saw no signs of beatings or blood or bruises on them, just a look of utter dejection. The major pulled Jannie out of the clearing and I followed. We made our way back to the major's hut.

"Those bastards are not worth feeling sorry for. I've seen rape scenes. Young Karen girls, no more than thirteen, left bleeding and dead. So don't give me shit about international conventions or fair treatment for these killers."

I kept my silence and made small talk as I let the shadow of death wash over me. Later, two sharp cracks echoed around the camp and I never saw the two dull-eyed Burmese men again.

The major said that over the last ten years, 45 of his soldiers had been killed. He rummaged through a pile of colour photographs on the tabletop until he found what he was searching for.

"She was only nineteen, but one of the best," he said, holding a graduation style photograph of a smiling young woman in a green military uniform.

"I get too close to my soldiers . . . it breaks my heart every time one gets killed."

The major moved through the pictures, stopped and stared at another of the same woman; this time she was lying on her back in dense jungle. The picture was slightly out of focus. The girl's lifeless eyes stared upwards, her young head framed by dead leaves and a massive halo of blood.

"There were seven days between these photos. She was on a mission and a stray bullet got her. Dressed as a villager, she'd go behind enemy lines with syringes filled with cobra serum and inject drunken SPDC officers."

It was hard keeping up with the major as he constantly took the story from hard fact, such as the dead woman, to the edge of credibility, with cobra serum.

"The really sad thing is, instead of fighting we could all be friends—if it wasn't for a few corrupt people. Instead of shooting each other, these kids should be out there playing soccer against each other."

The major stressed again that his unit's objective was not fighting SPDC coolies or low ranking soldiers. "We're going after those committing and ordering atrocities. We know their names and ranks and we'll get them."

The sounds and smell of dinner being prepared in smoke-blackened oilcans came from the makeshift kitchen. The night sky closed in and the men lit candles and placed them in windbreaks made of strips torn from plastic shopping bags. The flames threw yellow light into the shadows. Soon, chipped enamel plates with lumps of hot rice arrived. Two older soldiers joined us.

"This is Captain Tao and Captain Lay," the major introduced us. "Tao is the best radio man we've got. Give him eighteen hours and he can bust any frequency open. He's one of the reasons we've got the jump on the Burmese around here."

Captain Lay said nothing as he opened three tins of sardines and offered me one. I took it and spooned the oily fish onto my steaming rice. Plates of boiled potatoes and vegetables added to the meal.

Lay and Tao ignored the spoons and used their right hands to mash the fish and vegetables into their rice. They added dried chillies and used their hands to eat.

The major laughed and offered me the chilli. "In the front line they take a pocketful of dried chilli to keep them going when there's no food."

The major didn't eat but kept talking. "In camp we normally don't drink or smoke, but tonight, as we have a guest, we'll break the rule. We've got Russian and Chinese grenades or 'Karen Happy Water.' Your choice."

The three men cracked up at what was obviously a well-used joke. The major dug around in his small hut and emerged with three metal flasks. Opening all three, he poured generous amounts into the three screw-top cups. I said I'd try the Karen Happy Water, hoping to gain some points.

The drink was cloudy white and smelled like turned milk. It was fermented glutinous rice. It burned its way down to my gut where, hopefully, it killed any parasites I'd picked up during dinner.

As the drink flowed, the major was all smiles, jokes, and good-ol'-boy stuff. The conversation swung up the emotional ladder then down and back up again. It was hard to work out what was real and what was fantasy. He confided he had been in therapy in the US to help with his Vietnam ghosts, but stopped going when given an ultimatum to either give up the killing in Burma or his treatment. I asked why he was fighting with the Karen.

"They're the good guys. They're Christians, hate commies, and saved our ass during World War Two. I love them, I really do. And I want to give something back. Look what we did in Vietnam. Sometimes I wonder if I was fighting on the right side."

I asked the major if he liked killing.

"It's hard to kill. If you're looking down the sight on a scope, you see the eyes and they stay with you forever."

So why do it?

"The thrill and excitement of knowing that there's someone out there trying to kill me. Once you cross the line it gets easier, unless you have time to think about what you're doing or go home to the wife and kids. Soldiers are taught to hate: we live and behave like animals. We spend days hunting a kill, moving inches at a time, lying in our own shit, scorched under a hot sun, or wet and miserable in a rainstorm. We're taught to kill with a gun or a knife, a stick, a rock, plastic bag, anything, and then we get to go home. But you know something? There's no more home. We never leave the dead . . . they come with us. That's why I'm here. We're all in it together. Out here I don't have to justify what I do."

The major slumped and made noises about tomorrow's early start, when he planned to go upcountry to visit the commander of another brigade. I was welcome to tag along.

I was tired. The day had worn me out. The major asked Lay to take me to where I would be sleeping. It was a small, walled hut where the embankment curved with the river. Lay told me it was where officers slept, but it would only be him and me tonight.

Sitting on the bamboo platform of a long hut next to ours sat a group of older soldiers talking quietly. As we approached, they smiled a welcome and I asked if I could take their photos. As I focused and prepared to press the shutter, one of them stopped me, saying that a flash is sometimes used to trigger booby traps. To reinforce his point, he pulled from behind him a tatty cardboard box. Taking from it a plastic milk container and a coil of thin electrical wire buried in a white paste, he said quietly, "When this is primed with a detonator and the wires are joined, we can use a camera flash, mobile phone, or remote control to trigger it."

I promised I would always ask in future, given the amount of ammunition, land-mines, and other explosive devices in the camp. One of the soldiers started to pull and tug at one of the small round devices. He smiled and said don't worry, he was just disarming it. I did worry and, considering the number of maimed soldiers in the camp, I thought I had good cause to be. Arms, hands, or eyes were often lost priming or making mines or bombs.

I took some portraits of the men and close-up shots of the mines and booby traps, thanked them, and said I was going to bed.

They started laughing at something one of the soldiers said in Karen. When I asked to be let in on the joke, their laughter increased to a roll.

Lay translated, "They want to know if you're frightened of ghosts?"

I answered, "Depends on the ghosts? Are there any here?"

The men howled and Lay said, "Only new ones. Don't go down there to pee if you're afraid, because you'll wake the headless souls." He pointed down towards a gully. It was impossible to see beyond the small circle of light cast by a candle-lit lantern, but the men's meaning was obvious. I thought back to the two prisoners and the gunshots that afternoon.

I joked that I didn't think the ghosts would be coming for me, and that it would be them who had better take care tonight. My wisecrack chilled their talk, and Lay and I walked to our hut.

Lay was in the mood to chat. He was a tough man, but he was also prepared to reflect on what he was doing. He wasn't all bravado like some of the younger men. He admitted he got scared when fighting, and he missed his family. When that happened he usually hit the bottle, any bottle. It had cost him promotions and respect.

To me, it was surprising so few of these men tried to fragment their reality with alcohol, opium, or ganja. Their lives were full of pain, the future bleak. Lay said he was determined that his son would be a medic, farmer, or a teacher—anything but a soldier.

Lay said he was trained as a sniper, but the loneliness got to him. When he was out there alone, he had only ghosts to keep him company, and he drank to stop their whispers. He said if I really wanted to know about the Karen's war, the best person to help me would be a Karen not a *gawlawah* ('white person') like the major.

I asked him if he would help me.

"No, not me," he said. "I'm only a villager. I know only a little. You need to talk to one of our elders. I know one in Mae Sot. I'll ask him if he will help you. His name is Tha Ko."

We lay awake talking about our different lives. The contrast was obvious. My sturdy sandals lay next to his worn-out canvas pumps. My bed was a thin silk sheet sewn to make a sleeping bag; his was the bamboo floor and his arms over his head. I smothered myself in insect repellent, which he borrowed. His candle burned out and I used my steel Maglite to light the room. My Swiss army knife cut a new candle in half, while his blade was a piece of sharpened recycled steel, wedged and tied between two pieces of hand-worked wood.

I told him about my life in Sydney: coastal walks, ocean swims, coffee, wood-fired pizzas, newspapers, restaurants, bookshops, weekend barbecues, and movies. I talked about life as a journalist, travel, friends, and children. My children never knew an empty fridge, his never had a fridge to open.

Lay told me about his double life as a refugee and a freedom fighter. "My camp has 10,000 bamboo houses, each built on four metres of dirt. No lights, cars, or supermarkets. My son, like me, has never tasted ice-cream, been to a movie, sat on a train, or swam in the sea. I've no money. I've lived here since I was nineteen. I can't travel without getting arrested or paying bribes to Thai police. I am a simple villager, but I have to fight and kill. My wife and baby son, and her father and mother live in the camp. My family time is good. My job is winning freedom. My family's future is my job. We have to make sacrifices for those we love."

We stopped talking and through the open door I could see the stars and bats swooping between the huts and trees. A few candles slowly faded out, frogs croaked, and the river sloshed in the distance. I had visions of the Burmese army swarming downstream.

Earlier, the major had reassured me the Burmese wouldn't use the river to attack, but would try to sneak through the mountain pass that was guarded and mined. I lay awake and planned that, if we were attacked, I would swim with the fast flowing current to Thailand. Images of my bobbing head lit by an army flashlight stayed just beneath the surface as I slept.

The creaking and bending of the bamboo floor as Lay left the hut woke me up. He was outside whispering to someone. It was dark, but birds sang and the distant chop-chop of a blade against wood could be heard. I got up and folded the sleeping bag into its fist-sized cover. By the time Lay finished his conversation and returned with a cup of sweet coffee for me, I was packed and ready to go upriver with the major.

I took my coffee outside and was walking towards the camp-fire when I noticed one of the soldiers carrying what looked like an arm to the makeshift kitchen. Horrified, I followed, not wanting to believe what I was thinking. I had heard stories of cannibalism among both Karen and Burmese troops.

Unknown to me, my hurried pursuit had attracted the attention of Lay, Maw, and the major. As I neared the chopping block, I could see the scrawny fingers and bloodied forearm. I was just about to question the soldier when the major made me jump. "It's not what you think. It's a skinned monkey. A Karen delicacy. If you want, I'll get the boys to save you some for when we get back?"

The major was right. It wasn't a human arm, yet in the half-light and with my mind wired to expect horror, I was convinced I was about to see human flesh cooked and eaten.

Here was an example of my own confusion. What was real and what wasn't? What was I really seeing and what did I think I was seeing? I needed symbols to help make sense of the unfamiliar. Just as my photographs in the camp are proof of the existence of rebels, guns, and wounds, I still needed them to prove I had witnessed them. But I also realized I was in danger of collecting a number of easy-to-get clichés that would prevent me from seeing what was really happening to the Karen.

If I was to truly understand, I needed to be aware of my own preconceived perceptions and to try to avoid taking easy options to tell the story. I knew that a single trip to a KNLA training camp run by a *gawlawah* wasn't going to be enough. If I was to find out about the Karen resistance, I would need to take time and get beyond my mental shorthand. And that was going to be hard.

Anthropologist Edmund Carpenter wrote that it is hard to "experience the unfamiliar, the unnamed." Instead of saying "if I hadn't seen it with my own eyes, I wouldn't have believed it" we should say "if I hadn't believed it with all my heart, I wouldn't have seen it."

I needed to go deeper and find more than what I was seeing and hearing on the surface. I needed to talk with Lay's friend, Tha Ko.

The major moved Lay, Maw, Tao, and me down to the river and onto a boat. A heavy green kit bag was heaved onto rice sacks to keep it out of the water in the bottom of the boat. The four of them had changed into their street clothes. The major was dressed in jeans, scuffed Reeboks, and a US military T-shirt. Lay, Tao, and Maw wore a mismatch of ill-fitting trousers, jackets, and baseball hats.

Maw pushed into a fast midstream current before starting the engine. It sputtered into life as we moved low on the water. I was surprised to see that the current flowed south to north, the opposite direction to the hazy escape plans I had made last night. If there had been an attack, I would have been swimming against the current. Was this another metaphor of my confusion?

Morning mist clung to the mountaintops. Women washed children and clothing on the edge of the river, which was thick with foliage—an easy place for a Burmese sniper to idle away his time shooting up boats. I assumed the major and his men knew what they were doing and the risk of attack was low. After about forty minutes we moved across to the landing area on the Thai side of the river, where I hoped my car would still be waiting.

The men unloaded the boat and we moved up the embankment. The car was where I had left it. Radio man still fiddled with batteries in his lean-to. I opened the boot and Lay and Tao struggled to squeeze the kit bag into the cramped space.

I drove and the major sat up front with me while the three Karen shared the back seat. The major ordered me to drive north. The first checkpoint we passed through was unmanned. It was too early for soldiers to be up. I asked the major what I should say if we got stopped.

"Tell them you're a preacher or a teacher. Let Tao do the talking."

We passed through five checkpoints, where serious-looking Thai soldiers looked in and around the car. Red and white painted barriers had been set up across the road, and spiked tracks lay within easy reach, if needed, to burst the tyres of a suspect vehicle.

We drove past the three-kilometre front of Mae La refugee camp, where Lay's wife and family lived, and moved north through the heat, only stopping to eat *khao paad krapow gai*—rice topped with fried chicken and basil—at a roadside cafe. The men drank iced Cokes. When we were finished, the major handed me the bill. The early start, the food, and the heat made everyone sleepy. It wasn't long before I was the only one awake as we continued north.

I slowed down before another checkpoint and Tao leant over and told me to take the next left turn. We drove through a cluster of wooden houses, scattering black pigs, chickens, and dusty naked children. Tao pointed to a side road to the right. It rolled steeply down to a stream where two rotten planks supported by rocks made a bridge. It was going to be tricky getting up the steep bank on the other side. If I went too slow, I'd get stuck in the stream, but too fast and I'd crash into the embankment. If we got bogged down, we'd need a tractor to get out.

I considered offering to let one of the others drive. The major whooped and slapped his thigh as we slid in the thick mud, but keeping the car moving up the embankment earned me a few points from the men. As we cleared the crest, Tao told me to follow the track running beside the creek. I lost sight of the water as jungle claimed both sides of the track. It was a roller-coaster ride. Steep mud banks formed by the flooded creek in the wet season made it impossible to get out of the grind of second gear. Our vision was totally obscured by jungle.

It was another thirty minutes before glimpses of river, sky, and mountaintops could be seen. Automatic rifle fire and the answering thud of mortars could be heard as we slowly navigated the contours of the riverbank. I realized with some dread that our white car stood out like a dog's balls. My foot involuntarily pressed down on the accelerator pedal. The major and the others laughed.

We finally left the jungle track and entered a large, sunlit clearing, where I parked. The major, Tao, and Lay lifted the heavy green bag and dragged it towards a hut, where a group of soldiers carried it inside. An older man, neatly dressed with glasses, stepped forward and waited for the major to unlock the bag. I moved closer to see what was in it. The major took out four AK-47s, a black rifle, bandoliers of heavy ammunition, ten grenades, steel knives, two cloth-wrapped rifle scopes, and a flak jacket.

The major smiled and said respectfully to the man with glasses, "This should please the old man. Make sure Gai gets one of those scopes." He brushed past me out of the hut and said, laughing, "I see you're into gun running now."

I followed the major, Lay, and Tao to the shade of a large, open-sided bamboo hut on the riverbank, where four elderly men sat talking, smoking, and sipping coffee. It was a peaceful scene except for the shiny walnut handle of a Smith & Wesson .357 pistol that hung from a shoulder holster and sat stark against the bare skin of one of the old men—a KNLA colonel who had been fighting since 1949. The colonel was quietly putting the finishing touches to a plan to attack a Burmese outpost. His hard eyes sharpened as the major made introductions, and we waited for them to finish.

When the briefing was concluded, the colonel told me that even though the Karen were hopelessly outnumbered by the better equipped Burmese, his men compensated with their guerrilla skills. "The Karen have to win so all of Burma can have freedom, but we can't afford to fight head-on anymore," he said, echoing the major's strategy. "It's now more effective to attack specific targets, take equipment, and move out. We don't take positions, it's too costly. Now we hit those who are causing our people the most pain."

Outside the hut, battle-hardened, muscular KNLA men gathered around a low platform where young men and women were busy wrapping green banana leaves around a mixture of hot rice, fish paste, and yellow beans to take to the troops attacking the Burmese post. Smoke from a wood fire mixed with steam from the hot rice.

Just across the river, automatic gunfire stuttered and stopped. In the shadows of the hut, a man puffing on a thick green cheroot listened intently to static on a field radio.

Tao removed his baseball cap and sat down next to the colonel. They talked quietly, the old man's hand on the younger man's thigh.

Tao pulled what looked like a yellow mobile phone from his trouser pocket. It was a global positioning system (GPS), used to mark enemy positions and also where the KNLA had booby-trapped or land-mined an area.

Tao told me the old man was much loved by the Karen villagers.

"He has been fighting more than fifty years. He never stays in the same place two nights running. He's smart. He's adapted. He knows guerrilla tactics are more effective for us now."

Tao was concerned the colonel should have regular hospital treatment for his blood pressure, but the old man preferred to stay in the jungle and fight. "He never gives up protecting his people, that's why we love him."

The old man may have had high blood pressure, but he was intent on bombing the Burmese on the other side of the river. The radio operator spoke to the colonel, who allowed a small smile to crack his tight face.

"We're listening to the SPDC, and when they send reinforcements, we'll ambush them," he said.

Without warning, mortar shells announced that the KNLA had found the SPDC reinforcements just 500 metres over the river. The shells fell with dull thuds. Clouds of white smoke and plumes of yellow dust drifted up and over the tree-covered mountainside.

The old man's smile reached his eyes for the first time as the report came over the radio that his men had killed six SPDC troops and captured a large number of weapons.

The cash-strapped KNLA does it tough. Forget sophisticated equipment—there's barely enough money to buy decent knives, and their men have enough trouble trying to make the different bits of their uniforms match. Rubber thongs are worn by many of the troops instead of boots. But what works in their favour is that they are fighting for their cultural survival and to reclaim their sacred homeland. What they lack in equipment they make up for in loyalty, determination, and jungle skills.

A small man arrived at the side of the hut and waited as the colonel and the major enjoyed a few moments banter comparing and admiring their respective handguns. There was then a short but intense discussion between the major and the small man. When he left, the major said that the man was about to go on a mission. "He's a loner, but he's caused them a great deal of trouble." The man's scruffy T-shirt and Karen sarong belied his expertise as the unit's best sniper.

"Only he knows how many officers he's killed. He's the best I've ever seen and I'm glad he's on our side."

3 Food's Terrible, Pay's Lousy, The Hours Are Long

After the Burmese outpost was taken, I drove the major and the others back to the camp. The men greeted me with handshakes and grins. There was still no escape from the heat. The ground was hot, water was hot, and I was hot. Looking around the camp, it was hard to imagine how the men kept themselves motivated. They had lived there for ten weeks without a break, and cigarettes and alcohol were forbidden. Two men slept cramped together on each small platform, mosquitoes constantly bit, and the food was basic: two daily servings of rice, one of fermented fish, chilli, and lentils, and, if they were lucky, monkey, squirrel, bat, or bird. There were no books, radios, or any other signs of entertainment.

Their days were long, sometimes starting as early as 2:00 a.m. and continuing without sleep for another thirty hours. Their training ran from the mundane to the sinister. The major's battered training manual listed the skills they learned: camouflage and concealment; signals; AK-47s and M-16s; interrogation; target practice; map drawing; weather reading; mission planning; escape and evasion; first aid and hygiene; land-mines and booby traps; knife fighting, zero weapons, and silent killing.

The major insisted his recruits didn't need much motivation to keep fighting. "It's not like they have choices and can go out and get a job. They also know that their chances of survival are better with us. We go on dangerous missions, but we have the best equipment and training."

Later that afternoon I walked over to a group of soldiers talking with a Karen villager. Lay introduced me to the man, Saw Kwi Lar, a headman who had walked for three days to see if he could buy rice and fish paste for his village before the wet season started. His skin was leathery and he sucked on a wad of betel nut wedged between his cheek and teeth. Lay took us to a small shaded area overlooking the river.

I asked Kwi Lar about forced labour in his village. He replied that the Burmese army regularly took his people as porters. "It can be for one day or many weeks," he said. "We're made to carry food, ammunition, and wood, or to clean their camp. We have no choice. They treat us like animals. We get no food."

The Burmese send written orders to the village listing their demands, and these include things other than labour. "They want feeding and say they will pay later, but they never do. They take bags of rice and chilli. Their constant demands mean we have no time to grow or harvest our rice. If they take twenty or thirty people when we're preparing the paddy, we can't clear the ground or plant seeds. If it's during the harvest, we can't pick our rice. It dries and just drops to the ground to rot. We don't have enough to feed ourselves. It happens every year. That's why I have come to the border to buy rice."

I asked Kwi Lar if he could take me to his village.

"I can't," he replied. "If they found out, they would kill me."

The next afternoon, I was surprised to see an old, white-haired man ambling along a dusty trail leading down from the Dawna Range into the camp. He was wearing an oatmeal V-neck sweater back to front, a pair of Wellington boots, and leaned on a long stick for support. He stopped me and introduced himself as Thu Po Mu and proudly said he was 96 years old. His eyes sparkled as he spoke in broken English of his exploits fighting for the British during World

War II. This was no old codger romanticizing about the past. He was sharp and wanted to make his point to me—a white man who owed the Karen for their sacrifices.

Thu Po Mu said he had served with Force 136 under a British officer, Major Hugh Seagrim. He drew back his sleeve to reveal a faded ink tattoo. I could make out the number 136 and a rough crest amid Karen script. "Major Seagrim told me his wish was to be buried in the Karen State, and that's what happened. He was a good man and soldier. He loved the Karen. He said many times that when Burma was independent we Karen would be given our own state. We believed him. Why wouldn't we? We were both fighting the same enemies. That's why I served the British. We made many sacrifices for them. I was separated for seven years from the love of my life and I never did marry her because of the war. But many Karen paid much higher prices. I was a captain and saw a lot of fighting. It was tough. We had no drugs to treat malaria. We were away from our families, and the Burmans and Japanese took revenge on our villages for our supporting the English. Our fighting Britain's war didn't help our struggle for independence."

Instead of honouring these men, the British government, much to the disgust of some of its officers, handed control of Burma to Aung San, the country's nationalist hero, founder of the Burmese Independent Army, and father of Aung San Suu Kyi. Many of the Karen leaders today, their memories scarred by the destruction of hundreds of Karen villages and the slaughter of thousands of their people, find it difficult to understand how the British could have been so treacherous.

Few people in Britain today are aware of this treachery, but occasionally there are reminders. In the House of Lords, during a wider debate on Burma in March 1998, Lord Weatherill said that if the British government had fulfilled its promise to the Karen, there might not be civil war in Burma today. "Had they done so, it is unlikely that those courageous people would be engaged in a long and damaging struggle with the present Burmese government," he said.

Lord Weatherill called it a "debt of honour" and said Britain had an obligation to make amends by using its influence in the

European Union (EU) and the United Nations to bring heavy pressure on the Burmese.

To add insult to injury, few Karen who fought for the British colonial army ever received any pension. To their everlasting shame, the British government has conveniently swept its wartime debt and obligation to the Karen out of sight.

The Burmese military has forced as many as fourteen armed ethnic groups to sign cease-fire agreements, but the Karen still refuse, hanging on to their belief that a Karen homeland within a federated union of Burma is possible. This belief has come at a terrible price. The Karen lost most of their fixed territory during the 1990s, and with it most of their lucrative tax income from smugglers crossing the Thai border. All smuggled goods were taxed at five percent, and it is estimated that in the 1980s the gates generated 7 million US dollars a year for the Karen to pay for arms, uniforms, and medicine. During that time, the Wang Kha 'tax gate' north of Mae Sot on the Moei River resembled a bustling market town. French journalists André and Louis Boucaud visited during its heyday and described it in their book, *Burma's Golden Triangle*. There were Indian, Chinese, and Thai merchants, and each house was like a store: "stalls stocked with watches, alarm clocks, toothbrushes, toilet paper, cigarettes, radios, and cassette recorders. There was a hair salon, a movie theatre, cheap eating places, shoe stores, and an array of fruit and vegetables."

The brothers estimated that as many as 600 porters came through the gate each day, and on busy days as many as 1,000 men and 1,000 horses. The Boucauds described how porters were protected from bandits by the KNLA: "Each trader declared his goods, paid the taxes due, and received a receipt which acted as a pass for the other Karen checkpoints."

International aid agencies, including the UN, regard Burma as one of the poorest countries in the world, yet the generals spend at least forty percent of the national budget on the military; its only enemy is its own people. One three-minute piece of propaganda shown on Burmese television, picked up in Mae Sot, neatly illustrates this. A series of scenes shows soldiers storming beaches, ships firing shells at the coast, and jets blasting hillsides. As Burma has not been at war with any other country for sixty years, it can only be concluded that the military is attacking its own country.

Professor Desmond Ball, a military expert from the Australian Strategic Defence Studies Centre, has accused the regime of employing a special paramilitary unit to destroy the will of Karen villagers. Professor Ball told me, during a later visit to Canberra, "The 'Sa Sa Sa'—known as *Boung Bi Doh* or 'Short Pants'—are assassination squads. The closest equivalents I know of are the ones the Nazis used against Lithuanians and Ukrainians to wipe out villages."

The Sa Sa Sa comprises around 200 men divided into small units of four to six. They secretly roam particular regions torturing, killing, and burning villages. The other nickname given to them by terrified villagers is '*Shwit*,' the sound a knife makes when cutting through someone's throat.

"They worked directly for General Khin Nyunt [Burma's former prime minister and head of Military Intelligence], by-passing normal regional command structure," said Professor Ball. "They started operating about 1999 and they're real, very real . . . the nastiest . . . you really have to go back to the Nazis to find anything that compares. There's nothing, even in Africa or elsewhere, that is as evil."

According to a former Burmese army officer now living in Thailand, whom I spoke to, the Sa Sa Sa's objective is to terrorize. "They have been selected for their cruelty. When they enter a village they immediately kill. They cut off heads and stick them on poles. The villagers are herded under the severed heads and told this is what will happen to them if they help the KNLA."

The Karen Human Rights Group, based in Mae Sot, reports the Sa Sa Sa's "self-stated purpose is to execute every villager . . . who has ever had any kind of contact with resistance forces. They have been carrying out this function brutally, shooting, stabbing, and often beheading their victims and dumping their bodies in the rivers."

I later interviewed a woman at Mae La refugee camp who added a grim reality missing from the reports about the Sa Sa Sa. She said that her older brother, Thint Soe, a retired KNLA soldier, had been brutally murdered in front of villagers from Htee Po Neh in Thaton district. "My brother had returned with his wife, Naw Thet Moo, from working their paddy. Soldiers stopped them just outside the village. They said as my brother was once a KNLA soldier he must now be a KNLA spy. They tied his hands behind his back. One of them took out a large knife and stuck it in his chest, cutting down to his stomach. They pulled out his still beating heart and said, 'This is the heart of Kawthoolei. Is it yours?' His wife fainted and died later from shock."

The stunned villagers realized the couple's two young daughters, aged five and seven, were at risk, and hid them until they could be smuggled to safety in Thailand. The aunt, whom I spoke with, said that it took more than two months for the girls and their minders to reach Thailand. "The journey was hard on the girls. They had to walk at night from village to village."

When I met the girls some weeks after their journey, their legs were still cut and scratched and their feet cracked. Their emotional scars were invisible. "Sometimes they cry and ask for their ma and pa," their aunt told me. "They didn't see their bodies, so they're confused. Noises make them jump. Many times they just sit in the corner and cry. It's lucky they have each other to love."

It is the perpetrators of crimes like these that the American major was determined to kill. His men appeared to have plenty of arms and ammunition, and I asked him during a break in target practice where his unit got their weapons. His response was coy, yet he couldn't resist the urge to talk, even if his answer was cryptic. "We're always struggling but we do have friends. Many people owe the Karen. Who do you think is in the front line fighting the war on drugs?"

An article in *The Nation* on August 1, 2002 reported that Burma's Military Intelligence (MI, now disbanded) had angrily accused Thai authorities of giving arms and ammunition left over from the annual Cobra Gold US-Thai joint military exercises to KNLA guerrillas. A Burmese colonel, San Pwint, claimed the weapons (worth about 340,000 baht) were used to arm the Karen. I wondered if any of the guns and ammunition the major conned me into driving along the border came from Cobra Gold.

The major laughed when I suggested this. "Don't you worry yourself about any of that. More importantly, our generals are now giving us the best soldiers to train. We're comparable to any specialist unit in any country—and I mean *any* country. How many other units would train for sixteen hours a day and live like this," he said. "No disco, no R 'n' R, no pay, and two bowls of rice a day. Their camaraderie is high. This is their only family."

As we were talking, a young boy brought us cups of coffee, this time without the sweet creamy hit of condensed milk.

"Meet Chati," the major said, dragging the boy towards us. His army shirt fell down to his scuffed knees. He wore a pair of worn-down green flip-flops. I shook the boy's hand and indicated that he should sit. He looked at the major for his okay.

A shy Chati told me he was thirteen and wanted to be a soldier when he was old enough. The major interrupted to say this was like a summer camp and the younger boys wouldn't be allowed to join the KNLA until they were eighteen.

Chati preferred being here than at school. "I like shooting best," he said. "I live with my ma and pa at a refugee camp. Pa is in jail for taking wood from the forest. I miss him. I hate the SPDC for making us leave our village and live in a camp."

Chati was only thirteen and yet here he was talking about joining the army so he could take revenge. I asked him if he liked to play football, as I knew most Thai, Karen, and Burmese boys his age are mad about the game.

"I like it. I play striker in my school team. I've seen it on TV. I want to have real football shoes and a ball."

I asked Chati what he would prefer: a ball or a gun?

His reply was quick. "A ball."

But I knew that football would not satisfy Chati's need for revenge, and once he'd tired of that, he would be back looking for a gun.

Many of the soldiers in the camp had bullet wounds, horrendous scars, and some, like Sergeant Saw Ge, were missing a limb or two.

The sergeant had his leg blown off by a Burmese mine and now taught the recruits to defuse or arm mines, make pipe bombs, or plan an ambush.

As we sat on his platform, the sergeant slowly turned over a small section of blue plastic pipe with protruding wires and quietly explained how different devices work. "Mines slow them up. It will blow off a foot or break a leg of one soldier, but its real value is that it takes another three to look after him. It's a psychological weapon—they never know what's coming next."

Sergeant Saw Ge wrapped the pipe in a dirty plastic bag and placed it in a scruffy cardboard box. He placed a number of other mines on the platform. He selected one about the size of a household electrical adaptor. "This will blow off legs and blind them," he said. He pointed to another. "This is Chinese made and packed with metal bits. We've killed about 35 Burmese using these."

What the sergeant didn't say is that land-mines and booby traps are uncontrollable. Weather and time make them unstable. They treat friend and foe alike. Limbs are ripped off, sending dirt, stones, bits of clothing, plastic, metal fragments, and bone further into the wound and other parts of the body. Later this causes deadly infections such as gangrene. All this is deliberately built into the design.

Sergeant Saw Ge pulled out the KNLA home-made version of the US-made claymore, a devastating ambush device that throws out as many as 700 steel balls in a tight killing arc. The KNLA's home-made version is slightly smaller than the genuine US device and doesn't have the words "Made in the US" (or the obvious "Front toward enemy") stamped on it.

Mines are used by the Burmese as an effective means to control the civilian population. As usual, the Burmese military have taken it a step further. Villagers who step on land-mines are fined up to 20,000 kyat for destroying army equipment.

Most of the men I spoke with agreed that they were more scared of land-mines than fighting the Burmese.

Later, at dinner, I asked the major whether his unit also used mines indiscriminately. He replied he did not have the resources to waste. "We pick our targets. We don't use them where villagers might walk or farm. We save them for ambushes and for protecting our camps. Often we put claymores out at night and bring them back in the morning. Our home-made mines have a limited life span. A couple of months of rain renders the batteries harmless."

Soldiers might be able to locate and defuse mines, but for villagers they are lethal. Unless the victim can cross into Thailand for medical help, they die slow, agonizing deaths from untreated wounds. Even if they find a Karen medic, the jungle conditions make surgery a painful option. Amputations have to be done without anaesthetic. Medics often do not have proper bone-cutting tools and have to make do with sharp knives or hacksaws.

It was time to leave the major's camp and head back to Mae Sot. I thanked him for his hospitality and he grabbed my hand and shook it and then pulled me into a smothering bear hug. He said I was welcome back anytime. I said goodbye to the soldiers and Lay walked me to the boat.

Halfway down the embankment, Lay stopped me under a tall tamarind tree and said, "The major's got a good heart, but you have to understand the Karen always think the white man is their younger, smarter brother coming home to help them. The major's not the only one. We've had French, New Zealanders, English, Israelis, South Africans. Some have died fighting with us and we thank them for it, but it's our fight and it's our people who are being killed. You foreigners can always go home, you have passports, but we can't. If you want to know about the Karen, talk to us, talk to our people. We'll try to help you. It will take time, but it will be worth it."

He said I could start by talking to Karen people looking after the 150,000 refugees in camps on the border. He said many more Karen villagers resisted the regime's orders in jungle hide-outs, and he could arrange for me to visit them. Lay said I could also visit an illegal, but Thai-government-tolerated clinic run by a Karen doctor, Cynthia Maung, where as many as 80,000 Karen and Burmese were treated each year.

Lay promised to contact me when he got back to Mae Sot. Meanwhile, he said he would talk with his friend, Tha Ko, to see if he would help me.

"Tha Ko is old, but very tough," he warned. "If he doesn't like you, he won't talk with you. Lie to him and he won't come back.

Don't make promises you can't keep. Upset him and he'll have you kicked off the border. I'll talk to him and see what I can do. Don't thank me, he will make you earn your stories."

I boarded the boat and we moved away from the Burmese shore. I saw a ragged group of displaced Karen villagers and their children staring from the shadows at me. They looked like jungle ghosts as they faded from sight. I saw them, but knew they were still invisible to my world. They didn't exist, and fell outside our social and moral responsibility.

Many more Karen will die or be condemned to a life of misery before the world and its media considers their plight more newsworthy than that of a footballer's groin strain, a soap star's sex life, a celebrity's plastic surgery, or the banality of reality TV.

When we reached Thailand, I decided I was involved and I would try to report what I witnessed.

4 Caught In The Crossfire

When I got back to the Mae Sot guesthouse, I swung between feeling excited and deflated. I put my mood down to tiredness, the heat, and a need for another adrenalin hit. I had a 'shower,' scooping bowls of water from a big black plastic garbage bin, to remove the layers of red dust from my hair and skin. It took almost as long to swill away the gritty dirt from the cracked tiles on the bathroom floor afterwards.

Clean but already sweating from the heat, I went to the near-empty restaurant for cold water and food. A waiter handed me a menu and a glass of iced water. Ceiling fans turned but fought a losing battle. Mosquitoes bit at exposed flesh, leaving me swatting but always too late.

I ordered *gaeng ped gai* (red chicken curry) minus the small green chillies referred to as bird chillies in polite company, but known generally as 'rat shit' chillies, and looked through my notebook at plans and a list of potential stories. The red curry arrived, thick and creamy, and as I ate I put Dr. Cynthia Maung's Mae Tao Clinic next on my list of places to visit. Dr. Cynthia had received a bag of humanitarian awards for her work, including

Asia's equivalent of the Nobel Peace Prize, the Magsaysay Award. Locals and supporters boasted that she was the 'Mother Teresa of Burma.' Backgrounding her had not been difficult, as her media profile was high.

I finished my meal and returned to the room that I shared with cockroaches, geckos, and blood-fattened mosquitoes. It was a long hot night. The ceiling fan clunked but didn't provide any relief. An iced bottle of water soon warmed to room temperature, leaving a pool of condensation on the floor. The dry heat sucked all moisture from the air. For most of the night I hovered between sleep and a lethargic stupor.

Before sunrise, staff banging pots in the kitchen downstairs woke me. I trudged to the cubicle bathroom, where at least the water felt cold and sharp as I doused myself awake.

Slightly refreshed, I walked to the market, had a cup of café *bolan* and fried dough sticks slick with condensed milk. Despite the thick coffee, I still felt sluggish and wanted more sleep. Instead, I walked back to use the guesthouse telephone to call the clinic.

A young woman answered, and when I asked for Dr. Cynthia, she giggled and hung up. This happened time and time again until I was close to throwing the phone against the wall. I decided, in the end, to walk to the clinic, and asked one of the hovering waiters for directions. He said it was too far and too hot for walking. It would be better to hire a motorbike. But I still thought I could walk, and set off in the direction he pointed. By the look of amusement on his face, I felt I was about to do something stupid. It wasn't yet 8:00 a.m., but the sun had already cooked the road soft.

Scabby dogs lay on the edges of the road too hot to move. Some shuffled from one shaded spot to the next without finding relief. Morning vendors slowly turned their carts out of the sun and prepared to go home. After ten minutes I had left the town behind and was walking on a scorching strip of asphalt between dry rice paddies. Pulped toads, snakes, and flattened rats were part of the road surface. In the distance, grey smoke draped the Dawna Range. Like an impressionist painting, distant trees shimmered and blurred. The heat was unbearable.

The road fed into the Asia Highway—the future gateway to Burma, China, and India. Its promise had already generated a fair bit of fast money into Mae Sot as speculators gambled on Burma becoming trouble-free sometime in the future. A steady stream of vehicles sent dust and fumes in my direction. I passed a cluster of wooden houses, a petrol station, grilled chicken restaurant, and the airport before I realized I had gone too far. I was parched and considering going back to town when a motorcycle taxi stopped. The driver said something and nodded.

I said, "Dr. Cynthia's Clinic."

He grinned and indicated that I should climb on behind him, and in minutes we rode through the clinic's gates. I offered him money but he refused and waved me away with a smile.

The clinic was a cluster of rambling sheds fenced in by rusty barbed wire and a dusty track that no-doubt turned to mud when it rained. I asked an old man sitting on a low wall outside a large concrete house where could I find Dr. Cynthia. He shook my hand, offered me a sweet smelling jasmine flower, and replied in English that she was away for a week, but her office was inside the door behind him. I was told to find the thin man in a *longyi* (Burmese sarong) who spoke "English very good" and he would help me.

Inside the hallway, a scrawny man introduced himself in perfect, but overworked English as Maung Maung Tinn. He said he looked after foreign visitors. We entered the main room and I was instantly captivated by a young girl dancing to music blaring from a television. I stopped Maung Maung Tinn and we stood and watched her.

The girl was thirteen-year-old Naw Paw Thauk Kyar. Her long skirt billowed, caught in the air from a plastic fan. The music finished and she hopped to a pair of wooden crutches balanced awkwardly against a low bench. Before she could leave, Maung Maung Tinn introduced me to her and I asked if she would tell me her story.

Naw Paw had used crutches since a Burmese mine blew off her left leg four years before. She was nine at the time and was travelling with her mother to visit an aunt near the village of Pa Lu in the Karen State.

"We were living in the jungle," she said. "It was hot and I was hungry to drink. I was running to the river when I stepped on the mine. I lost consciousness. I heard the explosion but I can't remember feeling pain."

Naw Paw was taken to Dr. Cynthia's clinic before she lost too much blood. Her young face was haunted with the memory. "When I first lost my leg, I cried a lot. I'm used to it now, but I still miss not being able to play with my friends all the time."

Naw Paw said she got upset when she saw her friends running around and she could only stand by and watch them. "When I can't join in, I get cross. It's not fair. I watched my friends skipping and I wanted to do it. I practiced on my own for a long time. Now I can and I'm good enough to join in with the others. It hurts, but I don't care. I want to play, so I have to put up with it."

When the blood-spattered Naw Paw was first carried into Mae Tao Clinic, the Karen medics who treated her were amazed at her bravery. "She was very small," Maung Maung Tinn said. "We used to carry her everywhere. I've seen her do many things in spite of her pain. She plays football, skips, and tries to run. She's not only brave, she's kind and cares for the little kids at the school. She didn't have her mother to look after her—she only managed to come once or twice to see her daughter. Naw Paw cried a lot and still does."

Naw Paw's mother disappeared after her daughter's accident, but had apparently recently resurfaced, remarried, and moved to Bangkok. "I miss my ma. I cry when I think about her," Naw Paw said.

Our conversation was interrupted by the arrival of a *songtaew* (pick-up truck 'bus') to take Naw Paw and some of the other kids to their school on the other side of the Asia Highway. We agreed to continue our talk at the school during the lunch break.

Maung Maung Tinn said he would introduce me to some people he thought I'd be interested in talking to. We walked to a long building with a hand-scrawled sign above the door that read "Emergency & Trauma Ward." I was introduced to a young Australian doctor, Rebecca Foxton, and Karen senior medic, Law Gwa, who managed the ward and had cared for Naw Paw. I got their permission to hang around to see how they worked.

The trauma ward was a breeze-block construction on a bare concrete floor. Its tin roof caught the fierce summer heat, and it leaked in the wet season. Flies and insects buzzed through the glass-less windows. Beds were roughly built wooden platforms without mattresses or sheets, covered in lino for easy washing.

A list of ailments written on a whiteboard nailed to the bare wall told the daily story. Today it included kneebone destruction from a mine injury; forearm medial damage from a gunshot; another gunshot to the face; burns to a baby's face and head; abscesses from a land-mine injury; foot injuries.

Law Gwa, wearing a soccer shirt, sarong, and white gloves mopped up fresh blood and threw wads of ointment-stained gauze into a bin. Rebecca moved through the ward barefoot. Plastic bags held the patients' few belongings. Men and women sat cross-legged on the beds, talking quietly. A mother fanned her sleeping baby and a young man shook and bit his lip as a medic tried to inject him with a local anaesthetic.

Rebecca stopped next to a small woman and her baby. She removed a large pus-soaked plaster from the crying infant's head. The mother put the baby on her milk-swollen breast and the silence was immediate. Rebecca cleaned the baby's wounds, explaining to the mother through a medic interpreter to cut the baby's nails and keep the sores clean by using boiled water.

"The baby was only 26 days old when she was burned," she said. "The mother left her for a minute and a candle fell on her head. It's hard to stop it getting infected with all the flies." Rebecca was worried the mother would have difficulty caring for herself and the baby.

"I want her to stay at the clinic—she has breast abscesses that worry me. We need to watch her and the baby until they're both healed."

The mother shook her head and said she had to go back to Burma.

"If she goes, she'll see her traditional healer, and if that happens anything from cow dung to tree fungus will be put on the burns. We've had some horrific infections from wounds treated like that."

Rebecca lost the argument with the young woman, but struck a bargain that she would promise to return to the clinic in two days.

Soon, a small group was half-carried in from the cramped back of a pick-up—father, mother, aunt, and two small daughters. Their appalling injuries were caused when the father stepped on a mine.

Blood trailed the family into the clinic. Inside, two fans chopped at the hot air and bandaged patients stared as the medics lay the wounded on beds and assessed them while I watched.

"He's lost one foot, but will probably end up losing both," said Rebecca. "His wife got metal fragments in her abdomen and chest and has internal bleeding. Her sister has a piece of metal resting on her heart, causing blood to collect around her lungs. One of the daughters' fingers is blown off, and the five-year-old got metal through her femur, shattering it."

Rebecca already looked tired. Looking around the ward, it was hard to imagine her last job in an orthopaedic surgery in a fashionable suburb of Melbourne. After watching her treat bullet wounds, land-mine victims, sex abuse cases, and horrific infections from untreated sores, I was interested in why a young woman like her, who, on the surface appeared to have it all—she had played international water polo for Australia and had a promising career—would give up everything to volunteer here.

She said her friends thought she was ruining her career when she told them. "Out here I earn about 430 dollars a month [from an Australian aid agency]. Back home I'd get twice that in half a day, and we had the best resources money could buy." She said she planned to stay another year.

The clinic is cash strapped; even basic necessities like sterilized bottles and medical handbooks are regarded as luxuries. Instead, plastic bottles are recycled and used to store saline solution, and Rebecca made her own wooden footstools for leg injuries. Many simple medical procedures taken for granted in Western countries are too expensive for people who are barely managing to survive. But despite the meagre resources and makeshift facilities, people are grateful for the clinic.

"Most of the people who come here have no money. If I do an operation on someone, the word gets out, and the next day I'll have another ten turn up."

But Rebecca said she was no saint, and that many of the young Karen medics who worked with her were the ones who deserved praise for risking reprisals from the Burmese military.

"Many of the staff had to flee here for their own safety. They don't even know if their families in Burma are still alive. By working at the clinic, they endanger their families. We've had visits from spies—you never really know who you're dealing with. Somebody came into the clinic and attached a grenade to a window and the pin to a door handle so it would explode when the door opened. Luckily one of the patients saw a suspicious looking person and reported it. They found the grenade before anyone was hurt, but it was a close call."

Rebecca admitted there were times she missed the normality of life in Australia: "Sometimes I just don't want to see any more land-mine victims or people who are under constant oppression. I miss little things like being able to get in my car and go someplace without having to think of the ramifications.

"Sometimes I get pissed off with the lack of resources, but the problem's mine—my expectations are too high. You accumulate months and months of kids crying, being covered in blood, and trying desperately to save dying babies. At the end of the day, you have to know when you've had enough. Working here can be heart-wrenching, but I have to rely on using what resources I have to do the best I can."

At the school, Naw Paw sat in the patchy shade of a scrubby tree with her friend Hla Chit's head in her lap. Younger children clustered around, playing with her crutches, braiding her hair, or teasing her about boys. She blushed but laughed deep at one boy's cheekiness.

Naw Paw said she couldn't wait for the day when she could have an artificial leg fitted. "But it's cheap to buy shoes now. I only need one," she joked.

Nothing moved unless it had to in the noon heat. The sun-bleached patch of bumpy dirt and rocks where Naw Paw and the other kids played football would remain empty until late afternoon when it would be marginally cooler.

Naw Paw said that sometimes her friends still made her cry. "They make jokes about my leg or the way I run. I know they don't mean to hurt me, but I still cry."

Not surprisingly, Naw Paw wore a long skirt that hid the thick angry welts of scar tissue visible on her good leg. But it wasn't sympathy that this brave thirteen-year-old wanted.

"I'm normal. I can ride a bike. I can draw. But dancing is my favourite, and I do it very well," she said with a proud smile.

In spite of all the pain, taunts from other kids, and not being with her mother and brothers, Naw Paw was hopeful for her future. And she said she was luckier than most people at the clinic.

"I've seen people with much worse injuries than mine. Even babies die. I'm lucky, I get plenty of love and I've people around me who encourage me to keep studying. One day, I too will be a medic and help people like I was helped."

5 Borderline Stories

Captain Lay had not been in contact for some time and I was beginning to think he had forgotten about his promise to put me in touch with Tha Ko. To learn more about the Karen I was borrowing books and searching the Internet. I followed street kids as they rummaged through garbage trying to find enough plastic and cardboard to sell to recyclers. I wandered through the busy gem market, making contacts and trying to understand how it worked. I rode a bicycle to the river and watched smugglers bring over teak, giant prawns, and people.

Border towns have a restless edge, and Mae Sot is no exception. It is not unusual to see armoured personnel carriers moving troops through the crowded streets to border checkpoints. Dark-green helicopters hover overhead. Pick-up trucks with tinted windows hide drivers and passengers from scrutiny. Overloaded trucks bump axles against concrete as they rumble to illegal border crossings.

Rumours circulate about well-dressed embassy-connected men and women asking questions of local aid workers in café corners. Their large notepads, hushed voices, and furtive glances draw nothing but attention.

Nervous-looking backpackers trudge into town clutching their Lonely Planets. Sandal-footed aid workers ride their Chinese bicycles to collectively approved restaurants and bars for French fries, chicken burgers, pizza, and Heineken beer. Bored NGO officials, in their air-conditioned pallor, four-wheel-drive their way to account-paid dinners and listen yet again to monologue proposals from jaded field staff.

Dodgy looking adventurers slide around town looking for a way in and a fight—an easy way to pick up combat experience and, hopefully, a paid ticket to the next trouble spot. North American Christians loudly babble about putting up with insects, disease, uncomfortable beds, spicy-hot food, and never-on-time Karen leaders while battling to do God's work.

Academics on paid leave hustle for 'victim' interviews to add substance to their theses. On-the-make freelance photographers and journalists chase easy-to-sell stories of boy rebels with guns or doctor heroes. Gangs of ragged Muslim kids scavenge their way through the town's garbage, fighting rivals for café scraps.

One of the street kids I got to know was Mau Mye. He was eleven and hunted for anything he could resell; bottles, plastic bags, tins, paper, cardboard, and fabric were treasures to his experienced eye. He was one of the forgotten children of Burma. His story is common and thus considered not worth telling.

Mau Mye couldn't remember his mother, but he knew she was dead. His memories of his father were vivid but he didn't like to spend time on them, as he witnessed him being killed. The boy was only three when this happened. Mau Mye lived in a temple, but the monks still didn't know where he came from. He had grown to be bright, cheeky, and constantly on the lookout for something free.

At the Mae Sot dump, the child scavengers have to confront mountains of unstable, rotten garbage that attracts rats, which in turn attract deadly snakes. These are not the only dangers: others lie just beneath the surface of the festering refuse. Early one morning, Mau Mye was working the dump when the surface gave way under his bare feet. He sank up to his knees into smouldering coals, hot ash, melted plastic, charcoal, and hot metal. He suffered third-degree burns. Somehow he managed to get back to the temple, where the monks treated his legs with home remedies. But the burns were too deep and needed immediate medical attention. The monks took him to Dr. Cynthia's clinic. His grafted skin would never be the same again, but after eight weeks of pain, Mau Mye was back at work.

Mau Mye's story was only one of the many hundreds on the streets of Mae Sot. 'Little Legs' was another. I never got to find out his real name. He was in his late twenties, but smaller than a six-year-old kid and usually drunk. He hustled the town market, holding out his handless stumps for coins. His tiny feetless legs were tucked into a green pair of kids Wellington boots. Usually I gave him a ten-baht coin, but one day I decided to buy him a takeaway container of fried noodles with chicken. When I handed it to him, he was outraged. He threw the box back at me and locked his arms around my knees and tried to head-butt me in the balls. I jumped and he butted. This went on until I managed to shake him off. Our bizarre dance crippled the vendors with laughter and I never did get to find out Little Legs' story.

Three miles from Mae Sot, the muddy Moei River, snaking its way around the Dawna Range, marks the Thai-Burma border. Crossing the river is a road span—ironically named the Friendship Bridge—linking a Thai riverside hamlet, Rim Moei, with the Burmese town of Myawaddy. During the rainy season the river doubles its size. It is muddy, deep, swift, and dangerous. In the dry season when the river is low and sluggish, people wade or swim across, stopping to catch their breath on mid-river sandbanks.

These shifting sandbanks are a no man's land, and thus home to black-market hawkers of fake bottles of Johnnie Walker and London Gin, and Marlboro and Camel cigarettes. Flimsy cardboard shelters are built in the tall river grass. Rickety stalls are set up. Chickens scratch in the dirt, and drunks and drug addicts lie or sit on the hot sand.

At night, Rim Moei belongs to antique thieves, drug runners, smugglers, and packs of half-wild dogs. An antique buyer I had met in a Mae Sot restaurant told me that smuggling and trading was finished before sunrise, so one morning I set my alarm for 4:00 a.m. and set out for the river. I made sure to take a rattan stick, as

I wasn't willing to go up against the dogs unarmed. By the time I got to the river, my eyes were like saucers.

At Rim Moei, small boats from Burma slipped silently up against the riverbank, and groups of men hustled for the chance to unload their cargoes of furniture and bric-a-brac. Most of it was old and worn—remnants from the colonial past, remembered warmly by the threadbare Burmese upper and middle classes. Burma's dire economic situation has driven the once wealthy to sell their household contents. Well-dressed buyers from Chiang Mai and Bangkok ran appreciative fingers over the pieces before haggling.

Burmese temples are also ransacked, their religious artefacts hacked from ancient walls to fill orders from Europe and the US. The big city dealers became animated and territorial at the arrival of Buddhist icons. Their selections were wrapped and loaded into four-wheel-drive vehicles.

As the buyers drove to Mae Sot in search of breakfast, saffron-robed monks on their alms round broke the early morning grey. Steel roller doors were wound back to reveal cafés and restaurants. Gas-fuelled fires were lit by barely awake under-aged Karen girls. Huge pots of water for noodle soup and café *bolan* were brought to the boil.

I hopped on a ten-baht *songtaew* back into town, on the way passing warehouses filled with more Burmese antiques; unfinished four-storey buildings, built on spec; army units; the airport; and Dr. Cynthia's clinic. The *songtaew* was overflowing with people and stopped whenever passengers indicated. It finished its run behind Mae Sot's bustling market, just rousing itself for another day's trade.

Inside the *khao tom* shop, a small dark man gulped mouthfuls of rice and fish stock. His long black hair, flecked with grey, covered his weathered face. He could have been in his early forties, but when shadows closed down the light in his eyes, he looked older. The man's name was Sein (pronounced 'Sin'), and he had eagerly agreed to take me on a tour of the alleys and gem-cutting workshops around Mae Sot's main market.

Sein spotted me entering the shop, jumped to his feet, and rubbed his right hand clean on his shirt before shaking mine. His face rearranged itself into a huge grin. His checked shirt had been ironed but was at least twice his size. His shoes were too big and made him shuffle. Sein had all the attributes, except dishonesty, to have played Dustin Hoffman's scuzzy character Ratso Rizzo in *Midnight Cowboy*—always hustling for an opportunity but never missing the chance to help out someone worse off. During my months in Mae Sot, I had often seen him give what little he had to beggars or single mothers down on their luck, or, at risk to himself, advise stuck-up Westerners against getting ripped off at the gem market, where he operated as a bottom feeder, picking up small sales commissions on jade, rubies, sapphires, and synthetic fakes. Some days he made 100 baht, some days 1,000, others nothing.

It was a far cry from his youth. As a self-confessed wild young man in Rangoon in the 1970s, Sein upset his wealthy Sri Lankan family by getting into gang fights. Eventually, trouble led him to the border jungles where he joined and fought with ethnic armies until he was captured, accused of bomb making, and jailed for three years.

Sein had never asked me for anything other than a chat and a cup of sweet coffee, even when the gem market was slow and he was broke and hungry. He also understood that I know as much about gems as I do about smashed glass. He had indulged me in the past, taking the time to show me around the back alleys and introduce me to Muslim traders who had reached Mae Sot with their precious caches of hidden gems. Burmese miners who find stones worth more than 50,000 kyat are required to inform and sell the stones to the government. Many don't, preferring to risk smuggling them to Thailand, as they know the Burmese government will cheat them.

Sein finished his soup and we walked through the packed market. I asked him how business was.

"No good. People are aungry, very aungry."

I asked if they were 'aungry' because they were not selling enough to buy food.

"No! Not haungry! Aungry!"

I soon worked out the traders weren't hungry but angry. I asked him why, thinking police bribes, border closures, but not expecting his answer.

"Aungry at you! You never buy, only take pictures and talk. You talk, talk all the time . . . makes them aungry."

I had assumed I enjoyed a tolerated, good-natured banter with the gem sellers. I never thought, until Sein told me, that I was driving them insane with my questions and camera. I enjoyed watching the hustle and bustle as shoals of traders scurried from one potential customer to the next. I was curious how the deals were done, and was also interested to spot and maybe interview Burmese army officers who had come to town to offload ill-gotten treasure.

Sein stopped at a stall to say hello to his friend Rashid, a successful ruby trader from Mogok, home of the famous Burmese ruby mines. Over a cup of coffee, Rashid told me about high-priced rubies and sapphires he brought from Mogok to Moulmein and then on to Mae Sot. Rashid was originally from Nepal and said it was not unusual to see Indians, Chinese, Nepalese, and Westerners in Mogok buying gemstones.

"The best rubies in the world come from Mogok. The mines are hundreds of years old. Some are two kilometres deep and very cold. Men, women, and children from all over Burma work there. It's a big gamble. Some work for a boss, some get paid a share or a commission. But most just get sick."

Jade is the other sought-after precious stone making its way to Mae Sot. Burmese jade comes from the Kachin State, where Chinese mine owners and the Burmese military have dug out an entire mountain, shifted the course of rivers, and deforested the area in their lust for the 'heavenly stone.'

Today, Sein had offered to take me to a woman jade seller whose father had just arrived in Mae Sot from the Kachin State. We left the Thai section of the market, passing timber yards with their worn, but neat stacks of recycled hardwoods. In the Muslim quarter, street kids sold their scavenged waste, teahouse vendors piled hot nan bread into cloths, hot crusty samosas sizzled, and stacks of deep-fried sugar-coated pastries attracted small boys and flies. We passed a row of one-roomed houses. A man, his head and shoulders hidden beneath the huge span of a buffalo ribcage, still dotted with pink flesh, walked out of a doorway to an open-backed truck. He tossed the carcass in and returned for another.

I followed him in and asked Sein to ask him if it would be okay for me to take pictures. The two talked and laughed. I assumed that Sein had explained that I was stupid, but harmless.

Inside, the scene was bled of colour except red and black. Two men squatted on their haunches and, with long knives, sliced flesh from a heaped pile of thick bones. A single light bulb illuminated the room. One of the men smoked as he butchered. The floor was sticky with blood and offal. The stench left me gagging. As my eyes adjusted to the light, I made out the remains of the carcasses: four jawbones, the teeth still intact; four sets of buffalo horns; ribcages; and legs and hoofs. My sandals sticky with blood, I beat down an impulse to turn and run.

The men said that they usually slaughtered the buffaloes after midnight and worked through the night butchering before market. Most of the meat and bones ended up in the hundreds of bubbling Mae Sot soup pots. I thanked the men for talking and we left. Back outside, the hot, stifling air felt clean and fresh.

We took a short cut through a piss-stinking alleyway and stopped outside a shophouse, where Sein pulled open a sliding gate. He knocked on an open door and a grinning Burmese-Indian woman hurried from inside to greet us. Taking off our shoes, we entered a single room divided in two by a plastic curtain. Sein introduced Idress, 35, his wife Kaima, 35, and her father, Omar, 67. We sat on the floor and a young boy quickly fetched a big bottle of warm Coke and a bag of smashed ice.

Idress's family came to Mae Sot from Mandalay, where Omar had a gem business. He said his wife sold the stones while he looked after the babies. Kaima gave a cheeky smile and said their youngest baby was one week old. "I will go back to work today. It's hard if I'm not working."

Getting their precious cargo through all the different checkpoints coming out of Burma was difficult. "Everyone wants money," Sein complained. "If they see the gems, we have to pay or they just steal them."

Many of the stones passing through Mae Sot are worth millions according to Kaima, but she and most of the women selling them in Mae Sot would never get their hands on money that big.

"The good stones go straight to Bangkok. They're usually red-star or blue-star rubies, and good jade. They're sold in one of the big broker's houses. They never make it to the street. The commission on good stones is worth a lot, more than enough to start up your own business."

Idress said that smuggled gems are usually sewn into hidden pockets in clothing, secreted in the anus, or are swallowed. But smugglers know the Burmese are always suspicious.

"They shove a long thin stick up our arse, and if the tip hits something, they force us to shit it out. Thai police make us drink laxatives."

A senior surgeon at Mae Sot Hospital later told me that some of the swallowed stones are so big, the couriers have trouble passing them. Operating on smugglers to remove gems had become a weekly chore for him. He said anxious buyers who sponsored the stones paced up and down outside the theatre like expectant fathers waiting for their first child to arrive safely. He said he had done so many operations like this, he had enough to fill a medical encyclopaedia.

The small group exchanged animated gossip about the recent murder of a woman gem seller. They said she had come from Mogok to Mae Sot with top quality rubies worth about 750,000 baht.

"One piece was worth 100,000 to 200,000 baht," said Kaima. "She was a big . . . fat . . . it would be hard to kill her. She was garrotted with a steel wire."

"She was also stabbed," added Sein, making a two-handed jabbing motion beneath his heart.

Kaima suspected that the woman's boyfriend and his Mae Sot cronies had killed her. "She had one husband in Mogok and another in Mae Sot. Her Mae Sot boyfriend has disappeared. He's Burmese and has probably gone back to Burma with the stones."

But Sein thought the killing was the work of Mae Sot's Burmese mafia. Either story could have been true, but like so much else in Mae Sot, it would never be known what really happened

Omar shifted the conversation back to his gems, sensing that it was worth a try to get me to look at some jade he wanted to sell while I was still captive on his floor. Out of his shirt pocket he took some small plastic bags containing lumpy folded scraps of white paper. Unsealing the bags, he opened the papers to reveal polished pieces of jade. Some were light apple green, some dark racing green. He placed the pieces in my palm and pushed me into a splash of sunlight falling through the open door.

"Jade is the stone of emperors. Never buy unless you've looked at it in sunlight. If it's milky or cloudy, it's not so good. If it's cracked, it's no good. If it's too black, it's no good. The colour has to be clean. The Chinese value the lighter green, but the colour has to go deep. Jadeite also comes in different colours—white, pink, and white with gold."

Omar's animated pitch and the prospect of a sale attracted some bored neighbours. He handed me the rest of the stones. I tried to decline, saying, "I'm only looking," but the small crowd just laughed. I held a couple of the pieces up to the light. Again I said I wasn't interested in buying, but Omar was just getting into stride.

"Never mind, never mind. Present price for you. Now, last price you give me?"

He brushed aside my excuses and told me of the jade's quality, the hardship of smuggling, his daughter's new baby, and his heart problems in need of urgent medical attention. The expanding crowd looked at me in anticipation, their heads flicking to Omar and back to me. I decided to offer a ridiculously low price of 600 baht.

Omar shook his head and smiled before saying the pieces were worth at least 5,000. "No joking, Mr. Phil, your best price, never mind, how much?"

I upped my bid to 800 baht. Omar ignored it and said again how much. Then the haggling stopped while he talked to Sein. I speculated they were discussing either Sein's commission, or if I was likely to buy at all. I suspected a combination of both. Sein asked me to make my final price. I offered 1,000 baht, and before the words faded, Omar had wrapped the stones and placed them in my hand.

I handed over a 1,000-baht note, realizing I'd bought jade I didn't want. Naturally, I said to Sein to ask Omar if the pieces were real—at which Omar unleashed a torrent of theatrical abuse, lambasting Sein for his insolence. Obviously all part of the act.

I pocketed my stones and we left before Omar, now talking about rubies and sapphires and his mother-in-law's operation, could cajole more money out of me.

Mae Sot sometimes felt like a citizen's nightmare, a town of rumours and paranoia. Strangers were watched and whispered about. Most guesthouses, especially those frequented by Westerners and aid workers, had at least one waiter or a couple of regular customers supposed to be informers for the SPDC. They were mostly teenagers. They had family back in Burma, and if the Burmese wanted information, all they had to do was threaten their families.

As Burma was obsessed with watching its citizens, it should be assumed it kept tabs on foreigners working for and with their enemies—Karen refugees and anti-Rangoon activists. Thai Intelligence also kept a watch on local activists, NGOs, and aid workers. A Thai military source told me that defectors from Burmese opposition groups spied for the regime.

It was all a reminder that I would have to be careful whom I confided in.

6 Divide And Rule

In late 2000, after a trip to settle my affairs in Australia, I moved permanently to Mae Sot, and my wife, Kanchana, a nurse and child health specialist, followed a few months later. She volunteered to work at Dr. Cynthia's clinic and we found a wooden house halfway between Mae Sot and the clinic. It was small but suited our needs, and Kanchana worked on the garden, planting orchids, jasmine, herbs, and mango, banana, and frangipani trees.

Over the following weeks I visited various Karen organizations, and I was just entering the Karen Refugee Committee compound one afternoon when an older man pulled me aside and introduced himself as Tha Ko.

Here, at last, was the man Lay had spoken of with great respect. Tha Ko could have been anything: a senior army officer, professor, villager, shopkeeper. He looked strong and fit and younger than his 69 years. He wore thick-framed glasses, a tweed jacket, open-necked shirt, and a quick smile. As he pulled me aside he asked for my phone number and address. He spoke excellent English. He said Lay told him I wanted to know more about the Karen's struggle.

His next question took me by surprise. "What can you do for the Karen?"

I explained there wasn't much I could do to help, but I did want to write about their situation.

"Then why should I help you?" he growled. "Will your stories put rice on the table for our people? Can they end this conflict?"

I said I couldn't do any of that, but I wanted to understand what the Karen resistance was all about.

"It's simple," he said. "It's about suffering. We Karen are quiet people. Make no mistake, we have our bad people. We're not saints. But we're good at suffering. You could say we have perfected it. Others, like the Burmans, make lots of noise and get attention. The Karen remain silent. It's always been our way. We like to suffer, but keeping silent does us no good."

As he walked outside Tha Ko said he would be in touch. A beefy, scar-faced, one-armed man joined him, and Tha Ko nodded in my direction and said something, at which they both laughed. They got into a battered white pick-up truck that his companion drove away.

I asked the people I was visiting what they knew about Tha Ko. They said he was tough, abrasive, straight talking, smart, and worked hard for his people. As Tha Ko had so succinctly pointed out, my reasons for being in Mae Sot sounded weak. Even I could see why the two men laughed.

Months later I had my second encounter with Tha Ko. As I was sitting in my study clipping Burma-related articles from a pile of sun-yellowed newspapers, a pick-up truck pulled up outside. Tha Ko got out and looked around, uncertain if he was at the right house. He called my name and I went out to greet him. Kicking his sandals off, he began to sit down on the verandah bench, but I waved him inside where it was cooler. I pushed a cushion towards him, but he ignored it and sat on the wooden floor. We made small talk about Australia, international politics, and sport. He told me he hadn't seen his wife or children for nine years and that he spoke five or six languages fluently, including Chinese.

I already knew from experience that Tha Ko didn't suffer fools, and this included his own leaders. He was opinionated, but had earned the right to be. He was well informed, and it was no surprise to hear that reading was his passion.

"As a refugee, I have little or no money and few books here. More than twenty years ago an Englishman gave me a set of encyclopaedias. They're good, but old. I'm up to 'L'."

My wooden shelf groaned under stacks of books I had bought in Chiang Mai or Bangkok. I offered to make tea as Tha Ko went to the bathroom.

"How many people live here?" he asked when he returned.

I replied two and asked why?

"You have many shampoos and soaps. What do you use them all for?"

Our bathroom wasn't excessively stocked, I thought. But to a Karen who managed to do everything with one bar of soap, it looked like a supermarket. It was another reminder that, living in Mae Sot, I was constantly caught between parallel worlds of haves and have-nots.

Tha Ko admired our garden and said the Karen State was all fertile land. Our house was at the end of a small *soi* (lane) that backed onto a huge rice paddy that had lain fallow for a number of years. It had become home to a wide variety of snakes that now slithered through our garden to escape the machetes of farm workers preparing the field for the next planting season. The farmers had killed a couple of nine-footers and, since I had photographed the dead reptiles, they figured every snake they killed should be kept for me. They left them either curled in terracotta pots or hanging off the gate, almost causing heart attacks in me or our guests.

"Burma was once the rice basket of Asia," Tha Ko said. "The British made a fortune from our resources. Now, the military's madness has made land-mines and death our only crop. But they know how rich Karen lands are. Getting their trucks through the forests and mountains is a problem. There are no roads or bridges. But if they could, they would."

With great eloquence, Tha Ko explained how the generals do "dirty" business with warlords and Chinese businessmen. "They've carved Burma up. This one takes gems, this one drugs, this one sex, and this one timber. They work directly with profiteers—they call them 'national entrepreneurs'—well-connected people given special privileges. They don't pay tax or duty on imported equipment for logging and building. They get subsidized fuel. Their profit is from misery. They turn their dirty money into hotels, factories, fishing boats, and casinos fuelled with the sweat of the people."

Tha Ko was not describing some fantasy about an imaginary evil empire. It's Burma in the year now, a country with the second largest army in Southeast Asia and the second worst health record out of 192 countries according to the World Health Organization (Sierra Leone holds bottom spot).

"The generals are good at dividing people. They've signed cease-fire agreements with some ethnic groups in return for drug, logging, or mining concessions. But these agreements give their people nothing—only the leaders profit. The Burmese control them and use them as militias to in-fight and divide ethnic groups. These generals are evil—they're experts only in poverty and disease."

The US, UK, the EU, and the UN have all slammed the generals. Notable individuals like the Dalai Lama have urged the regime to stop the atrocities. But some countries are still happy to profit from working with Burma. Israel, Pakistan, China, North Korea, Singapore, and Germany have all, at some time in the last fifteen years, supplied weapons and intelligence used to hurt and kill Burmese people.

Despite Burma's pariah status and the diplomatic risks of flouting the arms and trade embargo imposed by Western democracies, there is an obvious economic motive. Ties with these nations gives Rangoon a sense of security and confidence that they can survive the sanctions.

I questioned Tha Ko about criticisms from NGOs that aid designated for Karen refugees is used to fund their war effort.

Tha Ko glared at me before answering. "Are you accusing the KNU of using the conflict for political and economic gain? What do we have to gain from watching our people living off hand-outs in camps? Some leaders have made money for themselves and their families from border trade. Like all people, we have those who are selfish, but many of our leaders earn just 2,000 baht a month, others nothing. Our people help our resistance. Some carry supplies or medicines, others are medics, and some are soldiers. We don't have choices. We can't live in our own country in peace and we don't have freedom in Thailand. Westerners come here and say they'll stop funding our schools, clinics, and refugee camps if we use their money to protect our people. What will that achieve? If some rice or medicine is skimmed off refugee supplies, where do you think it goes? We want the fighting to end. Foreign journalists like you come here and say our leaders are too old and corrupt. Who have you been talking to? Look at all the human rights reports on the Burmese [dictators] and ask yourself who is the cause of the suffering?"

Tha Ko fiddled with his teacup and stared through me. He sighed as if letting go of something difficult. "Who do you think controls UNICEF's [United Nations Children's Emergency Fund] immunization programme in Burma? Do they immunize children in ethnic areas? What about all the others [NGOs]? They're all controlled by the regime. Aren't they being used as a weapon? We don't ask you for much, but what you do give, you make us beg for it."

Tha Ko and I sipped at our tea and sweated. I couldn't help feeling a sense of hopelessness at how difficult and complicated the Karen's situation was. Tha Ko refused my offer of lunch.

"I'm a refugee. We only eat twice a day," he said, not missing a chance to make a point.

Understanding Burma's political situation is complex; understanding the ethnic diversity and the racial tensions even more so.

The official government map of Burma shows seven ethnic states: Chin, Shan, Kachin, Rakhine, Mon, Kayah, and Kayin (Karen). Tha Ko complained that the map has neatly pushed the Karen into the mountain regions on the Thai-Burma border.

"But many Karen live in the Irrawaddy Delta region and have done so since before the Burmans. This is a deliberate strategy to shrink our territory. Our Karen flag has nine rays, each one representing one of our divisions. Our people in the delta and upper Burma are persecuted. Our language is forbidden in schools, and Karen with government jobs are denied promotions.

Tha Ko pointed out that even though many Karen admire Aung San Suu Kyi, the confidential 'democracy talks' between her and the regime exclude ethnic groups, and there won't be a resolution to Burma's conflict if they are not included.

"There's no doubt Suu Kyi has a good heart and good intentions, but if democracy means majority rule, that is the Burmans and the NLD—it will be *their* democracy. If ethnic people don't get their rights, it will be more of the same."

Tha Ko said that, in spite of Aung San Suu Kyi's goodwill and opposition to the dictatorship, the NLD has a dark side. Before Burma could savour its independence victory, Aung San was assassinated by his political foes. Before his murder, he had tried to unite Burma but had indicated he was in favour of Karen autonomy. But for many Karen, a grim shadow hangs over Aung San's BIA that fought with the Japanese.

"There are current members of the NLD, ex-BIA soldiers, who are guilty of atrocities against Karen villagers during and after World War Two."

Tha Ko claimed the BIA were more brutal than the Japanese to the Karen. "They were trained by the Japanese on the Thai border. They then marched together to Rangoon, raping and looting as they went. They took Karen women as sex slaves. There is not one Karen family who escaped them.

"She's not our leader, but we regard Suu Kyi as a genuine and legitimate Burmese leader. We don't trust the people around her. We have to be very careful when we work with her, for she isn't walking alone. Some of the NLD and the SPDC have the same military backgrounds. These are the same men who fought and killed our people.

"The talks with Aung San Suu Kyi have been going on for more than fifteen years without any change for the Burmese people."

As the talks are always secret, with no publicized agenda, Tha Ko said they serve no purpose other than window-dressing to appease the international community.

"These generals learned well from the British to divide and rule. They started talks with some of our leaders while ignoring others. If we are not careful, they will split us."

Tha Ko accused the regime of having in place a political and institutional framework to keep control if and when the switch to democracy is eventually achieved.

"Their people run the police, all state institutions. They are cutting up the political and territorial cake and distributing it to their regional commanders. Everything looks like it has changed so they can keep everything the same."

I asked Tha Ko if the Karen would ever be able to put their differences with the Burmans aside.

"Our struggle started long before 1988. We have suffered much under this Burman 'master-race' syndrome. They expect us to forget and forgive, but for those who have been abused and violated, it is hard. Of course, for the perpetrators it will be easy to forget."

Tha Ko spoke with pride as he described the Karen's migration from Mongolia to Burma and their settlement of most of lower Burma and along the Thai border. "We have our history, our language, our culture, and our land. By nature we are quiet and peace loving. We try to be honest, moral, and work together whether we're animist, Buddhist, or Christian. We don't like fighting or arguments. If we have disputes we are likely to leave the village and settle somewhere else to avoid disharmony. There are many different groups of Karen, but most of us belong to either the Sgaw or the Pwo. I'm Sgaw. Most Pwo Karen are animists or Buddhists. But you'll find most of the Christians are Sgaws. Our schools taught Karen language and literature. We had plans for a Karen university, but this regime made it illegal to teach our language. Our struggle is for social justice and equal rights. If we get that, our fight is over."

Tha Ko paused to catch his breath, then leaned forward. "In 1969, the Burmese began their 'Four Cuts' (*Pya Ley Pya*) offensive against us. Their strategy was to stop community support to our resistance. Their aim was to cut off food, money, information, and recruitment. All contact with our army was illegal. Whole communities were relocated if they were found in military designated 'black zones.' Villagers caught in black zones were shot on sight. Homes, crops, and animals were stolen or destroyed. Villagers were used as porters or human shields to protect their soldiers.

"This scorched earth policy was meant to crush Karen villagers' support for the KNLA. People hid in the jungle. If they went to other villages to look for food, soldiers shot them. The army mined or sold Karen land to businessmen to log the timber. When they torture or kill, it's a message to other villagers—'help the KNU and this will happen to you'."

Reports by human rights groups such as Burma Issues document thousands of incidents of torture and abuse by the military. In just one, a Major Theung Kyi from Military Intelligence had a Karen villager stretched between two trees like a hammock. He was tied face down, his arms tied to one tree and his legs to another. The major forced villagers and soldiers to use him as a hammock. He died two days later. The man's two-year-old daughter was hung upside down by her legs and a fire lit under her. Another villager had a rope tied from his penis to around his neck, so that when he moved his head he would be in excruciating pain. When the soldiers tired of this, they spread and tied his legs to posts; his scrotum was tied with rubber straps and then set on fire. His penis and scrotum were burned off.

A Burmese army deserter I met later in Mae Sot told me torture was common. "We put plastic bags over people's heads and filled them with water, we cut people, pushed hot bamboo sticks down penises, cut off ears, and cut off fingers for rings."

Tha Ko said the Karen don't torture their enemies. "We kill them on the spot or let them go. But maybe that's because we can't afford to feed them," he joked.

Talking with Tha Ko was fascinating. He brought up topics at random, and then introduced another complexity—religion and political factionalism.

Religious differences were skilfully exploited by the Burmese in 1994, when approaches were made to dissatisfied Karen Buddhists who wanted a bigger share of Karen political and economic power mainly held by Christian leaders. About 1,000 Buddhist soldiers, encourgaed by a monk, U Thu Zana, deserted from the KNLA and formed the Democratic Karen Buddhist Army (DKBA). It was a masterstroke for Rangoon, and a body blow that temporarily crippled the KNU.

The deserters blamed Christian Karen leaders for discriminating against Karen Buddhists, but it is far more likely the Burmese took advantage of existing discord to divide the Karen. The Karen leadership's inability to counteract the generals' strategy of playing Christian against Buddhist, Karen against Karen, provided Rangoon with a crucial victory. It also set the scene for the Karen's greatest symbolic and military loss—the KNLA headquarters at Manerplaw on the Salween River.

Manerplaw was not only an important symbol of the Karen's resistance, but was one of the last pieces of fixed territory they held inside Burma. The headquarters was also a safe haven for Burmese opposition groups. Past attempts by the Burmese army to capture Manerplaw had failed, and they had lost thousands of soldiers in the process. The Buddhist deserters, with their knowledge of the secret jungle paths and surrounding minefields, led the Burmese army directly to victory.

I was later told by Professor Desmond Ball just how terrible a blow this had been: "It was not Burmese military supremacy that captured Manerplaw, but the treachery of the DKBA. They knew their way through the stronghold's defences. It was a devastating piece of bastardry on their behalf."

Today, the DKBA still does dirty work for its Burman masters. In early January 2004, DKBA soldiers from Battalion 999 forced villagers in Pa-an district from their homes and farms at gunpoint and used them as slaves to build roads. As it was harvest time, most of the villagers' rice crop was left to rot.

Tha Ko explained how the DKBA leadership is well rewarded for their loyalty to the Burmese with cars, drug trafficking and logging concessions, and a constant supply of arms to attack villagers under KNLA protection. He dismissed the DKBA as nothing more than traitorous bandits. "They have no political history, no political philosophy, no political agenda, and no political mandate. What do they stand for? It's certainly not for the Karen. They are like warlords, robbing, raping, and killing innocent villagers. They say they're Buddhist, but if that were true, they wouldn't kill. How can you have a Buddhist army? Buddha would be horrified."

Tha Ko explained that if discrimination was a problem, it was more about educated elites being in control of the KNU. "Christians are usually better educated because they get help from Western missionaries. Buddhists and animists do not have the same opportunity."

Today, former KNLA corporals and sergeants are DKBA colonels and generals. For them, it has paid off. But regardless of the rhetoric from both sides—grievances about religion, promotions, pay, new-gotten wealth, and nepotism—the only winners are the Burmese junta. The split made it easy for them to bluff the international media and community that the fighting is nothing more than an internal Karen tribal squabble.

Tha Ko stopped talking when he became aware my attention had wandered. I could hear loud snoring. It felt close and I asked Tha Ko if he heard it? He looked puzzled, but slowly he collapsed into laughter.

"It's Bo Gyi, my driver," he said, struggling to his feet. It was his signal to leave, and he shuffled his shoes on and said goodbye until our next meeting. Bo Gyi's head jerked forward as Tha Ko opened the passenger door of the pick-up.

Since the split, the Karen State has divided into zones controlled by either the DKBA or the KNU. To verify what Tha Ko had told me about the DKBA, I arranged an independent visit to a jungle hide-out inside the Karen State to meet medics staffing a small clinic. I talked with a number of villagers hiding there about the DKBA. An elderly woman stood on the edge of the small crowd that gathered to listen while I interviewed a land-mine victim, and when we finished talking and the crowd dispersed, she hung back.

She said her name was Naw Mu Haw ('Crying Girl'), and she had lived on the run for four years since Burmese and DKBA soldiers destroyed her village.

"I have to live like this whether I have dignity or not. I can't go back to my village. I have no money, no work, no fields. I miss my land. They took my cattle. I have nothing to sell and nothing to buy. They burned what little we had. Our only shield against them is the KNLA. The DKBA are mad. They don't care what they do. We used to eat together, live together, now we fight, Karen against Karen. If we continue to hate and kill each other, it will be difficult for us to come back together. There will be much pain and bitter tears between us."

On another trip to check the DKBA story, photojournalist Jack Picone and I drove north of Mae Sot to try to find evidence of

DKBA activity. About an hour out of town, we pulled in next to a Thai military post on the Moei River to stop for lunch. A couple of Karen men approached our table and, speaking English, asked us who we were and what we were doing. We told them we were tourists having a look around. They offered to take us upriver. As we were just across the river from the DKBA Special Forces 999 headquarters, I felt they had to be connected to the DKBA, and with some trepidation, we accepted their invite.

We passed several boats piled high with large bags of charcoal. Out of sight of the river, machine-driven saws screamed and churned through hardwood. Our guides told the boatman to pull in at a jetty near where a large group of men tumbled massive teak logs from boats onto the sandy beach. Standing guard, a stern-looking sergeant in DKBA uniform carried a sniper's rifle with scope. His badges marked him as a member of Special Forces 999. He smiled a welcome and in slow but passable English said his name was Soe. We made small talk and he told me his family had strong KNU ties, but he had decided to join the DKBA.

"My father is a KNLA officer and my brother works for the KNU," he said. "I joined the DKBA because I didn't want to live like a refugee. I wanted to live here in Kawthoolei, my homeland."

Soe wore his DKBA uniform with pride but said, "I don't want to fight my brothers, my father. I'm worried that one day we will be shooting at each other. It's wrong we're divided. I want the killing to stop. It's enough."

Our guides were keen to show us a sawmill and factory producing wooden furniture. We followed them away from the river towards the sound of machinery in a large wooden building crammed with carved doors, tables, and machined planks. Inside, uniformed men hovered over unprotected saws and planes, machining rough wood to finished product. One guide proudly showed us a photocopied furniture catalogue, in Thai, and said we could order anything we saw in it. In the background, Indian and Chinese businessmen did deals with a hard-faced Karen over a bottle of whiskey.

Outside, men struggled to load huge logs onto a truck. The guide said the truck was destined for China, as were the huge piles of logs stacked around the factory. The amount of activity and cut timber added credibilty to Tha Ko's claims about the spoils the DKBA had been given as a reward by regime.

By this time I had agreed to work on a book about the DKBA with Desmond Ball, so I needed to research and interview them. It would be risky and it could also have jeopardized the trust I had built with KNU/KNLA leaders and soldiers. After a series of on-off meetings, a Karen acquaintance with access to the DKBA made arrangements for me to interview Major General Maung Chit Htoo, the infamous leader of the DKBA's Special Forces 999 Battalion, who had featured in many human rights reports. I was anxious. On my past trips into Burma, the KNLA had provided the security to protect me against the people I was now planning to meet.

A car took us to a crossing on the Moei River, where a big long-tail boat waited at a jetty. I was tense from working the interview over in my head. The powerful V8 engine coughed and we moved away from Thailand only to stop at a sandbank six metres into the river. The boatman told us to walk the rest of the way over series of planks and sandbars to the other side. On the opposite bank, I could see an armed guardhouse. Burmese and DKBA flags fluttered on either side of the hut. I smiled as guards approached us. We were politely told to wait.

Bored teenagers and cheroot-smoking men stared openly at us to break the monotony of their day. In the distance, the sun bounced off an approaching four-wheel-drive as it came down an unsealed road. The vehicle stopped and the driver rolled his window down and ordered us inside. We drove in silence towards a large concrete house and a row of wooden huts. A translator for the DKBA told me it was the home and headquarters of Major General Maung Chit Htoo.

Groups of heavily armed soldiers in black or camouflage uniforms hung around the main house and its empty swimming pool. Black tattoos ran up their bare arms. We were ushered into a big room like a guesthouse reception area. Vinyl sofas and lounge chairs surrounded a glass table. Servants brought plates of spongy cakes and cans of Coke and Fanta. I asked for hot coffee, fumbled with my tape recorder, and silently re-read my prepared questions for Maung Chit Htoo.

He entered the room and introduced himself and his wife. He was younger and shorter than I expected. His rank, uniform, medals, expensive handgun, and jewelled fingers contrasted with his youthful appearance. The former KNLA sergeant was doing well. To be fair to him, KNLA soldiers I had talked to spoke highly of his battlefield skills and bravery. His welcome was cordial and I began with soft questions about his age and rank. He told me I was the first foreign journalist to interview him.

Slowly, I built my questions to where I put allegations of rape, illegal logging, tax gates, and drug trafficking to him. The alleged rape had happened while he was with the KNLA. The question didn't please him, and I had to keep at him as he evaded answering it.

The tension built as Maung Chit Htoo's eyes hardened. "It wasn't rape," he eventually responded. "It was a boy-girl problem."

I stared. Nobody drank or ate, and the tension remained.

"What do you mean 'boy-girl problem'?"

His wife chipped in and said she would also like to know. Maung Chit Htoo was proud of his wife and was not shy about promoting her prettiness. Photographs lined the wall showing her in DKBA uniform or brandishing an AK-47. Along her arm a thick scar disappeared into her blouse—the result of a recent assassination attempt on her family by the KNLA. The attack killed their young son and left Maung Chit Htoo with a score to settle.

Her question made Maung Chit Htoo angry and he looked everywhere except at me. I waited for him to fill the silence.

"You know!" he said.

"No I don't. Did you rape her?"

The tension drove the rest of the group to pick nails and stare into glasses. Finally he said, "I had sex, but didn't marry her. My commander accused me of rape, jailed me, and demoted me to private."

Maung Chit Htoo then made snide cracks about KNLA leader General Bo Mya. He said he was proud to be Karen and that his hero was the KNU's revolutionary leader Saw Ba U Gyi. He boasted that his picture of Saw Ba U Gyi was bigger and better than Bo Mya's.

Intrigued by this weird diversion, I asked to see it. He said it was in his bedroom. I said I would like to get a photograph of him with it, so our entourage trooped into the bedroom and there, hanging above the bed, with its stuffed toys and frilly pink bedcovers, hung a large framed picture of the revered KNU leader.

Maung Chit Htoo said, "I have more respect for Saw Ba U Gyi than I do for some of the present KNU leaders. It was them who caused our split. But I admire Bo Mya. We have similar backgrounds, except he was better off than me. I had only one year of study to his nine. I also still respect the KNU, but if they attack me I will fight to protect my area. Some villagers are with us and some are with the KNU. But they can't even collect leaves for their houses because of our mines."

I asked Maung Chit Htoo about the DKBA's involvment in the drug trade. He took his time to answer.

"I strongly oppose it, but we do have some bad people who deal in drugs and who rape, but I have made a policy to change this. Some DKBA leaders are not good. In the future we will get better."

Maung Chit Htoo admitted that he and his men made money from logging, cattle, taxing villagers, and smuggling cars. "We get support from the SPDC, they let us do business and use the roads for our bus services, boats, and tax gates."

For most of his 39 years, Maung Chit Htoo had been fighting: seventeen years with the KNLA and nine with the DKBA. I sensed he had had enough and would like an easier life.

"Yes, I want peace. I want to be a farmer. I have the same aim as the KNU: the unity of all Karen. I love our Karen flag. My aim is to see our freedom from the Burmans. Our problem is easy to fix—we have to stop fighting."

But I got the impression that the profits and power would be hard for Maung Chit Htoo to give up.

"The KNU say that if we are to be together, we have to return to them. But if we do that, we will be refugees, and if we fight the SPDC there will be a lot of dead Karen. But Bo Mya has said to us, 'you're with the SPDC, so you're the enemy.' This is the problem."

Maung Chit Htoo blamed the KNU and the foreign media for the DKBA's bad reputation. "Foreigners only report good from the KNU and bad from us. They never talk to us to find out our story. You are the first. I don't like it."

Maung Chit Htoo wanted a break and said he had organized for me to be given a tour that took in the hospital and school, and a stop for lunch. He said I would always be welcome at his camp.

After the tour, I crossed back over to Thailand. In Mae Sot, I met Tha Ko and told him about my trip. He said that because of individual ego battles between the Karen, the resistance had suffered and had at times degenerated into petty corruption and destructive power plays.

"It takes more than one piece of bamboo to build a house," he said. "If there's one man who can make all the Karen one, I will call him leader. Until then, we will not be the political force we could be."

7 Living In The Shadows

Nobody can accurately say what the population of Mae Sot is, but local officials joke there are 60,000 Thais and around 70,000 Burmese. Karen and Burmans outnumber Thais in the narrow walkways of the town's market. Take into account the 140 or so factories fuelled by Burmese sweat, and the population has to be closer to 250,000. This institutional blindness to the number of Burmese is deliberate. Thailand needs cheap labour, but is unwilling to publicly say so. This creates a grey zone where Burmese workers are never sure of their legal status. It makes them easy prey for corrupt officials wanting bribes, and bosses wanting labourers for factories and farms; it also ensures the workers remain passive and compliant.

But not all the Burmese are prepared to take it without fighting back. One day as I was walking around Mae Sot, I strolled through Wat Chum Pon, a large temple used as a short cut from the market to the Asian Highway. Behind a large pagoda, in a wooden shed, novices were chanting at the feet of an older monk. I wandered over, and a younger man introduced himself as Arkar. My initial reaction was that I was about to be hustled for money. But my cynicism was unfounded. Arkar told me he was Burmese and was organizing factory workers to renovate the temple by giving small donations from their meagre wages to buy building materials. He wanted to show Thai people that migrant workers could contribute to the community. Arkar also ran safe houses for Burmese workers in trouble with the authorities.

Arkar was 32, his small frame buried under a baseball jacket and cap. He spoke without bravado of how he had survived four years of a seven-year jail sentence in Burma's notorious Insein Prison for distributing political leaflets, and being sold to a Thai fishing boat. Arkar was not his real name, but like many Burmese in Mae Sot, he used an alias for security. We talked for about an hour, I took some photographs of the monks and the filthy canal that looked tranquil in the setting sun, and arranged to meet Arkar again at a market teashop he ran with his family.

The next day, I walked to the market in search of Arkar's teahouse.

Like most Asian markets, Mae Sot's can be eye opening and stomach churning. Plastic bowls filled with squirming eels compete with buckets of flapping snakehead fish and tied bunches of still-alive, disembowelled frogs. Women take live fish and push the end of a cut-off broom handle down the open mouth to the tail and scrape off the scales. Trays of deep-fried insects are placed next to bamboo racks of roasted rats. Locals like to munch fried worms, grasshoppers, silkworms, beetles, and cicadas with their beer.

Rows of red, white, pink, and yellow roses make a sweet-smelling break from the pungent onslaught and the wriggling mass of live food. Exotic orchids as tiny as a fingernail, others big with drooping blooms, are sold in bundles for as little as a few baht. Groups of dark-eyed Burmese girls, arms linked, shop for colourful sarongs, bananas, green vegetables, and mangoes. Sharp-eyed youths drift and loiter around the girls. Both groups paint their cheeks with *tanaka*, a yellow powder made from grinding a piece of *tanaka* wood on stone. Mixed with water it creates a fine yellow paste used as protection against the sun. The intricate patterns add a touch of style and highlight their eyes with mischief.

Near the open channels of stagnant drain water that criss-cross beneath the fish stalls is the undercover area of the market known as 'Burmese Alley' with its rows of teahouses and karaoke bars.

Large aluminium pots bubble with oily yellow and red coconut curries. Hungry customers munch on chunks of crispy battered pumpkin, sweet potato, and grated papaya dipped in a mixture of crushed peanuts, sour tamarind sauce, dried chilli, and sweet dark molasses. Rotis sizzle and smoke on hotplates. The aroma from cooking basil, garlic, and palm sugar fills the air. Eyes water as a wok full of crushed chillies catches on the wind from a fan.

Young men sit cross-legged on plastic stools smoking green cheroots and sipping coffee and tea oversweet with condensed milk. Muslim gem dealers take a break from the hustle of the market to chat, gossip, and debate. Dull-eyed, pot-bellied Burmese Intelligence agents hide behind fake Ray-Bans fooling no one, as drug dealers slide small plastic packets of *yaa baa* ('crazy drug'—methamphetamine) to eager users.

To the casual tourist, Burmese Alley is an exciting walk on the wild side. But beneath the exotic surface, the Alley has a dark side.

I had arranged to meet Arkar at his "Morning Flower" teahouse, but I couldn't determine which one it was, as all the scripts above the identical shopfronts were in Burmese. I looked into the interiors as I passed each one, hoping to see him or him to see me. This got me nothing but curious or hostile stares from the busy tables in and outside.

Giving up on the teahouses and fazed by the stares, I wandered to a stall to look at a motley spread of poorly printed Burmese books and magazines. Flicking through dictionaries, comics, and government propaganda, I felt a slight pull on my arm. It was Arkar. He smiled, gently shook my hand, and ushered me into his busy shop. Inside, it was all noise and steam. Small boys wiped tabletops with dirty rags and placed hot glasses of coffee and tea in front of customers who stared at a television fixed high on a corner wall. Just above and to the side of it, a spirit altar was home to a picture of a wizened old monk, several pieces of fruit, a can of Coke, and a garland of pink plastic flowers.

Arkar sat down and removed his baseball cap. "My younger brother, mother, and sister all work here now. Upstairs there's karaoke. Want to see?"

I declined and instead ordered coffee and Chinese tea.

Arkar said that many of the young Burmese people in the teashops worked in Mae Sot or were looking for a lift to a higher paid job in Bangkok. He knew from his own experience that Burmese workers were easy prey for the human sharks cruising the Alley.

"When I first came to Mae Sot I worked in a restaurant for 800 baht a month. Seven days a week, no days off. I saved my money. A 'carry' (job agent, so nicknamed by the Burmese because they often used the 'Carryboy' minivans) offered to take me to Bangkok and get me 6,500 baht a month serving petrol. But first I had to pay him 8,000 baht. I worked in Bangkok for eight months."

Migrant Burmese workers pay 'carrys'—often rumoured to be police or other officials—thousands of baht for a job and safe passage through the border checkpoints.

Arkar was doing well, saving money and making friends. But it wasn't long before he was approached by another carry offering better opportunities in Malaysia.

"He said he would take me and eleven other Burmese workers to Malaysia if we paid him 10,000 baht each. He promised us jobs that would pay 25,000 baht a month."

But the carry had no intention of taking them to Malaysia. The first sign that all was not well was when the van pulled into the fishing town of Pattani, 1,100 kilometres south of Bangkok. Lots of cheap labour is needed for the hundreds of trawlers and fish factories of southern Thailand. As many as 80,000 illegal Burmese people are used to service such industries.

"The carry hid us on a boat and told us to keep quiet while he contacted his friends who would take us to Malaysia. We had to hide under piles of stinking fishing nets. The carry never came back. Another man found us under the nets and said we'd be arrested if we were found. He said he could help us find work in Ranong if we paid him 3,000 baht. We had no choice, we gave him the money."

Arkar and his friends were sold to a fishing boat owner.

"It was a large factory boat, three storeys high. There were thirty men. We fished for fifteen days. It was the worst time of my life. I was throwing up all the time. I considered suicide every day. It felt worse than the four years I spent in jail. Each time I thought about throwing myself in the sea, my mother's face would appear."

Arkar's gentle face belied the anguish and fear he lived through in prison and on the trawler. His voice dropped as he described life in jail, squeezed into a squalid cell with eight other prisoners and being tortured, beaten, and starved. How a couple of overflowing, stinking bowls served as toilets. No light entered the damp cell. Denied medicine and with no protection against cold or heat, many prisoners died.

The regime jailed unionists, political opponents, university students, and even school students. An Australian, Leo Nichols, was tortured and died in a Burmese jail. His official crime was to have owned an unregistered fax machine. Comedian Par Par Lay was given seven years hard labour for telling a joke about the regime. Legally elected politician Daw San San, sixty, received 25 years for talking to the BBC. People have even been jailed when their car broke down.

After the fishing boat returned to Pattani, Arkar decided to run away. "I couldn't stand to go back to sea, so I made plans with another worker to go back to Bangkok. I got paid 1,400 baht for the fifteen days' work, but I had little left after my boss had deducted my food and other stuff from it."

Moving around Thailand for Burmese workers is difficult. Blamed by Thai authorities for everything from spreading disease to drug running, they get little sympathy from police or villagers.

"We caught local buses to the train station and bought tickets with the money we had left. We were scared when a policeman on the train asked for our tickets. We said nothing, but he ordered me to read the front page of a Thai newspaper. I couldn't. I thought he'd send me to jail, but he was kind and told us not to worry, keep quiet, and he'd help us get to Bangkok."

Eventually Arkar made his way back to Mae Sot and got another job in a Thai restaurant. But his experience in Pattani had scarred him.

"One of my best friends was robbed and killed. We have no rights in Burma or in Thailand. We are robbed by the police and even by fake police. The only difference is, real police take 300 baht, but pretend police take everything we've got, even our lives."

The "pretend police" Arkar feared belong to one of Thailand's many paramilitary groups or volunteer militias. The Burmese are hassled constantly by police, army, immigration, forestry rangers, village volunteers and paramilitary groups, and other Thais posing as officials. Uniforms and insignia are easy to buy in Mae Sot, as are accessories and even weapons. Fake ID cards are also easily obtainable. What makes the 'fake cops' dangerous is that they are prepared to beat, rape, and kill migrants once they've robbed them.

Arkar's ordeal made him even more determined to help his people.

"I worked hard and saved enough to open this teahouse. I can now afford to run two safe houses to help workers in trouble."

Arkar admitted that at times he thought he had taken on more than he could cope with. "There are a lot of political groups in Mae Sot, and many compete with each other. How can we help our people when our organizations cannot work together? Some groups get money from overseas. They buy mobile phones, motorbikes, and computers. They live well on this money when it should be used to help workers. They use it for their own political or propaganda purposes. Workers earn seventy baht for twelve hours work. Some activists spend 200 baht a night on beer—that annoys me. Migrant workers don't even know these organizations or people exist. They don't meet with workers unless they're bringing foreigners to see how workers live. You say it's not much money, but it's a waste. I know because I have to go to the police, hospital, and factories to help workers."

Arkar's enthusiasm was tangible, and the venom directed at Burmese activists was real. His criticisms seemed justified as his own words, deeds, and achievements spoke for themselves.

"I want to show Thais we can help ourselves. To show them Burmese workers aren't only takers but that we can also give to the community."

Arkar enthusiastically outlined his plans for a workers' health clinic that would be self-funded through donations of five or ten baht a week. Seed money had already been raised by Australian trade unionists. It was operating illegally, a day-to-day proposition dependent on the tolerance of local Thai officials.

Burmese migrant workers or refugees are not allowed to open bank accounts in Thailand and have to rely on the Alley to send money home.

Workers used Arkar's café to phone and send or receive messages. To be able to run a café in Mae Sot, one needed connections. Security had to be bought and, unfortunately, it didn't come with guarantees.

A few weeks after our interview, I was riding my bicycle through Mae Sot when I had a phone call from Arkar. It was hot and I was sweating. I juggled my mobile phone out of my shoulder bag and continued riding one-handed. I wasn't in the mood to talk, but Arkar was.

"Phil!"

"Arkar. How are you?"

"Phil . . . where are you now?"

"Mae Sot. What do you want?" I was hot and sweaty and really didn't want to talk.

"Phil . . ."

"Arkar, I can't hear you," I lied, with frustration and enough irritation to silence him. "I'll call you later."

Arkar hesitated before answering "okay...." and his voice faded.

I forgot to call Arkar back until much later that night. There was no answer. I tried again the next day, the day after, and the day after that. His phone was dead. It wasn't until a week later that he phoned me.

"Hello, Phil."

"Arkar, how are you?"

"Good."

"I'm sorry I couldn't talk last week. What was it?"

"I was in jail. I needed 200 baht to get out."

A few days later, Arkar came to my house to talk to me. I left him with a cup of coffee while I searched for my notebook. When I came back, Arkar was bent low over some coloured photographs I had been given of Karen children murdered in Dooplayah district in Burma. I was puzzled why he was bent away from me until I realized he was crying. There was no sound. But tears tumbled from his eyes.

Arkar had brought his own photographic nightmare to show me. He had three photographs of a young man laid out in a coffin made from packing crates; black stencil marks were still visible on the rough wood. The man was Arkar's friend, Naing Lin. Arkar told me he was from a small village called Taw Ku, not far from Rangoon. One afternoon, Naing Lin had just finished playing in a soccer game between Mae Sot factory workers. He was walking home when four motorbikes slowed and drew up next to him. Each bike carried two men. One of the pillion riders fired a gun. The bullet hit Naing in the forehead and exited through the top of his skull.

Arkar pointed at the picture and said, "Naing was only 25. Anybody can shoot Burmese workers and there's no problem. We took him to hospital and the doctors called the police. Naing died. The hospital wanted 12,000 baht before they would release his body."

Arkar and 100 of Naing's friends took the body to the temple and prepared it for cremation. Naing was poor in death as well as in life. His friends used a back-to-front shirt as a shroud. His head was shaved, washed, and wet talc rubbed on his skin. In the picture, the red-brown bullet hole was still stark on his forehead. Small coins had been placed in his mouth to help him pay his way when he got to the other side.

Arkar asked me if I knew what Burmese workers say when they see smoke over Pro Phra district (south of Mae Sot)? I shook my head and said no.

"Another Burmese worker is being burned. Thais say it takes three car tyres to burn a Burmese. The police don't care. Migrant workers have fewer rights than street dogs."

8 Saint or Sinner

It was a long time before I finally arranged to meet Dr. Cynthia Maung, and even then I had to wait until she returned from one of her many overseas conferences. I was shown into her sparse office that she shared with other staff. Papers sat unfiled, faded colour photographs of her children and Aung San Suu Kyi were glued to a wall.

I sat facing Dr. Cynthia across a low wooden table. Her thick black hair was pulled tight and tied at the back. She nodded, smiled, and waited. I asked about her life before the clinic.

"In 1988 I finished my studies and was running a clinic in a Karen village of about 20,000 people. Like everybody else, I just wanted democracy for my country. The military made our demonstration a crime."

By taking part in democracy demonstrations, Dr. Cynthia was placed on the military's hit list. With colleagues, she fled to the Thai border. "It took us seven days and nights. We could only travel at night because the army hunted us. We arrived in Mae Sot in February 1989 and set up the clinic as a temporary shelter for students who had fled the violence in Burma. They were very young. When we first started, we had only ten people. Word spread and many more arrived. Then in June and July there was a lot of fighting north of Mae Sot, and the Karen leaders sent their sick."

She laughed as she remembered how the clinic started. "It was only intended as a safe house. I never planned for it to be a hospital or even a clinic. It was just an old wooden storeroom made from scraps of wood left over from an old sawmill. In our first year we delivered six babies, and now it's more than 2,000."

Dr. Cynthia relied on donations from overseas Burmese and the local Thai community to keep the clinic running. "They gave us blankets, plates, and pots. Local Thais helped us a lot. They brought beans and oil. The local Catholic church and Thai businesses supplied rice and medicine. People brought us charcoal, blankets, and mosquito nets. Every month something always turned up. I only carried some basic equipment from Burma. I had my stethoscope and some small items. I've been here sixteen years. I came for three months, then I thought it would be three years, and then five, but the situation in Burma got worse. Our contract for the lease of the land and the buildings is always for one year to the next."

Since those early days, the clinic has outgrown its humble beginnings. It now spreads over an area the size of a couple of football fields and takes in 80,000 patients annually. But Dr. Cynthia doesn't want this to be mistaken for a sign of success. "It just means we are seeing more suffering. It is very difficult for our young people working here. They see social and cultural problems that can't be treated. They see too many abandoned children and babies. They see older people homeless, women with husbands in jail, and drug addicts. It's hard for our young medics to cope with all this sadness. They need to see some happiness and be able to treat more than just hopeless cases. All they witness are broken communities, broken families, and broken people."

Dr. Cynthia paid tribute to her young medics for making the clinic work: "Every medic wants to do something to help. All our workers have had family members killed, imprisoned, or tortured. Many of them are from displaced villages and were brought up running from jungle hide-out to jungle hide-out."

Karen teachers and community leaders select people who they think have the commitment and attitude to be trained as medics.

"They have to be motivated. It's not money that brings them here. A junior medic earns 800 baht a month and a senior medic with a family gets 1,100."

Dr. Cynthia is grateful to Thailand for giving her the opportunity to set up her clinic, but said the problems in Burma cannot be fixed until the dictatorship lets the people take part in the political process.

"The solution to our problems is not here in Thailand. We have no rights here, it's not our country, we're stateless people. But we need to build partnerships with Thai people while we live in their country."

We left her office and Dr. Cynthia took me on a slow tour of the clinic. We passed a queue of anxious faces outside the out-patients department. Many of the women carried babies bundled in faded sarongs. Those too sick to move folded like thin shadows over metal benches.

"People in Burma are too busy struggling with daily survival. They don't have time to deal with or even think about the severity of their situation. The main killer is malaria, and we also see many malnourished children."

Malaria has had a devastating effect in Burma. Médicins Sans Frontières (MSF) claim it is the country's biggest killer, and the Thai-Burma border is where the world's most resistant strains are found. Medical experts agree that the best way to prevent malaria is to sleep under mosquito nets treated with an insecticide. But even the most basic precautions are beyond the reach of people under siege.

"Many of our people have been forced from their homes. They are always moving to avoid capture. It's impossible for them to buy nets or insecticide, even if they were available."

Many of the terminally ill who come to the clinic for treatment are scared to die in Thailand because the Burmese military refuses to let relatives take the bodies home. Burmese families are dirt poor and can't afford the cost of a funeral—transporting the body, buying a coffin, and paying for a ceremony. People have become pragmatic about death and simply make their goodbyes saying, 'You take the body, and we'll take the soul.' The clinic pays Mae Sot Hospital 500 baht each time they have a body to burn.

It is no surprise to Dr. Cynthia that Burmese national health indicators are catastrophic, especially when the UN notes that the regime spends 222 percent more on its military than it does on health and education. UNICEF reports that as many as 1 million Burmese children are malnourished.

Dr. Cynthia worried that, under the regime, Burma had become a country divided by race, religion, education, arms, and wealth. "If you want a healthy society, all people have to be treated as equals. It's important we have different ethnic groups involved if we are to rebuild our country. If people are to live and work as equals, the barriers that divide them have to be removed."

Inside the door of the clinic's nutrition ward, a small gaunt child, her ribs visible, lay still on a plastic mat. Her four-year-old body weighed only 5.6 kilograms. A disposable nappy swamped her tiny frame. Her finger-thick arms and legs were motionless, but her eyes tracked me as I bent to photograph, and she smiled. Standing behind her, nine-year-old Kama watched as a medic checked the frail child. Kama was also malnourished. Her shaved head and powdered face gave her a haunted look. She weighed sixteen kilograms, about a third of what she should.

A small chubby man poked his head inside the door and spoke in Burmese to Dr. Cynthia.

"Saw Eno has just come from Burma," she said. "He's a nurse in the TB ward of a large Burmese hospital. He'll talk to you if you change his name and the name of the hospital."

I asked him why so many Burmese crossed the border to seek treatment at the clinic.

"In Burma we have no drugs; we have nothing to give. Every day I see forty people with TB. Some are young, some old. Our government says there is no HIV, but it's a lie.

"I earn 5,000 kyat a month. It only pays for food. We have no time to grow vegetables. Our time is spent working, going to meetings, and doing volunteer government work. We have no choice. If we refuse, we're fined.

"We work for the next meal. If we try to buy medicine on the black market, we can be arrested. If we speak out, we're arrested. We never speak without first looking over our shoulder, and when we do speak, we look at the ground. The generals keep a sacred white elephant as a sign they're strong and have the gods on their side. We know it's pink, but if we say it's not white, we're arrested.

"It's very depressing. Talking to you is a jail sentence. Our country is sad. Many of the diseases could be prevented if we had the means . . . that's why we have so much malnutrition. It's especially hard on babies and children."

As a mother of three children, it is not surprising that Dr. Cynthia has made the welfare of children one of her priorities. "Our young children," she said, "have seen too much violence. If we don't solve the problems, they will be passed on to the next generation. That's what keeps me motivated. I want a better world for my children and the children of Burma. I ache for the day when at least our children can go home to a peaceful Burma."

A young woman approached, and Dr. Cynthia said she had to go back to her office, as some people from a large Western NGO based in Bangkok had arrived. We returned to her office, where a group of four women in business suits sat waiting outside in the comfort of their air-conditioned hotel minibus. The doctor smiled as she scanned the women for clues as to who they were. She led them to her office and the delegation shed their shoes at the door. Their neat row of leather shoes was out of place among the pile of worn-down plastic sandals and flip-flops belonging to clinic staff.

While Dr. Cynthia dealt with the NGO women, I wandered and chatted with some of the clinic's staff and patients. Rain started to fall, and soon a torrent ran from the unguttered roofs towards the packed in-patients ward. People and possessions were jammed between beds and floors. A bright-eyed older man mashed rice and fish as his sick wife lay still on a wooden bed. The man washed her, changed her clothes, brushed her hair, then organized the tiny space around her bed, everything grouped on a wooden box that acted as a bedside cupboard. The couple had obviously known better days, before old age and Burma's generals caught up with them. The man smiled as young children pushed past him. He slowly raised his wife to a sitting position and cradled her in his arm. With his other hand he fed her.

A tangible sense of love and humanity permeated the ward. An eight-year-old boy ran and ducked between beds as he fetched rice for his scarecrow-thin father, reduced to skin and bone by some disease. The boy propped his shoulder under his father to try to get him up to walk. As the exhausted man slid to the floor from the effort, the boy bent down and hugged him.

The packed ward may not have been run according to Western standards or expectations, but it lacked nothing in regard for the well-being of its patients. Unlike in Western hospitals, the medics allowed the patients' family and friends to be there at all hours. Families slept under and beside beds, prepared meals, and tended their sick. Instead of disinfectant gagging the air, the smell of cooking rice and curries added a sense of nurturing to the room. The feelings of angst and powerlessness that pervade Western hospitals was also missing.

An hour later, the driver took the NGO delegation back to their hotel, Mae Sot's most expensive. I was told by one of Dr. Cynthia's colleagues that the women had come to assess if their money was being well spent. During their meeting, they had grilled Dr. Cynthia about the clinic's "mission statement," "objectives," and "strategies." I thought, if they had taken the time and ignored the mud, a quick tour of the wards would have answered their questions.

NGO management plans sound and look good on paper, but from a local reality fall short of what is needed. Frustrated staff told me the 'non' part of the NGO badge is fast becoming obsolete as more and more organizations comply with rules laid down by governments. If they don't obey, they miss out on funds. Another point of contention is NGO consultants charging up to 1,000 dollars a day plus hotel and expenses. Up close, the jealousy and rivalry between consultants and local staff gets ugly.

The UN and larger aid agencies with infrastructure in place are funded to manage crises caused by natural disasters or war. Their Western staff are paid huge salaries and fly in to evaluate projects like Dr. Cynthia's clinic. But it is important to distinguish between highly paid international career aid workers and NGO consultants, and volunteer humanitarians. The latter give their services for low wages based on local conditions. The careerists and consultants often milk their position for all it's worth. Once their salaries, expenses, and per diems are paid, there is nothing left for the people they are supposedly employed to help.

Mae Sot aid workers regularly savaged one particular UN careerist working with refugees for his extravagant lifestyle. Their vitriol was based on more than envy. They contrasted his Jaguar car, wine cellar, large air-conditioned house, and expensive clothes with the conditions refugees lived in. It wasn't hard to understand their resentment, especially when people in refugee camps are fed a daily diet of rice, fish paste, and mung beans.

According to the Thai-Burmese Border Consortium annual report, the total cost of looking after and feeding a refugee is 4,600 baht a year, equating to thirty US cents a day for each person. Next to the consultants' salaries, cars, and luxury accommodation, that figure is obscene.

When Dr. Cynthia re-joined me, I asked her about the attitudes of NGOs and consultants working in the region. She took a more charitable attitude toward them than I now do, saying Mae Sot is not an ordinary town and living there is difficult for everyone.

"There are so many political groups and NGOs to deal with. There are lots of power struggles between the different interests and egos. But we can't separate our people from that struggle. We have to keep putting their interests before our own. Many [consultants] have travelled to a lot of countries, but not very far from their own comfort. I feel, because of this, they are not participating fully or being fulfilled as human beings. I've seen so many careers made by diseases."

Dr. Cynthia fixed me with a blank stare and let the silence hang. Finally she said that prejudice at all levels had to be broken down and it would take time to change attitudes.

In spite of some local resentment and bureaucratic hassles, many Thai people in Mae Sot are proud of the international acclaim Dr. Cynthia and her clinic have brought to the town. Local people from all walks of life have offered support. Dr. Cynthia's reputation means she is also in high demand at overseas conferences. I asked her why she hadn't taken the opportunity to move her family to a more comfortable life away from the poverty, disease, war, and the never-ending line of sick refugees.

"I've been asked to live in Canada, Britain, the US, and Australia, but what would I do? It would be a good opportunity for me and my children, but what good would it be to my people? The world is the same over. Wherever you go, people have problems and poor health. How to fix those problems is the question?

"People keep telling me the international community will step in and stop the regime. But they haven't. I don't know if it's because the Burmese people are patient or just passive. The people are brainwashed." She gave a forced laugh at the suggestion that she was a saint, and bit back at people who wanted to beatify her. Then her tone turned to anger. "I feel more like a leaf in a storm when I have to deal with all the factions who want me to work to their agendas. You need to clarify what 'saint' means. What are the qualities? Who determines them . . . you, the media? Rather than making me or Daw Aung San Suu Kyi a saint, people should take responsibility to do something themselves. Burmese people need to become mobilized. Making a few responsible for solving the world's problems is not a solution. As in holistic health, people have to take responsibility. The situation in Burma has made the people irresponsible; they constantly look to someone else to do it for them. What she can do [Aung San Suu Kyi] is limited. Everyone respects her and believes she is a good leader, but how much can she do? How much has changed since 1988? The decline in the economic situation means people can't even think about politics, they're too busy trying to feed their families. The education system is strictly controlled, there are no NGOs allowed in unless they are compliant."

Our interview was again interrupted. Dr. Cynthia had another visitor, and she told me to carry on in the wards and we would continue later. Hovering in the doorway, a tall bearded backpacker stood waiting for me to leave. He pushed past me and I walked towards the trauma ward.

Inside the ward, the senior medic, Law Gwa, was examining the raised leg of a man lying prone on a wooden bed. His leg was encased in a metal frame to keep it still and its weight off the bed. Law Gwa's hands were rubber gloved as he slowly dabbed with a piece of gauze held in scissors at the side of the man's leg furthest from my view. I moved around to get a better look at the wound and then wished I hadn't.

The man's upper thigh had a hole, big enough to insert a fist, that ran from above the knee to just below his hip. Most of the flesh and muscle was missing, exposing the entire length of the thigh bone. I asked Law Gwa what had caused the injury, expecting his reply to involve a land-mine.

"His leg was sore and he went to see his traditional healer. The healer only found a pimple. He treated it with one of his potions and gave it a massage. After a few days the spot turned into an open ulcer and the healer put more potion on it. It then rotted away to leave what you see now. He also has osteoporosis, and when his healer massaged his leg, he broke the bone."

The wound was terrible, making it hard to conceive what caused the flesh to rot. According to Law Gwa, the healer could have put anything from a buffalo-shit poultice to a home-made mixture of jungle plants on it. Law Gwa had the man on intravenous antibiotics and had cut away the rotten flesh to try to save the leg.

In a small room at the back of the ward, a young Karen man was being prepared for an operation. He had been working with elephants, moving logs out of a forest, when he stepped on a mine. The man's foot was blasted to pulp and bone fragments. The medics needed to amputate the foot and lower leg. A cutting line had been drawn just below his calf muscle, the black ink cruel against his brown flesh. In the dim light, he looked crucified on the raised bed in the makeshift theatre. The combination of anaesthetic and the fear of losing his leg made his eyes bulge in anticipation as the medics waited for the painkiller to kick in. They assured me that though the man would be conscious he would not feel pain, but would hear his leg being sawed off.

The man told me he had been on the job just three days when he stood on the mine. As he hadn't finished the work his boss had contracted him to do, he would not be paid. To add unbelievable insult to his injury, the Burmese army had fined him 10,000 kyat for destroying military equipment—the mine!

He whispered to me that he never thought his "life would be so cruel." I agreed, and declined the medics' invitation to watch the amputation. I walked back to the office.

Dr. Cynthia had just finished with the backpacker, who was shuffling his feet into his well-worn Birkenstock sandals. Dr. Cynthia was grabbed by one of her staff before we could resume our talk. Instead I asked the backpacker a few questions. He was from the US and had come to Mae Sot to get his Thai visa renewed at the border. He'd read about the clinic on the Internet and, as he had studied naturopathy, he believed he should share his knowledge with the clinic. He thought the clinic relied on Western medicine and needed to embrace alternative healing. He wasn't donating money, medicine, clothes, or even his time. His attitude or beliefs could not be shifted, and he dismissed me as another "straight." I suggested he spend time working in the trauma ward to get some perspective.

A constant stream of Western tourists go to the clinic demanding Dr. Cynthia see them. Many are unaware of their own insignificance in the overall scheme of the border situation, but have enough front to insist, like one photographer, that Dr. Cynthia spend ten hours being photographed "to enhance my portfolio."

One of the medics, who had seen me talking to the backpacker, wished she had the money spent by visitors getting to the clinic. "We don't need more people coming here, but we could use their holiday money to treat more people."

With my encounter with the 'new-age healer' still fresh, I asked Dr. Cynthia her views on how traditional and modern medicine compared. Before answering, she gave me another of her stares that passed through me and finished up about a mile away.

"Because people in remote areas in Burma cannot get good medical care, they rely on traditional methods. Sometimes it makes their condition worse. Traditional medicine has to walk side by side with science. For example, the traditional birth attendant [TBA] thinks a newborn baby's life force is in the placenta, so immediately after birth they tear it out. In modern medicine we wait, otherwise it can cause massive bleeding and collapse the uterus. It could also kill the mother. Traditional birth attendants don't let new mothers eat eggs or give their babies breast milk for three days. We know mother's milk at this stage is full of colostrum and builds the baby's immunity to infection.

"There are many misconceptions that can cause conflict between health workers and traditional healers. Using buffalo shit on wounds is dangerous. Eating monkey brain is also believed to be good to fight off mental illnesses, but would you do it?

"We need to know what works best in both systems. The health worker needs to learn more about prevention, and we have to build on the respect the traditional healers have in their villages. The ideal is to teach traditional healers to combine scientific methods with traditional remedies that work. We have seventy backpack teams that go inside Burma to give care to over 100,000 displaced people. They also work with village leaders and traditional birth attendants and healers. Given appropriate training, they can be important in improving health."

Dr. Cynthia responded to my interjection to "tell me more about the backpack team" with the stare, more silence, and finally a frown. Her patience had run out. She said if I wanted to find out about the backpack team, I should talk to them myself.

Dr. Cynthia's children arrived from school with a clatter and swarmed over their mother. The clinic was winding down for the day. Medics left the wards to go to their small, shared rooms to relax, have showers, or play football. Outside the gates *songtaews* waited to collect passengers. A huge red sun dropped over the trees that fringed the back of the clinic, and clouds of insects rose from the rice paddies to chase the last of the daylight. Stray dogs gathered in packs for the night's mischief.

Back in town, the day market had closed, its empty wooden stalls left to the rank smells, rubbish collectors, beggars, and muggers. A large rat scurried among the garbage. Brothels switched on their fluorescent striplights. I made my way to Kung's Bar—a favourite haunt for backpackers, journalists, aid workers, and activists—for today's latest rumours and an ever-present shot of Mae Sot paranoia.

9 Backpackers

Dr. Cynthia gave me the name of a Backpack Health Workers' Team (BHWT) leader to speak to. As I had trouble pronouncing his name, Hsernai Moo, I had to ask her to write it in my notebook. She also gave me a copy of their annual report.

I made an appointment to meet Hsernai Moo at his office near Mae Sot's airport. When I got to the single-storey house, it was deserted. I was early. I took off my sandals and entered a large room. On the walls, hand-drawn maps marked territory covered by backpack teams, and faded photographs captured the horror of their work. Land-mine victims lay in jungle huts with scorched flesh. Children silently howled as syringes were squeezed into their tiny arms. Porters lay dead, their faces twisted in grotesque death masks.

A cough interrupted my self-conducted tour of the office. A tall man wiping sleep from his eyes knotted his red and blue sarong and introduced himself as Hsernai Moo. He laughed and said if I wanted to remember how to say his name, just think of the sun and moon. He resembled a figure from an old sepia photograph of North American Indians. I stopped examining his face and asked him about a photograph of people standing on a riverbank with reed-and-bamboo panniers.

"Visitors think we use canvas backpacks like travellers. We have to use big bamboo baskets to carry medicine and supplies. They're cheap to make and last a long time. We carry up to forty kilos in each one. Sometimes we need elephants to move it all."

Sunny Moon and the backpack medics provided health care to people living rough in jungle hide-outs. It's hard to get an accurate number of the people displaced in the Karen State, but he estimated it to be as many as half a million. Getting medical supplies to them is difficult. The further the backpack teams go, the less medicine they have, as villagers along the way need treatment.

"These people are at risk from all sorts of diseases. We only reach about ten percent. We take in a six-month supply of medicine wrapped in sugar or rice sacks, and plastic in the wet season. We carry our personal items in small army packs. Karen villagers volunteer to help. We're all working for the same thing—our freedom."

As we talked, Sunny Moon was never far from laughter. He fiddled with his long hair, finally smothering it under a gnome-sized beanie. He said that the ideal way for the backpack teams to travel was in a large group. "If the situation is quiet, we go together, but if there's fighting at the villages we split up and run. During the last two years we've had eight medics killed and one arrested. The one who was arrested, we don't know if he's alive or dead. Shells, shooting, or mines killed the others, and a woman medic fell into the river during the rainy season and drowned. She could swim, but the river was stronger."

Sunny Moon said he had 250 backpack medics divided into seventy teams providing for 150,000 people. The youngest backpacker was 22 and the oldest sixty. There were more men than women. Grinning, he said that the women were better at keeping records than the men. But his laughter hid the seriousness of the work.

"It's dangerous, but more so for villagers. Every day they have to live with the reality of the SPDC, who wage war against them. Mines start at the feet, but blow up into the rest of the body, even causing blindness. Soldiers usually attack the villagers after the wet season when they're harvesting their rice. This happens every year.

They plan it. It's a race to see if the villagers can get their rice in before they're attacked. They now ask us for land-mines to protect their crops, but we can't help with that, we only have medicine."

Sunny Moon became a refugee in 1997 after it became too dangerous for him to live and work as a medic in the Karen State. "I go in and out of Burma at least four times each year," he said. "We help everybody, even the SPDC if we come across their sick soldiers. If they're holding guns, we don't care for them. Men who carry guns for reasons other than protection are mentally sick. Often their soldiers are very young, as young as fourteen. They want to escape, but are afraid or don't know what to do. If they're caught, they will be punished and killed by their officers. We try to avoid the fighting, or wait, but if there is a battle, there will be wounded soldiers. Often we are asked to go to the front lines, but we prefer that injured people are brought to a safe place."

The medics have to cross SPDC territory at night without torches. They have to move slowly. Sunny Moon was not young, but looked fit. He laughed and modestly claimed he was getting too old for the job. "I'm now 53 and it's getting hard to keep up. I fell down five times on the last trip. There are mines to avoid, but our villagers guide us, and without their help we couldn't go. We have to play hide-and-seek with the SPDC."

Sunny Moon had worked like this for more than 25 years and had got used to most of the dangers, including the ever-present risk of malaria and other natural hazzards. "Snakes are no problem. Tigers stay quiet—they must know they're prized on the black market. We take our own hammocks to sleep in. In the rainy season we stay in villages where it's safer."

Sunny Moon blamed the wet season for delivering his worst nightmare—leeches. "I hate them more than snakes, mines, bullets, or Burmese soldiers. They suck your blood and you don't know they're doing it. They like warm places, especially your groin and armpits. Big river leeches grow to six or seven inches. I really hate them!"

To fight them off, Sunny Moon made his own lotion, a mixture of lemon and tobacco that he rubbed on his socks and arms. "Sometimes it works. Small yellow leeches go for the legs, and the little green ones wait on leaves and go for the upper body. But when sleeping they drop on you, and you wake up with your eyes filled with blood and you can't see. I take an eyewash to clean the blood from my eyes."

After 25 years on the front line, Sunny had developed a simple view on the world. "People of all races are basically the same. The body temperature is the same, the blood's the same colour. Health work, more than any other job, lets me treat people equally. When I was young, I was very sick; my mother prayed for me and promised God that if I recovered I would do good work. I don't want to break my mother's promise. I'll keep going until I die, because I believe in the work I do."

Sunny Moon suggested I talk to a woman medic to get another point of view, and said I could meet him and her for lunch the next day at a roadside stall near their office.

I arrived early at the 'restaurant' and Sunny Moon was already there with a Karen woman he introduced as Ruthie. The food had already arrived—Thai Isaan style—and Sunny Moon had ordered enough for all of us: *gai yang* (barbecued chicken), *som tam* (tangy green papaya salad), *khao niao* (sticky rice), *nam tok* (pork neck mixed with mint, onions, garlic, and chilli), and plates of raw vegetables. We ate first and then Sunny Moon said he was going to a meeting at Dr. Cynthia's clinic.

Ruthie said she was uncomfortable about the interview. "It is very dangerous for us if we're recognized, even here in Thailand. I was only sixteen in 1988 when the big demonstrations took place. I joined in. One of my friends was a student leader. Our teacher was a government spy, but we didn't know. My friend was arrested because of this teacher. All he did was take part in a march. My parents were betel-nut farmers. When the SPDC came, they beat people and killed our headman. We had to hide in the jungle for two years."

Ruthie came from a big family. She had eight brother and sisters, and she was the second youngest. She said she hadn't been scared, as she was used to sleeping in the jungle. The KNLA would warn them when the SPDC were coming, so they could hide. But she had never known peace.

"When I was two months old, the soldiers attacked our village and my grandmother named me 'Quick SLORC Come'."

SLORC (State Law and Order Restoration Council) was the name the Burmese regime used before they changed it to SPDC. I was to discover that the Karen often named their children after events, places, or even out-of context ideas.

"I hated my name, but the whole of my life was spent running from the Burmese. We never had doctors in our village. When people got sick, we used traditional medicine. But when my brother died, I thought I should learn about medicine."

Ruthie credited her uncle for getting her involved with the backpack team. "He was a local KNU leader and told me about the training run by Dr. Cynthia. She came to a 'secure area' and trained some villagers. I thought I could help my people, unlike when when my six-year-old brother was ill and I felt powerless. My ma gave him paracetamol, but it was no good. He kept calling for our father. I ran to get Pa. It was a long way, and when we got back five hours later, my brother was unconscious. He died soon after. That's why I'm a medic."

Ruthie avoided my eyes as she took her time to come back from where she left her dead brother. She dug in her bag and took out a banana, peeled it, and handed it to the small son of the 'restaurant' owner.

"After my training I was sent to a rural clinic. The SPDC attacked us and we had to run. We couldn't take anything. We evacuated in fifteen minutes. We saved some medicine but lost all our equipment. They took our records and found out all our names. If they had caught us, we would have been tortured and jailed. One of my friends was caught. She was jailed for two years and her husband executed."

Ruthie hadn't seen her parents for more than six years. "It's too dangerous for me and for them, so they don't want me to take risks. They're proud of my work and me. We all hope to go back to our country one day. It may seem hopeless, but we dream. I miss being with my ma, especially now she's getting old. But when I see people suffering, it makes my problems seem small. I witnessed one of our student comrades being tortured and killed. He was a boat soldier carrying food for villagers. I was hiding and saw them torture him with a knife until they killed him."

Ruthie started to cry. She made no sound as tears fell down her face. In the background the boy played with a disinterested dog.

When she recovered, she offered to show me some photographs from her trips. She kept them at Dr. Cynthia's Clinic, so we walked over there to get them.

As we walked past the clinic's reproductive health ward, a medic rushed over to say there were two young women with complications resulting from abortions. Ruthie invited me to tag along with the proviso that I kept in the background and didn't take photographs.

"I train traditional birth attendants in modern delivery procedures. Too many Karen babies die unnecessarily because the TBAs have poor knowledge of health issues. One TBA told me she never washed her hands before a delivery, only after, because to wash hands before a birth is regarded as bad luck. Many of the mothers and babies get infections."

A single fluorescent strip threw light against a green cloth covering the wire-meshed window. Inside the small room, two young women sat on wooden beds. They looked scared. Ruthie smiled to comfort them.

"The TBAs in their village gave them abortions and they weren't done properly. These women worried about telling us because we might blame them or deny them help."

Ruthie took their temperatures. "Their fevers are down and the bleeding has stopped." Then she ushered me away from the beds and out of the room. "They are both lucky they were close to the clinic."

Ruthie took me to another room and showed me a large collection of sticks, rusted steel needles, hooks, and other objects that had been inserted in women to induce abortions.

"Sometimes the clinic is a five-day hike for these women. If we're working in a village and need to send a woman out, it's difficult and dangerous. We might have to carry her over rivers, mountains, past army security posts, and minefields. If we can, we prefer to operate where we are. But for that you need to have an experienced medic with a team who can do amputations and other surgery."

Ruthie stared at the bagged objects. "Getting an abortion is dangerous. In Thailand it's illegal. Many women are ashamed to go to the hospital or to come to us. They'd rather use an underground abortionist or a home remedy."

I asked Ruthie to explain what she meant by "home remedy."

"These women are scared. They can't afford medicine, so they look for cheaper options. They buy herbs and other plants in the market, and put the leaves in their vagina. Sometimes it works and the girl aborts. If they go to an abortionist, it costs about 200 baht if they're one month pregnant or 500 baht if they're two to three months. Some factory owners sack their workers when they're pregnant."

We left the ward and Ruthie invited me to the room she shared with two other medics. She pulled out a cardboard box. Inside were bundles of photographs. Ruthie handed me one. On a mat inside a bamboo hut, three young children sat at the side of their mother. The woman's eyes were closed and blood streamed from her mouth onto a larger stain spreading across the shoulder of her yellow shirt. The children looked stunned. Their ragged clothes hung off their thin bodies. Ruthie said their mother died from eclampsia during pregnancy.

"Pregnant women inside Burma are usually malnourished and anaemic. If they survive the birth, their milk is inadequate. In desperation they feed their babies sugar water."

Ruthie passed me more photos: a malnourished man, his bones poking through paper-thin skin; a man on a green garbage bag, his arm punctured by a bullet, blood-soaked bandages in a puddle underneath his arm; charred remains of houses, schools, and rice stores collapsed into ash; an old man dead in his green underpants, shot in the back of the head while fleeing from soldiers.

Ruthie rifled through wad after wad of horrific pictures: disembowelled women, foetuses torn from them; worn-out porters killed for being unable to work through their fatigue; children and elderly people suffering from a range of diseases and wounds;

more destroyed homes, burned crops, and bloated dead animals. "Their only crime is that they're ordinary people—who the SPDC see as their enemies."

We walked outside, where three mangy dogs battled over a plastic bag of throwaway food, fangs ready to draw blood. An old woman aimed a kick at the nearest dog, causing it to go from scowl to scuttle. A younger woman puffed on a fat cheroot. A father used a child's small umbrella to protect his wife and newborn baby from the hot sun. I thanked Ruthie and left her with her photographs, as I was unable to deal with any more.

In the clinic, I spoke to Dr. Tom Lee, a member of Global Health Access Program, who confirmed how difficult and dangerous it is for the backpack medics. Dr. Lee worked in emergency care in a large Los Angeles hospital, but for the last nine years had trained and brought donated supplies and equipment to the backpack medics.

"They are highly skilled in treating malaria, land-mine injuries, gunshot wounds, and a whole host of diseases," he said. "The health situation in the Karen State is a human rights issue. Child mortality figures are up there with the worst in the world; one out of four kids will die before their fifth birthday. Child mortality in Burma is ten times as high as Thailand."

Dr. Lee was worried that the tendency for NGOs to engage with the regime would derail the backpack team's work.

"There's lots of international aid money available, and it may take health programmes away from indigenous people like the backpack medics. The backpack team has a health structure that works. The last thing they need is some gonzo regime-organized group taking over health delivery. That would be a disaster. The regime rips aid money off NGOs. They have to exchange their dollars at outrageous rates; at least fifty percent of the budget is eaten up this way.

"Under very difficult circumstances, the Karen have set up cred-ible health systems. The surge of aid money to Burma is worrying, as about half of it goes to the generals. NGOs working inside Burma give legitimacy to the regime, and they're being used as a weapon against ethnic people. Funding the regime to tackle health problems ignores the fundamental question that it's the regime that causes Burma's health problems in the first place."

Dr. Lee stopped, carefully considering his words.

"If we give them the benefit of the doubt, NGOs are being duped. Many of them drool over the money earmarked for Burma. All of them, MSF, Doctors of the World, UNICEF, are contained, restricted to the areas the regime allows them to go to. It's unethical."

The doctor believed that many aid workers start out with a cause but get addicted to funding, going to conferences, and ego tripping at meetings. "They start to lose their heart and the reason why they wanted to do aid work in the first place."

Despite the need to improve their medical knowledge and get rid of their harmful superstitions, Dr. Lee was keen to use traditional village healers as a resource the medics could use. "Giving them something as basic as a plastic bag containing soap to wash their hands and a clean blade to cut umbilical cords saves lives. Herbal tea is not going to fix land-mine injuries."

Each year, Dr. Lee said he looked forward to his time on the Thai-Burma border. "Coming here is kinda like a holiday, it's so different. Working in an emergency ward of a large US hospital is a madhouse of violent crime. But even in our flawed system [US], in an emergency, we treat everyone regardless of their ability to pay—but in the Karen State, people just suffer and die."

As part of his border training in Mae Sot, Dr. Lee prepared live pigs for practicing mine amputations on. At the end of the amputation training, the pigs are cooked and eaten after they've served their medical function.

"We do a lot of pig surgery. One in twenty-five of all deaths are from a mine. The backpack teams have 20,000 baht for 2,000 people. This is just pain medicine. There was a time when they did amputations with a knife or hacksaw. A knife won't cut through bone, so legs or arms had to be taken off at the joint. We've brought in wire saws, but there have been incidents when medics had to use the small saw in their penknives. Karen people are incredibly brave. Women don't take pain medicine in childbirth, kids getting shots don't cry. Show a child in the US a syringe and they scream."

10 Death Town

On the surface, Mae Sot is a normal town; those doing the smuggling, extra judicial killings, and informing for both Thai and Burmese intelligence agencies seem ordinary. They're all neighbours. They are the people who stop for a chat and are always willing to lend a hand or a bit of advice. The young motorcycle taxi driver I hired on a regular basis once disappeared for a couple of months. When he turned up again, I asked where he had been. His casual response was that he had been jailed for people smuggling. He didn't consider what he had done as wrong. He thought he was helping people get out of Burma and finding cheap labour for Thais. Getting caught was his problem, as he now had to cut the police in on his scam.

Understanding Thai police culture for an outsider is complicated. The Thai police are corrupt because they are so poorly paid. The police structure has too many levels to support, authority is centralized, officers are rarely punished for their own crimes, and there is no outside assessment of their performance. A policeman starting out at twenty earns about the same as a manual labourer;

by the time he is ready for retirement at sixty, and if he is still at the same rank, his monthly wage will be around 7,000 baht.

Karen and Burmese migrant workers are trapped in a vicious circle surrounded by exploitative Thai employers, corrupt cops, Burma's poverty, and Rangoon's military barbarism. They are easy prey for human vultures out to make a killing. And often they *are* killed.

In February 2002, police found the bodies of seventeen Karen farm workers (the final number was twenty) floating in the Moei River. What the Bangkok newspaper reports did not say was that the men, women, and children had been blindfolded, stabbed, and had their throats cut. Locals told me later that the bodies were pushed back into the current to take them away from Thailand, to avoid the mountain of bureaucratic paperwork and all the un-answered questions. I happened to be on a cross-border trip with Tha Ko around the time of the killings. We were on the Moei River when he pointed to a small creek where some of the bodies were found. He said the youngest was eleven and the oldest about 45.

"They were a family looking for work in Thailand. We think they were killed by carrys who had promised them jobs," he shouted above the noise of the engine.

In March 2002, thirteen workers were dumped on a garbage tip with plastic bags tied over their heads. A smuggling gang admitted getting rid of them after they had suffocated when hidden under vegetables in a truck travelling to Bangkok.

"Our people are cheap labour," said Tha Kho. "We have no rights here. Many factory and farm owners often refuse to pay our people for their work. We can't argue or go to the police."

Tha Ko told a story of an elderly man from Mae La refugee camp who had both his daughter and his son-in-law murdered by a farmer.

"The landowner had promised the couple accommodation, food, and 3,000 baht if they worked for one year. When the year was finished, the farmer gave them 1,000 baht. They protested but took the money and left. The couple later went back to argue with the farmer. When they hadn't returned to the camp, the old man went to look for them and found them with their throats cut but their baby still alive. He buried the couple and took the infant back to the camp."

Local businesses in Mae Sot are underpinned by exploited Burmese labour. There is no escaping it. Every meal cooked, shirt washed, road or house built, rice paddy planted, fish caught, garment sewn has been done by migrant sweat. Hotels, manufacturers, construction companies, government officials, and police all take advantage by either underpaying illegal migrants or stealing their money. Tourists, aid workers, and people like *me*, reap the benefits of this by enjoying cheap food, accommodation, cleaning services, and transport.

Hotel and construction workers are paid around 1,200 baht a month for working twelve-hour days. Factory workers get between 500 to 2,000 baht a month for a ten-hour day with maybe one Sunday off a month. If the workers sleep at the factory, accommodation and meal fees are deducted. They are fined for sickness or leaving their machines to attend to family problems. Domestic servants are often paid nothing, only getting their board and keep, and are at risk from physical abuse and rape.

Mau, a Karen domestic at a Mae Sot guesthouse I often ate lunch at, worked seven days a week and had a work permit. Chatting with her and her colleagues one afternoon, I asked them if they had ever been given drugs to make them work harder. One often heard stories of migrant workers being given amphetamine-laced water and food.

Mau laughed and said she was one of the reasons her boss didn't need to invest in expensive machinery. "You want clothes washed, just give them to your Burmese washing machine. Want the grass cut, get out your Burmese lawnmower. If you want us to go faster, give us *yaa baa* or coffee and if we break down there's plenty more from where we came from."

Mau didn't have a bank account to put her money in, so had to leave it with her boss. The longer she left it there, the harder it would be for her to get it. When she did get paid, Mau usually sent her money to relatives.

Burma's inflation rate is out of control, but denied by the regime. The official exchange rate is pegged at 6.5 kyat to the US dollar. On the black market it sells for between 900 and 1,150 kyat.

As a result of Burma's economic woes, the number of women entering the sex industry is also growing. After some months of asking, Arkar agreed to introduce me to some of Mae Sot's prostitutes at a brothel used by factory and farm workers. Arkar picked me up at 3:00 p.m. one afternoon. Mae Sot was quiet and the heat had chased most people off the streets. Arkar took me through the lanes behind the market and into a dead-end alley with a row of mouldy concrete houses. Outside one, a fat middle-aged woman sat talking to a man. Arkar spoke to the woman, nodding in my direction. The mamasan said we could talk to the girls, if they were willing.

I smiled at the mamasan as I passed, and she laughed. Inside, two young women combed their wet hair. I explained through Arkar that I was interested in their work and why they did it. The tall, more attractive girl shook her head, pointed to my camera, and shouted at us, "No!" The other girl, however, told Arkar she would like to talk. I told Arkar to explain that she didn't have to answer any question she didn't want to, or be photographed. She smiled and said it was okay.

Naj said she was seventeen, but she looked only fourteen. She took us down a corridor to the drab concrete room where she sold sex. Her tiny frame made the dingy room look large. Today, she said, she would have to have sex with as many as ten men.

"It's never enough. I'm a disappointment for Mamasan. She says I'm no good. She wants me to work more. I don't like this work but I have no money. I borrowed from Aunty and I can't leave until I pay it back."

Many of the estimated 40,000 Burmese prostitutes in Thailand borrow large sums of money to help their families pay for a funeral, hospital care, a failed harvest, or a debt to a money lender. Naj was brought from Burma to Mae Sot by a carry and had to pay him about six months' wages to do so.

The room that Naj worked from was empty except for a grimy plastic mat on the bare concrete floor and a pink nylon mosquito net suspended from a green plastic hanger. An empty brown bottle supported a stubby candle and a stick of incense. A graffiti heart was the only decoration on the sad, unpainted walls. As Naj talked, she clutched a grubby pillow.

"I get 100 baht from each man and Aunty gets 100. There are five girls working here. Mamasan's favourite girl hates me [the girl who refused to talk] and always picks on me. Life here is hard. If I don't earn enough, Aunty makes me go with cops when they come for their 'present money'."

Arkar seemed edgy and urged me to put my camera away. I asked him what was wrong and he replied that taking a Western journalist into such a brothel was dangerous for him. The mamasan shouted something and Arkar translated that I had to pay Naj and her 100 baht each. It seemed an opportune moment to leave, so I handed over the money and we made our way out. Arkar said he was told that a policeman ran the brothel and was on his way over, or, he said, the mamasan just wanted us out of the way.

Burmese migrants with no job, work permit, or money, if stopped by the police, are taken to the border to be returned to Burma. If they do have a job, but are 'illegal,' their employer is fined. Naturally this is deducted from wages and the worker ends up working for nothing. Illegal crossings into Thailand appear easy to prevent—the trips are usually made in full view of border posts—but as one local Thai official acknowledged, "If there are no Burmese, who's going to fill all the factories? It's easy money for the police, Immigration, and the rest—that's why they keep it going. They [the police] are only active when Bangkok orders a crack-down on 'illegals,' for publicity."

Money is not the only price many refugees and illegal migrants have to pay. Many are beaten, raped, and murdered. I was at Dr. Cynthia's clinic when Nang was carried into the trauma ward. Nang, thirty, had been working on a farm harvesting rice and picking tomatoes and corn for a Thai boss. It was early April and Songkran was approaching. Nang was making plans to see his family and wanted to buy new clothes. He asked his boss for his money, as he had not been paid.

"He wouldn't pay me. He swore at me and walked off."

Nang followed and again asked for his money.

"He hit me on the head with a piece of wood. I fell down and he shot me [in the thigh] with a pistol."

Nang's face was black where the blood had gathered under the skin. His lips were swollen deep purple, and there was a bullet hole in his thigh. He was lucky the artery was not severed. This attempted murder was over 1,000 baht.

I asked Arkar if he could arrange for me to visit a factory. He seemed more comfortable with this than the brothel, but said we could only go while the boss was away or at lunch.

Once again I climbed on Arkar's motorbike, and we rode ten kilometres out of Mae Sot through dry rice paddies to a series of large concrete compounds out of place in the flat fields. The buildings inside were protected by high walls topped by barbed wire and broken glass.

Arkar drove slowly through the gates of one factory as the Thai motorcycle taxi drivers loitering outside stared at us.

The workers were on their lunch break. Women cooked curries in blackened pots on outside fires. Some cradled babies. Arkar led me to a large wooden shed and introduced me to a young man in a tight white T-shirt and Elvis haircut. His name was Min and he leaned against a doorframe, cigarette dangling from his mouth. He was all macho attitude.

Min came to Thailand illegally. He worked in a knitting factory just outside Mae Sot for eighteen months, but for the last six months had run this factory's teashop.

"Here we do have a lot of trouble, but it's still easier than Burma," he said. "I like it here. In Burma there isn't any work."

Min said he saved the money to open the shop. "I pay the boss about 3,000 baht a month to use the building and sell food to the workers."

This factory, manufacturing underwear and T-shirts, was small compared to the big concrete structures protected by armed security guards. The 300 workers and their children lived on the premises in wooden and concrete shed dorms. Each shed held as many as sixty two-tiered wooden bunks, each about a metre wide. Single men and women lived in separate dorms. The single women had attempted to decorate their dorm with pictures torn from magazines. Compared to the women's, the men's shed was bleak. No photographs or coloured sarongs brightened the dark space. The walls were bare except for stains.

The married quarters were stifling hot. Couples and their children had sewn plastic rice sacks together to create privacy around their two-metre spaces. There was no room for personal belongings except on the floor. Outside it was hot, but in the family room under the plastic rice bags it was like a sauna.

Two bath-sized concrete troughs provided the only facilities for washing people and clothes. A single tap ran into each of the troughs. The sides were stained with mould, and pools of grey water lay all around the bathing area. A stagnant pond separated the teahouse from the living quarters—a breeding ground for mosquitoes.

Min poured us tea from a large blackened kettle into smudged glasses. "I enjoyed being a student," he said, "but I never finished. I would like to study more, but now that I'm married with two kids it won't be possible.

"Some workers from here went back to Burma to visit family, but when they came back, their jobs were gone. If you don't have work in Thailand, it's expensive to live here."

Male workers enjoying their break milled around the shade of the teashop, smoking green cheroots, reading newspapers, and drinking Thai caffeine stimulants. The thin sound of Burmese popular music squeaked from a small Chinese cassette player. One of the men took a communal cigarette lighter attached to a piece of string, lit a cheroot, and butted into Min's narrative. His name was Aung and he had worked at this factory for about six months. He said the conditions were not as bad as other places he had worked in.

"At some factories they only give you bad rice and not even much of that. Here we get rice three times a day; curry we buy from Min. I pay him 300 baht a month—for that I get curry and coffee twice a day."

But, Aung said, child workers only get paid half the wage of an adult. He said the youngest worker in his section was only thirteen years old.

Min described Burma's dire economic situation and I asked him why the Burmese people don't turn on the regime. Min stared hard at me before replying. He said the slaughter of 1988 was still fresh in their minds. "They won't protest. They hate to die more than they hate to starve."

The machines and electric fans started up in the windowless factory, and reluctantly the workers folded their newspapers away. I was relieved when it was time for us to leave, as I wouldn't have been surprised if someone had informed the boss and security guards that I was there.

The use and abuse of Burmese workers puts everyone in a self-created web of silence. It works on locals and foreigners alike. Plenty of people are willing to talk, but not if what they say is to be sourced and quoted. Locals are compromised by profits, and the Burmese migrants can't rock the boat if they want to stay and work. This environment in which Burmese workers are treated as sub-humans validates the remorseless beatings and lets rape and murder go unchecked or unpunished—diminishing the gravity of the crimes.

On August 29, 2004, however, roles were reversed when two Burmese women killed their Thai employer and her baby. The women, aged twenty and fifteen, had planned to rob their boss after her husband went to Bangkok. The girls crept up on the sleeping woman and hit her on the head with a handsaw, but only succeeded in waking her. The younger girl then pulled the woman's head back while the older one cut her throat. To stop the baby's cries, they drowned him in a plastic washing-up bowl. They were later caught with 32,000 baht, five mobile phones, a wristwatch, and gold jewellery. In a bizarre but standard Thai police procedure, the girls were forced to re-enact the crime for journalists and television camera crews.

If it is bad for the Burmese workers in Mae Sot, living in Burma is a lot worse.

Over dinner one night, a doctor friend of mine introduced me to a woman who had just entered the restaurant. He asked her to join us. The woman was a Burmese NGO worker and said she had just arrived in Mae Sot from Rangoon. Her English was excellent. She ordered coffee and said she was willing to talk, but only if I agreed not to identify her or the type of work she did. We agreed to call her 'Nee.'

Nee was employed by a Western NGO working in Burma and had come to Thailand for a workshop. In spite of the economic hardship and extreme politics, she liked living in Burma. "It's my home. I live in hope that one day there will be changes for the better. I can move freely inside Burma, but I don't discuss politics except behind doors with close friends. We have no access to any real news, only propaganda. There's nothing in the newspapers and we don't have access to the Internet. The news on TV is shit. We skip it and watch the Chinese movies. We only hear rumours about what is happening, but then the rumours tend to be right."

A major problem facing Burmese opposition groups is their inability to get information to their people. Many in remote areas still don't know who Aung San Suu Kyi is. Opposition groups have no radio stations or regular information to distribute to their supporters. The regime uses the national media to defame its critics and confuse people.

"Corruption rules Burma. If I leave the country, I have to surrender my passport when I return, then I have to pay bribes to get it back. A professional such as a teacher earns around 5,000 kyat a month from their government salary. Manual labourers get about 1,000 kyat a day."

Teachers, civil servants, police, and doctors have to make up for this bizarre financial disparity through corruption—by charging fees for forms, medicine, tuition.

"Inflation and taxation is bad," Nee continued. "Farmers are taxed by the government as much as thirteen 'tins' [about one acre] of rice per harvest. Many run away; they have no way to pay."

Nee managed to finish her studies but said it was difficult: "The university was always being closed down. The government always blames Burma's problems on insurgent groups like the Karen. Many Burmese people feel they're troublemakers and think of them as terrorists. People know they shouldn't believe what the government tells them, but they do. Only the middle class is aware of what's happening. The other forty million don't care. The government tells us we have no forced labour in Burma, but we see child workers everywhere—building roads, working in hotels, even in government offices and gardens."

Getting sick in Burma is a problem for everyone. "We have hospitals, but there is nothing inside—no medicines, no treatments. If you're involved in illegal drugs, it's okay, but if you're talking politics, it's not. It's a lifelong sentence for you and your family. You won't be able to get a job or education. But if you're involved in drugs you can always buy your way out of trouble. Drugs are available everywhere—heroin, opium, and amphetamines; we even have people buying expensive cough syrups from India that contain lots of codeine.

"There are many informers. Most are not paid, but they do it to get privileges for their families. I know of a public-service family of six. They earn 7,000 kyat a month but need 700 a day to live. Sometimes, instead of eating they go out to watch a video because it costs only five kyat and it takes their minds off food."

The poverty is one of the reasons many Burmese women turn to prostitution. There's very little work, and if all you can get is twelve hours in a prawn-freezing plant for next to nothing, it's understandable why women sell themselves. Nee said that sex is one of the boom industries in Rangoon: "All the bars, karaoke places, beer stations are places to buy sex. Many Chinese and Japanese come to Burma for the cheap sex."

Nee laughed when I asked her about Burma moving towards democracy. "We have to have some form of peace process first. Look, our government even puts monks in jail. First they disrobe them and then jail them like common criminals. If monks aren't safe in Burma, what chance do we stand?"

Monks have indeed felt the wrath of the generals. The Buddhist Relief Mission (BRM) reported on their website that monks disgusted at the regime's lack of respect for Buddhist precepts and values showed their dissatisfaction by demonstrating.

"On August 8, 1990, more than 7,000 monks and novices walked through the streets of Mandalay. Soldiers confronted them and opened fire, killing two monks and two students and wounding seventeen others. One novice disappeared."

In response to the killings, the Sangha Sammagi of Mandalay declared an *attam nikkujjana kamma*, 'overturning of the bowl,' a protest of refusing alms from the military or their families. The boycott drew nothing but contempt from the military leaders who said their killing of monks was justified and the thought of going to hell held no fears for them.

After my interview with Nee, I met a Buddhist abbot at Umpiem Mai refugee camp who had protested. The abbot was a bowling ball of a man. His massive arms caught at the folds of his robes as they threatened to come undone. He ripped into Burma's human rights record and said it ensured the generals were destined for hell.

"They're afraid of the people—that's why they want to destroy us. Even monks are killed. It's hard for monks to collect alms when the people have so little to eat themselves."

The abbott said that when he was younger he witnessed the brutality of the military close up. "I was nineteen when I first protested. I wasn't afraid. I followed the Buddha's path and Aung San Suu Kyi. But I was shocked. After the killings they used fire engines to wash the blood off the streets."

I wondered out loud how Burma, a Buddhist country, managed to spawn this regime.

The abbot responded with a huge belly laugh. "When they get old, they believe that by building pagodas it will be enough merit to get them to nirvana. But it won't. By breaking the Buddha's precepts they have condemned themselves to many lifetimes of hell. They'll be back, time and time again, to suffer."

11 Bleeding Hearts

When wandering Mae Sot's dark side, it's important to remember that there is also light. Many Thai people care and want to help stop the abuse against migrants. The *Bangkok Post* and *The Nation* regularly run stories about abuse and trafficking. A teacher at Mae La refugee camp told me of Thai forestry rangers catching a Karen man illegally cutting wood to make charcoal with his son. The man was blind and missing an arm from a land-mine injury. The rangers, instead of arresting him, emptied their pockets and gave the man what money they had.

But still, most illegal workers are forced to live and work in Mae Sot's shadows. A report on Burmese migrant workers for Médecins Sans Frontières by Duncan McLean offers an insight.

> . . . *Mae Sot is infamously corrupt with a climate of fear generally pervasive within the migrant community. Direct abuse usually takes the form of extortion during arrest, detention and deportation, while indirect abuse includes corruption and negligence in the running of trafficking networks, brothels and oppressive labour practices on the part of employers.*

Sadly, McLean concludes what many of their local critics say is the inability of NGOs in Thailand to protect the oppressed. "MSF, like most of the NGO community, has been relatively silent, and advocacy has not been emphasized with regards to those who fall outside traditional refugee concerns."

People working for aid groups usually come from backgrounds with a well-developed sense of their own rights or, as Tha Ko succinctly put it, "They're people who are relieved when they see a policeman. In their own country, that works—there, they have rights. But here those rights no longer exist. They don't know how to operate [and] when it's your ability to pay that determines how much security you're entitled to, it shuts them up."

When the weather cools, just before Christmas, Mae Sot is crowded with academics, freelance journalists, missionaries, and fund-raisers. Guesthouses are taken over, cafés fill, and refugee camps, clinics, and activist groups are put on a 'must-do' list. Locals and new arrivals exchange territorial scowls as favourite café seats are taken and food service slows to cope with the demands of the newcomers. Restaurant staff are suddenly projected into the spotlight by cries of 'remember me' and a central role in a long-forgotten incident.

Mae Sot is a town full of rivalry as well as bribes, con tricks, and rumours. And that makes it dangerous. Wanting to know who's who and who's doing what to who can be risky, and Western aid workers, activists, volunteers, and adventurers are sucked into the local intrigue. Like kids trying to out-scare each other, they all relay their best worst horror stories. Voices whisper and brag about decapitation, stolen camp funds, spies, extortion, gambling, guns, drugs, sex, corruption—bigger shadows to throw against the wall.

In reality, NGOs and Westerners in general have little to be scared of. Military Intelligence on both sides of the border know who works for who, and NGOs are not targetted for teaching, feeding refugees, or bringing medical care.

The real problem is that international aid agencies and NGOs are addicted to institutional funding from governments, the UN, the EU, and churches. The emergency aid business has grown into a giant unregulated industry worth billions of dollars a year.

Lamon

The major's camp

Sergeant Saw Ge (planting booby trap)

Thu Po Mu

The four principles

Naw Paw (left) and Hla Chit

Mr. Sein

The butcher

Scavengers

Mau Mye

Little Legs

Gem market, Mae Sot

Kaima and Mr. Sein

Deportation

Burmese migrants, Mae Sot police station

Friendship Bridge, Moei River

Vendors, Moei River no man's land

Major General Maung Chit Htoo

Arkar (right)

Naj

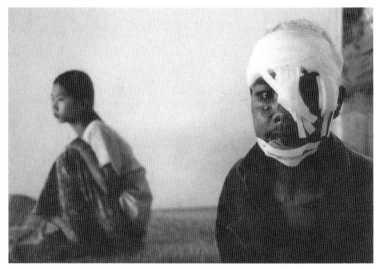

Trauma ward, Mae Tao Clinic

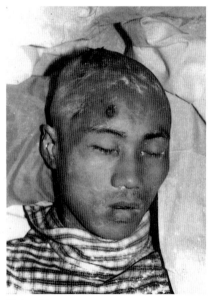

Naing Lin

Dr. Cynthia Maung

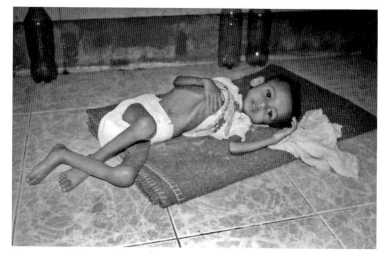

Four years old

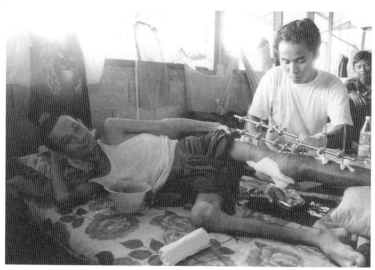

Senior medic Law Gwa and patient

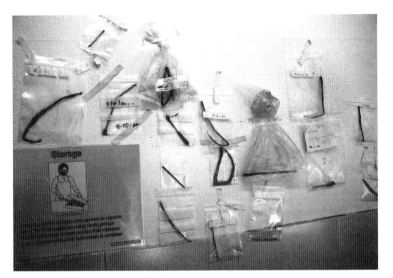

Abortion sticks, Mae Tao Clinic

Backpack medics

Moe Moe and Let Let Win

Beak and friends

Ma Nweh and daughter, Hnin Hnin Way

Ba Sein, Car Htoo and Ma Htun

Mae La

Jungle school

General Bo Mya

Kho Noc with Kar Kur and Dih Klee

Dih Klee

Aung Naing

The Bible and the bullet

KNLA guardpost

Colonel Ner Dah

KNU drug rehab

Portrait of Saw Ba U Gyi

Padho Mahn Sha (left)

55th Karen Revolution Day

Phu Tah Moo and Thu Po Mu

Rescue party

Blacktown (white T-shirt)

Alan Dawson, a columnist writing for the *Bangkok Post* (December 10, 2004) ripped into the International Federation of Non Governmental Organizations (IFNGO) meeting held in Burma to discuss and run workshops on Prevention of Drugs and Substances Abuse. Dawson lambasted the IFNGOs for staying in "lovely" five-star hotels and keeping "murky financial records." He claimed most NGOs had become "outsourcing arms of government."

Dawson attacked the NGOs for failing to criticize the regime's abuses, the jailing of Aung San Suu Kyi, or—considering their reason for being in Burma—its dependency on drug money: "The vast group of NGOs went to ASEAN's [Association of South East Asian Nations] most drug-ridden, drug-dependent nation and sat placidly in five-star, buffet-breakfast satiation and contentment."

Journalists coming to Mae Sot often allocate only a couple of days to get the images and interviews they want. Transport is expensive, getting access to rebel camps and finding someone to translate interviews is difficult, and getting an understanding of the local situation takes time. Most freelance journalists don't have funds to cover any of this, and rely on NGOs to help. It's an uneasy alliance.

Self-interest and self-preservation drives NGOs as their humanistic ideals are pragmatically pushed aside. Local volunteers are brought up to date about expected policy changes at hastily arranged workshops to prove 'we hear what you say' and 'we consult.' Disillusioned local staff label the workshops 'rubber-stamping exercises' to push unpalatable political policies. New arrivals to the NGO scene in Mae Sot endure a series of mistake-riddled knowledge tests until they drop out, get it right, or are accepted. Social gatherings are defined along class lines. High-ranking officers, doctors, consultants, and UN staffers on bloated salaries hang out together, plan theme parties, eat and drink imported food and wine, and shop for antiques.

Expat lifestyles are segmented along salary levels, eccentricity value, and links that offer bragging rights. Activists and volunteers on local wages and freelance journalists mix together out of necessity and the dire need for information. Long-serving veterans smugly float above the rest, comfortable that there's nothing to be gained from doing conversation laps with newcomers.

I asked Tha Ko for his views on Western NGOs.

"They're like children competing for our attention," he said. "It's ironic because we consider them to have the answers. Most don't stay long. When we disappoint, they leave. But we didn't change, they did. It's the same when they don't speak out against corrupt Thai officials, or plan to transfer their programmes to Burma. Time and time again they let self interest push their conscience to the side."

Many foreign aid workers and volunteers arrive in Mae Sot bristling with good intention, revelling in the ethnicity of the Karen, and discovering the town's dark side. But after failing to understand the Karen power structure and the KNU's need for secrecy, they start to demonize or canonize. The competition for attention from visitors and approval from the Karen gets ugly. Alliances are formed between the hurt, and together they unravel their original professional motivations for being in Mae Sot into personal issues. As they prepare to leave, they talk about corruption, laziness, self-serving activists, despotic armed leaders, and are dismissive of long-term volunteer doctors, nurses, and teachers who are doing a good job without fuss.

Tha Ko felt that because the problems are the Karen's, they have no right to make demands. "When we look at our situation we can see who is helping us, and it's mainly white people. Thailand says it's doing a lot, but they get plenty back from the Karen. We feel we have no right to make demands on our donors. We see they have problems. Some come for their careers, some to make money, but there are plenty who care for the Karen."

There are as many as fifty different NGOs working out of Mae Sot, but still the number of Burmese and Karen in and around the town who are jailed, beaten, robbed, raped, and killed increases each year. Tha Ko claimed NGOs, including the UNHCR (United Nations High Commission for Refugees), have been silenced. They don't speak out because they fear reprisals from Thai authorities or local influential crime figures.

Kathleen, a long-time survivor in the business of delivering aid on the border said the Karen are not without blame. "Strategically they play foreigners against each other, but they ask for it. Aid is a billion-dollar industry that has yet to be given a name. Some NGOs put minimum staff and effort into the Burmese problem but use the terrible stats on health, AIDS, and land-mines in their reports to generate funds."

Kathleen was so angry she was almost crying. "It makes me mad. Many have been here years. They stay silent, whispering among themselves in bars and restaurants, back biting, acting like stamp collectors with reports, refusing to give them to people who might make a fuss."

She said another failing of NGOs is their 'fact-finding' visits from head offices to the borderline camps. "Understanding the complexity of living as a refugee is impossible to assess from a two-day visit. We had a foreign embassy staffer visiting Mae La camp who said it looked better than what he'd seen in a Thai-Karen village."

Kathleen said the man failed to understand the restrictions refugees live with. "They can't leave to find work, hunt or fish, forage for vegetables, or go to Mae Sot to post a letter or to shop. It takes at least three days for the camp officials to approve an application to travel, and if they don't have it they get arrested and deported."

Kathleen named a US-funded international aid group paid to work with the Burmese migrants that was copping a fair bit of stick from their own jaded workers.

"They've got a boss on a huge salary and lots of new staff. They've bought cars and rented air-conditioned offices, but there's no money left to set up or run their family health programmes. All they can do now is talk to the migrants about not having unprotected sex—and they can't even give out condoms or pills."

Over beer and coffee in a Mae Sot café, Aung Naing, a former Burmese student leader, said that in his sixteen years' experience of working with NGOs, their training for medics, youth, and women had been the most useful. But otherwise, he was scathing.

"NGOs don't care what we want. We'd like to know how much funds are used on salaries, expenses, and management. They're not open. We used to think this was the life of all foreigners—cars, big houses, maids, computers, video cameras, eating at restaurants every night. It's not very different from the old colonials, and we didn't realize the money for all these luxuries is donated to help us. Consultants are brought in to train local trainers, but there's never enough to pay the locals when the consultants have left."

When I put it to Aung that consultants must bring some benefits, he was dismissive. "They fool themselves. They're like vampires sucking our blood. They leave nothing behind but hot air. They've become experts in other people's despair—ours. They spend large amounts of money, but what has changed for people in the camps? When their conferences and workshops are over, what do they produce, besides more reports? I used to think the reports would do something, but it's just another way of burying us."

Aung lashed out at expats who criticized Burmese workers. "They complain about us drinking beer, but if an NGO wants a 'fact finding' meeting with you, they always arrange to meet in nice bars or restaurants. I used to think they were kind because they paid for my meal and drinks, now I know they just use expenses." He stopped and laughed. "But that's better than meetings with Thai Intelligence; they get us to pay the bill and then take the receipt so they can claim it as an expense."

Mae Sot can be dangerous, but the further we are culturally, psychologically, and geographically from the flashpoints, the more deadly they seem. Imaginations go into overdrive, distorting fears and twisting realities. The talking becomes addictive. And some people build on layers of mischief, not realizing how easy it is to endanger those who are involved. Those remote from the guns, land-mines, smuggling, drug manufacturing, or crime have a tendency to crave exotic or dangerous stories. They don't realize, because of the volatile and often illegal nature of conflicts, the distance between calm and death can be only seconds apart. In Mae Sot, an innocent package of medical equipment donated to the 'wrong side' can easily be distorted by gossip to 'supporting the enemy.' A Western volunteer, trying to ingratiate herself with the Karen, almost got a young Burmese doctor killed. She gossiped to a Karen soldier that the doctor might be a spy. I'm uncertain if the volunteer realized that her accusation, perhaps only idle chat, could have been a death sentence for the doctor.

12 No Place Like Home

Borders mean more to people than just lines scratched in the dirt by politicians and government officials. Borders can mark the point between justice and injustice, freedom of speech, disease, persecution, torture, hunger, poverty, imprisonment, and the break-up of family. Crossing borders may offer the hope of a better future for the poor; for the persecuted the chance to escape oppression. But for those caught in the border crossfire it means death and injury. After each clash between the Burmese military and the KNLA, Karen villagers cross the Moei River in their tens of thousands to take refuge in Thailand. This infuriates the regime. They see the refugee camps in Thailand as KNU strongholds and have, on a number of occasions, crossed the border illegally to attack and burn.

Forced out by Burmese atrocities, as many as 19,000 refugees live in Umpiem Mai, 86 kilometres south of Mae Sot; 10,000 more are in Noh Poh camp, 224 kilometres along the twisting mountain road referred to as 'Death Highway.' Sixty-six kilometres north of Mae Sot, Mae La camp is home to as many as 45,000. Further north, Mae La Oo camp takes care of 15,000 refugees, and 14,000 more live at Mae Ramalueng camp. But many more thousands of

Karen are refugees in their own country, having fled the fighting to makeshift camps on the Burmese side of the river.

It is ironic that both Burma's military and international NGOs accuse the KNU of using the camps to organize their resistance. One Burmese officer, Major General Kyaw, actually whinged in the *Bangkok Post* that the camps were KNLA strongholds. "These so-called refugee camps are in fact bases from which the KNU plan their attacks inside Mynamar [Burma]."

International aid agencies make similar claims. They accuse the KNU of using the camp food to feed their soldiers, Karen medics of taking medicines to go on active duty with the KNLA, and Karen soldiers of using the camps to recuperate in while away from the front. Some NGOs even accuse the KNU of keeping refugees imprisoned in the camps to ensure the food supply is maintained. What they forget is that the Karen people don't have choices. They're at war, whether they want to be or not.

At Ler Per Her, about 100 kilometres north of Mae Sot on the Burmese side of the border, 840 people lived in a haphazard collection of small bamboo huts overlooking the Moei River. Because Ler Per Her, like all IDP (internally displaced people) camps, was on the Burmese side, there were no international aid agencies or refugee programmes.

Tha Ko arranged for photojournalist John Hulme and me to visit the camp. We drove north of Mae Sot in a loaded pick-up truck, passing the three-kilometre stretch of huts that is the home of the 40,000-odd refugees of Mae La camp. Just north of Mae La, we slowed to zigzag through the red and white barriers of a Thai army checkpoint. We turned off the highway onto a dirt road that climbed through a dusty Thai-Karen village hugging the hillside, then cut through bean and corn fields and stopped under the shade of a big tree. A rotund man with a huge smile greeted us, and Tha Ko introduced him as Soo, Ler Per Her's headman.

We unloaded the truck before taking a path down to the river, where a longtail boat sat on the sand. We climbed aboard and squatted among the donated sacks of rice, dried fish, watermelons, and medicine. Tha Ko nodded at the sacks. "There's nothing over there. Everything has to be brought in. They have no rice, no medicine, and no guarantees there will be anything tomorrow or the next day."

To supply the 8,000 kilograms of rice needed to feed the 840 people for a month cost 60,000 baht, and it all depended on unofficial donations.

We chugged upstream towards a half-submerged bamboo 'fence' stretched across the river. Our boatman slowed and aimed at a small opening in the middle. I braced myself for the impact of arm-length pieces of bamboo sticking out of the water, but to my relief they bent and swished along the bottom of the boat.

Tha Ko laughed as I photographed the fence. "Is it the first Karen fishing trap you've seen?"

I admitted it was, as the boat glided up to the shoreline.

We were met by a group of villagers who pulled the supplies ashore. They wrapped sarongs around the sacks, strapped them to their backs and across their foreheads, and trudged barefoot, half a kilometre, up a steep bank to the village. The porters maintained a steady pace. A sleek lizard crackled through dried leaves. A black snake twisted away at our approach.

We stopped at Soo's house for a break before meeting the villagers. John got permission to photograph, and he wandered off with a gaggle of children in tow. We left the shade of the house and walked through a row of bamboo lean-tos. In one of the huts, a mother, Naw Doo, and her two teenage children sat on a bamboo platform about the size of a single bed. The slanting roof was made from layers of large dried leaves, and was so low that nobody could stand. The dwelling was smaller than a child's cubby house, with no furniture and no visible possessions except for a cane basket, a mat, a mosquito net, and a plate. Outside there was no shade and the soil's green cover had long been worn down to sand.

Naw Doo was getting dinner ready for her family. She laid out two white bamboo flowers, a tight handful of green leaves, one wriggling insect like an earwig, and four live shrimp, each about an inch long. These would be added to a small amount of rice, some chillies, and, if they were lucky, some pungent *plaa daek* (raw pickled fish).

Naw Doo said she and her children were used to going without food: "Many times we only have rice and chilli. We eat twice a day. In our old village there was plenty of food."

121

She smiled as she listed all the fruits and vegetables she used to grow in her old life. "We had carrots, corn, rice, pumpkins, gourds, peas, beans, mustard, cabbage, chilli, bananas, mangoes, and jackfruit. Now I survive on what I can get from the forest. We get sick, but that's normal for people here. Look at how thin I am."

Naw Doo said that her husband had joined the KNLA. "We ran away from the fighting, we don't want to go back. We've left all our memories and our ancestors behind. We don't want to live in a refugee camp in Thailand. We want to be in our own country, our own village. I get sad, but it's our life."

Naw Doo stared hard to stop the tears and turned her head away to keep her sorrow private. I asked if I could photograph her catch of shrimp. To give an indication of their pathetic size, I placed a ten-baht coin next to two of them on my notepad. I finished photographing and was about to put them back on the plate when suddenly they wriggled and fell through a crack in the bamboo floor. Embarrassed, I had to scrabble through dried leaves to retrieve them. I had no way to replace Naw Doo's food. Money was useless, as there were no shops or supplies. Finally, I located the shrimp and, red-faced, handed them back.

Tha Ko and I walked towards the bamboo clinic dug into a hill high above the river. We crossed a log used to ford a dried stream. Tha Ko said that sanitation was poor here, and malaria rampant, especially in the long wet season from June to October. Respiratory illnesses killed both young and old. Already fragile immune systems were weakened further by poor diets.

At the clinic, a mother and father waited patiently for the medics to finish treating a seriously ill child so that their one-and-half-month-old baby could be examined. Their infant was malnourished, her tiny arms and legs lifeless, her huge eyes staring. Her mother and father had hiked for two days from their jungle hide-out after the baby, Eh Paw ('Love Flower'), had fits. The couple had nothing except hope expressed in the naming of their baby.

I asked Tha Ko about the Karen custom of giving their children strange names. During my time on the border I had come across 'Quick SLORC Come,' an 'Umbrella,' 'Eric Clapton,' and a family with a 'Comma,' 'Exclamation Mark,' 'Full Stop,' and 'That's Enough'—in English.

"It depends on the situation," he said. "Old people are cautious about names. Some say if the name is beautiful, it might attract a spiteful spirit, so if you hear of a child called 'Dog's Vagina' you'll know it has been given a hideous name to protect it."

Kahor, Eh Paw's father, wanted his family to stay in the camp because he feared the Burmese would take him as a porter or kill him. "They made me carry rice and other supplies," he said. "I was beaten and had to find my own food. They treated me like an animal. I was lucky I escaped."

Next to baby Love Flower, another young mother, Naw Moler, lay exhausted. She was pale and her clothes were worn out. She had just trekked for five hours to the clinic. Her baby had chronic diarrhoea, a temperature of 42 degrees, and cried non-stop. Her weakening condition made the two young medics rush, as they tried without success to find a vein big enough to attach a saline drip. Neither mother nor baby had eaten all day. Naw Moler said she was too worried about her baby, Ma My Nit, to stop to search for food. "I tried breast-feeding, but she kept throwing up. I brought nothing, I have nothing, but I can find friends here to feed me."

A naked toddler entered the open clinic and a thin stream of diarrhoea squirted out of him. His mother rushed to get water and a cloth and swilled the mess away with her bare hands. Meanwhile, the medic, Hla Ey, slapped baby Ma My Nit's foot, hoping to raise a vein. "She's dehydrated," he said. "If we don't get a drip into her, she will die. Mothers only come here when it's really serious. If they came earlier, we'd have more chance of saving them. Our people need education about basic health care."

The baby howled as the medics decided to insert the drip into her foot.

"Taking out bullets and doing amputations is easier than this," Hla Ey said.

Tha Ko suggested we leave the medics to work, and he took me to meet a Buddhist abbot whose village had been destroyed by the SPDC.

"The military arrived at the end of the wet season," the abbot told us. "They went around catching chickens, ducks, and pigs. They got drunk and wanted young girls and food."

The terrified villagers ran away after the Burmese soldiers raped a deaf and dumb woman and murdered her husband.

On Christmas Day, 2002, a few weeks after our visit, Burmese and DKBA soldiers attacked Ler Per Her village, shelling and burning and forcing the villagers to escape across the Moei River. None of the refugees were killed, but mines placed on the edge of the camp by the KNLA as an early warning defence killed seven SPDC soldiers and alerted the people.

I returned to Ler Per Her with Tha Ko a week after Christmas. Headman Soo met us on the Thai side and took us downriver, past the burned-out patch of ground, all that was left of Ler Per Her. The clinic, school, and everything else was gone. Soo said that at least sixty soldiers had come from the south, while fifty came from the north. "This is the fourth time we've been attacked. They also fired shells at us when we reached the Thai side. They started burning in the afternoon. In two hours it was all gone. It was three days of continuous fighting and shelling."

People had already returned over the river to the Karen State and set up a new camp in a dry creek bed five kilometres downstream from their bombed-out and now booby-trapped former homes. When we arrived, family groups sat in patches of shade with no food and only the clothes they wore.

Tha Ko shook his head, angry as he surveyed his people sheltering under the bushes. "They will have to start again. They have no tools, but they will have to clear the land and build new homes."

We walked through the dry riverbed, following the sounds of children talking and drinking from sections of bamboo dipped into a bubbling spring. Over their shoulders hung bulging Karen tote bags containing everything they owned. The kids were on their way to 'school.' But their school had no building and no desks. In small groups they clustered under the shade of a large teak tree and listened as their teachers—three women and two men—read to them from early-learner books. Two blackboards were propped against the trees. As I crouched and took photos, I was ignored, no competition to the teachers or their storybook.

After 'class' I spoke to one of the teachers. Her eyes were dark from lack of sleep and her face was dotted with mosquito bites. "I, like the children, have everything in my bag ready to run," she said. "It's difficult to keep the school going like this, but if we stop now, it will be a waste. We can't lose any more moments. Time is precious for our children. We have eighty students. They are good, but our biggest problem is malaria. Even then, it's hard to stop them coming to school. They burned all our tables and benches, but our children are safe. It's only wood, we can build again."

On the trip back to Mae Sot, I could feel Tha Ko's anger.

"We don't have enough soldiers to make an impact," he said, "and we don't have enough international persuasion to make the UN or the US do anything."

He showed signs of fatigue. Seeing his people huddled in the riverbed had taken it out of him. The magnitude of their suffering was enormous. And the coming wet season, while bringing relief from the heat, would only add to the disease. Unless shelters were built on the high ground, they would be cut-off by the flooded river.

After our visits to Ler Per Her, I wasn't to see Tha Ko until the first rains of the wet season, when he took me to Mae La camp.

Mae La is the size of a small town. It is overcrowded and the bamboo huts resemble a shanty, but the will to survive with dignity among the people overrides all else they have to battle. Hospitality shown to strangers is humbling. Plates are borrowed; rice is cooked and water boiled; eggs, coffee, beans, and vegetables are offered. The refugees try to live normal lives despite the conditions, working as labourers if they can, weaving for extra cash, making music, socializing, and sharing what little they have. The Karen I met in the camps had pride, not because they're proud of where they are, but because of who they are.

Tha Ko guided me through muddy lanes and over log bridges fording streams. We stopped at a bamboo stall and picked up some of the products on display. Most of the use-by dates were old by at least a year. Tha Ko said the camps are a dumping ground for merchants with damaged or outdated stock they couldn't otherwise sell. "We don't have much choice. Beggars can't be choosers. They [Thai or Burmese merchants, often Muslims] come here selling diseased chickens, out-of-date medicine, and unlabelled tins of food."

Around us the hustle and bustle of life went on. Chilli from woks filled the air; people sipped muddy tea at ramshackle 'cafés'; men played draughts on a home-made board using bottle tops as markers; and schoolchildren chanted lessons back at teachers and ancient blackboards.

The narrow lane lead us to a junction, where a series of large bamboo huts stood on the edge of a big muddy circle. A stream of women and children passed in and out of one building with a faded sign above the doorway, "KWO." Tha Ko led me inside, where a young woman sat at a table writing in a ledger and chatting with an older colleague. The young woman's name was Moe Moe. She was 24 years old and the secretary of Mae La's Karen Women's Organization.

Moe Moe worked with refugee women left without family support. Some were widows, some the victims of domestic violence, others had been abused by employers or escaped from brothels.

"It's a big responsibility," Moe Moe said. "There are 22,500 registered women living here. That doesn't include the children. Many have had a difficult time getting here. Often a family member has been killed or raped. We also have many orphaned children."

Some of the women had come to the camp to stay with relatives, but because of their abused backgrounds and the cramped living spaces, the situation deteriorated.

"There's trouble because of children. Relatives sometimes discriminate between their own and the newcomers, and there's sexual tension between the men and the single women. This causes fights."

To deal with the issue, the KWO set up a number of safe houses and an orphanage. Moe Moe said the orphaned children can cause trouble in the camp: "They come here with many hurts . . . they're not normal anymore. They steal and have violent tempers. They've been abused, their parents killed. It makes it difficult for us. We're not qualified. How do we start to treat mental problems?"

Moe Moe herself is the oldest of three sisters. Her colleague at the other desk was actually her mother, Let Let Win, who was the KWO vice chairwoman.

Tha Ko said the work Moe Moe and her mother did was invaluable. "They don't get paid, and they have to organize workshops and training for the women. Let Let Win rents out videos to help." Tha Ko smiled with mischief. "But she's aggressive, belligerent, and has an acid tongue. She's tough, and a great motivator. Men have no say in this place."

He went to one of the shelves and pulled out a battered book and rifled through the pages until he found a photograph. "Let Let Win was a KNLA commander with three platoons of women soldiers feared by the SPDC."

The picture showed a younger Let Let Win in KNLA uniform posing with her M-16.

"I joined the resistance when I was sixteen," she said, "and worked as a teacher in Kawthoolei and underground for women's organizations.

"I was married at 22 to a Karen soldier who worked deep inside Burma blowing up military targets. I stopped working for three years and had my three girls."

Not long after, Let Let Win got news that her husband had been captured by the Burmese after a mission went wrong. "They told me he was tortured and killed. I was devastated. I came back to my village with my daughters. Because of my political background, I couldn't contact my parents. MI took me in for questioning. I told them I had finished with the revolution for my children's sake. I had no one to help me. I was completely alone. I stayed in my little hut, fished, hunted, and foraged for vegetables in the forest. I got back in touch with the village defence groups and the KNU and became an undercover agent.

"I became a KNU organizer and recruiter. After about ten years, I was well known to MI. One day, I got information from the KNU that the Burmese were going after my babies because they couldn't get me. That night we fled. I took nothing but my sister, mother, father, and the girls. We went to KNU territory and I put the girls in school. I felt it was time I became a soldier. I did one year of training and three months as an officer. I formed a women's unit."

Let Let Win's unit became notorious. The Burmese intensified their efforts to capture her and boasted about what they would do to her.

"I was to be taken alive and they said they would kill me without letting out any of my blood—they intended to rape me to death. Their threats made me more determined to fight. We were good. There was one officer renowned for his cruel abuse of women. He used them as porters and for sex. We tracked his men down and killed them. We left a warning that molesting women would not be tolerated. Women make excellent soldiers. We can do anything. I used only the toughest. The rest were trained as medics and radio operators. At that time the KNU was strong. We were used as decoys in ambushes by the male units. Our last big battle was in 1992 at Mwa Wah Soo. The Burmese used heavy artillery and their soldiers were drugged. They kept coming and coming, we couldn't stop them. They captured our base. Men were supposed to join us, but they had second thoughts about taking orders from a woman."

Let Let Win found that looking after her children and being the commander of a fighting unit was difficult to manage. "I'd leave them with my parents while I fought. Moe Moe was always in trouble. Because the Burmese found out about them, they had to keep moving and changing schools.

"Our people are hurting. They have to eat roots, leaves, and insects. They have no medicine, no shelter to protect them . . . why wouldn't I fight?"

Tha Ko laughed. "She was fearless. She'd still be there if it wasn't for her children's safety. We hear the Burmese still ask if that Karen woman still fights."

Not long after she hung up her gun and settled into life as a refugee, Let Let Win was delivered a kick in the guts.

"I bumped into my husband's best friend. He acted strange when he saw me, then he said my husband was alive and living in Singapore with a new wife and family. I was shocked. He had been given shelter by a Burmese woman and they escaped together by boat to Singapore."

Let Let Win got up and walked outside, away from my eyes and my questions. She took her time to wipe her tears and return.

"In my heart I knew he wasn't dead. I sold everything I owned to search for him. I'd hear a rumour he was buried in such and such a place and I'd raise the money to get there. I visited many graves. Moe Moe dreamed about her father all the time, she still does. I felt very betrayed, but now I can accept it as my fate and let go."

Tears spilled from this tough woman's eyes to reveal the cruel price she paid for love. Where lesser mortals would have collapsed, she gathered her strength and her children and used her energy to help her fellow refugees.

Rain began to crash heavy against the leaf roof. Small candles were lit and I noticed, for the first time, a young boy sleeping wedged between two big bales of fabric. His arms and legs were splashed with dried mud. His too-big T-shirt hid a baggy pair of adult shorts. His bare feet were calloused and his scrawny legs twitched as he dreamed. Moe Moe said his name was Pad De Klo, meaning 'Restless, Never Still.'

"He sleeps under the huts like a dog. He never uses a mosquito net and is never sick with malaria or dengue. He's a miracle. They [doctors] should examine him."

Moe Moe added that he was always hungry. "Sometimes he doesn't eat proper food for days. He goes wandering off in the hills and survives on berries and roots. His favourite place is the graveyard; he loves funerals. He has just come back from working as a herder. He got no pay and slept with the cows. No one knows his history; he has no parents. He says he had an uncle, but he didn't want him."

Tha Ko nodded and said, "Not all Karen are good people. It's important you see us for what we are. Some Karen steal children and sell them if it will make them money."

Moe Moe interrupted him before he got on a roll and introduced me to Hnin Thi Da Myint, a pretty girl just turned fifteen. Her father was Pa-O and her mother Shan, but both had been dead for five years. An elderly neighbour adopted Hnin, gave her the Burmese part of her name—Myint—and then sold her to a carry who took her to Thailand.

Hnin was smuggled to Bangkok and sold to a rich Thai family as a domestic servant for 30,000 baht.

Hnin spent three years with the family without any pay. "I was sold to them," she said. "They didn't have to pay me. I ate with them. They loved me. I went to the shops and restaurants with them. They taught me how to eat with chopsticks and a spoon and fork."

In spite of feeling loved and being treated to restaurant meals, Hnin said without bitterness that the wife got upset with her when she was 'mischievous.'

"I broke seven plates and she got angry. She threw the broken pieces at me and cut my head." Hnin moved her fringe to show a scar on her forehead. "I was also beaten with a leather belt when I made mistakes. They beat me but loved me," she said without irony.

Even though the conditions were reasonable at the house, it upset Hnin that she did so much work and never got paid for it.

"One day the man and his wife went out and the children were all watching television. I took three dresses off the clothes-line and left."

Hnin's story became unclear, but while on the run in Bangkok she somehow met a man who spoke Burmese. "He took me to a house where many Burmese people were waiting to go back to Burma."

The man was another carry, who offered to take Hnin to Mae Sot.

"We went by car and when we arrived I was sold to another Thai family. I was supposed to cook, but I didn't know how, so they taught me."

The family of seven included five children, all older than Hnin. Once more she worked for no pay.

"It wasn't fair. I did lots of work and got nothing. The old man would fondle me. I didn't like that, so I escaped."

Hnin gave the impression that the old man did a lot more than just fondle her, but she wouldn't elaborate with so many other people now in the room.

When the man sent Hnin to buy chicken, she took the money and kept going. "I met a Burmese man and he took me on a *songtaew* to a house near Umpiem refugee camp. I stayed a night and the next morning, then the man told me to go to the camp and say I was a refugee."

At the camp, Hnin was taken to the women's boarding house.

"I was sent to kindergarten. I was the biggest, but couldn't write. The girls teased me and called me names. After three fights I was expelled."

Hnin punched one of the younger kids, made her nose bleed, knocked her unconscious, and then kicked her in the stomach. She was sent to Mae La into the care of Moe Moe and the KWO.

Hnin said she had had enough school: "I'm too big. I don't want to go to 'kindy.' I want a shop to sell shaved ice, snacks, and cold drinks."

Let Let Win had 'showered' and now sat on the floor combing her wet hair. A tiny girl half crawled, half pulled herself across the floor to her lap. The girl couldn't talk and her body movements were a series of uncoordinated jerks. As Let Let Win reached out to her, she beamed.

Let Let Win told me that the girl's parents had abandoned her and she was found foraging for food scraps under a hut. People called her Naw Bet Koh—'Beak'—because of her misshapen head. Let Let Win pulled the girl into her lap and massaged her skinny arms and legs. The girl relaxed and her eyes shut with the contact of Let Let Win's hands.

Children were not the only ones receiving help from Let Let Win. Ba Sein, his wife Ma Htun, and their three children had suffered twenty years of misfortune at the hands of the Burmese military, who had targeted Ba Sein for portering.

"If I couldn't go, they fined me 1,000 kyat a month," he said. "When I couldn't pay, I ran away, but they caught me. They gave us one cup of rice a day. After about four days, I was following the lead porter and he trod on a mine. The two in front took the full blast and died. I lost the sight in my left eye.

"For ten years I was lucky. I worked for them but nothing bad happened. Then, in 1997, they took me again to build a fort. We cut timber and cleared land. I was sick, but still had to work. I went to the forest to cut bamboo. The load was too heavy, but they made me carry it. On the way back I fell down and was impaled on spikes used to protect the fort. The load held me down and my good eye was punctured. We had no money for treatment. I went to the traditional healer and he put herbs on it. My eye healed but I was now completely blind. Some people die, some get well, that's life."

With her husband unable to work, the responsibility of feeding the family fell on Ma Htun. Two mines had exploded in two days near their village, but she decided to gather leaves in the forest. "I walked off the path. The mine blew my leg apart. I fainted and my friend tied my sarong to slow the bleeding. I was lucky. It only took two hours to get to a hospital. Now we are both disabled and it's difficult to work. Before I lost my leg, I could get work pounding rice; now my husband does it with our guidance. I weave clothes and my eldest son tends cattle. It will take all day to tell you my troubles, they're endless. We wanted our children to grow up and live some life without hardship. For us, they're our hope. I don't want my son to work. I want him to go to school."

Car Htoo Heh was only eight years old, but his young face showed he took his responsibilities seriously. "I'm happy I can help my ma and pa," he said. "When people need water in the camp, I find some in the hills and sell it to help ma."

Ma Htun nodded. "He's a good boy, he takes nothing, he gives me all. We depend on him, we need him."

Car Htoo swelled with pride. "I'll do any kind of work that will earn money, but I would like to become a teacher."

The group of adults listening to our talk laughed at his ambition, but the boy, anxiously twisting his hands, was serious—and so far he had helped put food on his family's table.

Moe Moe called to the shadows for a young girl to come and talk. Ma Nweh looked fifteen, but she didn't know her age. Her story was like something out of a Dickens novel.

"When I was small, I remember my ma and pa, but Pa went away and Ma gave me to a Buddhist nun. I stayed with her for ten years until, one day, a Burmese woman made friends with us. She said she wanted to look after me and adopt me. The nun didn't want me to leave, but I was fed up of begging. She said she would teach me, so I left with the woman. She lied and sold me to a brothel in Mae Sot. I cried a lot. One of the men told the police they used under-age girls, so I was taken to the police station and my adopted mother was also arrested. We had to pay the police. The woman paid for herself and said she'd come back for me. She didn't. I stayed three days and was released. I went to a house where my adopted mother used to go. She took me to another brothel and sold me. I ran away and went back to her. She sold me again. This time I stayed three months and wasn't paid. They used us like slaves. I escaped with an Indian girl and we went to her mother's house, but her mother sold me to another brothel in Mae Ramet [35 kilometres from Mae Sot]. I was there one month when the cook said that if I agreed to be his wife he would help me; if I didn't he said he would kill me. We left and came to Mae La to his family. He made me work and give him money. I got pregnant and he got addicted to *yaa baa*. I bought a lottery ticket and won 5,000 baht. He took all the money and went to Bangkok without me. His uncle and aunts beat me and called me a prostitute. The KWO found me and took me from them. When my baby was born, my husband returned from Bangkok and I went back to him. His aunts tried to give my baby away, but I couldn't let them, I love her. My husband left to go north. I followed him and found him with another woman. He drove me away, so I came back here.

"I've had a poor life. I've suffered much and I didn't know where to go, but I am happy with the KWO. People in the camp don't like me because I was a prostitute. Some are cruel. Some men are nice to me, but they just want sex."

Ma Nweh drew her baby, Hnin Hnin Way ('Floating Mist'), close, and stroked her face and hair before continuing, "My baby is exactly one year and seven months old. I never knew my age, so it's important that I know my baby's. I want her to have a good life. I am learning to sew and weave while I'm still young."

But in spite of her baby and the weaving lessons, Nweh said she found it hard to feel good about herself: "I don't trust people. Men, I hate them . . . they hurt me bad. I know I can't fight them, I can only hate."

Outside, as if on cue, a group of men began to argue. One of them leaned through the open door, drunk but not unpleasant. Let Let Win moved quickly and took the man by the arm and led him back outside into the darkness. Minutes later he was back. This time she gave him a mouthful of rough talk. Shamed, he stumbled away.

Let Let Win pulled the bamboo door closed and bolted it from the inside. She smiled and touched Ma Nweh gently.

Tha Ko nodded and laughed again. "Let Let Win tells it straight. Some people say her delivery is rude and aggressive, but she has to be. So many women and children need her protection."

13 The Hardman

General Bo Mya was the acknowledged hardman and defence minister of the Karen National Liberation Army. After 55 years fighting the Burmese, he lived in guarded exile in Mae Sot. Rumours and innuendo flew around border towns about the old general. Academics, human rights activists, NGOs, journalists, Burmese opposition groups, barflies, and Burma know-it-alls threw all kinds of labels at him. He has been called a warlord, a despot, a nationalist, a conservative, a killer, a tax collector, and a cruel dictator, and has been described as corrupt, uneducated, and backward.

Bo Mya has been a thorn in the side of the Burmese for decades. Hated, but respected, by the dictators, they have painted him as a despotic leader in the mould of Conrad's Colonel Kurtz. On one occasion they published, in their national media, dubious, blurred pictures they alleged were of him bayoneting his own soldiers.

I wanted to interview General Bo Mya to see which, if any, of the labels stuck. He was one of the last of Southeast Asia's old style minority leaders still fighting.

Asians generally expect interviews to be friendly chats. Confrontational questions are not appreciated. It would not be considered polite to question the old man on rumours, best-forgotten incidents, or flaws in his leadership.

I was driven by his son, Colonel Ner Dah, to a secure house outside Mae Sot. We sat outside at a large teak table. A poster of Stallone's Rambo and another of a waterfall framed the wall on either side of the general as he sat down. Hot Chinese tea and biscuits were served by a muscular man. In the background, KNLA men sat around talking and chewing betel nut. The old man kept still. He wore a Karen sarong, military vest, and kept a stout cane by his side. Initial appearances were fearsome. His eyes sat hard in his jungle-ravaged face. This was a man who feared no one, at peace with his god.

I asked the general about his earlier life, and he slowly and carefully chose his words. He was one of twelve children born to a poor hill-farming family in Papun district in the northeast of the Karen State.

"My parents never thought they would give birth to a soldier. In my village, people didn't lie. Our headman taught us not to steal from our neighbours and to help each other. If someone was bad, no one wanted to marry into their family."

Bo Mya's father died when he was young, and he credited his mother with bringing him up. "She always taught me to love our Karen people. Even when I was a young commander she'd say, 'look after them . . . make sacrifices for them . . . work for them.' She told me she was proud of me, and that meant a lot."

Bo Mya joined the Karen resistance when he 21. "It was during the war [WWII]. What happened under the Japanese occupation shaped my thoughts. The Burmese collaborated with the Japanese, but instead of fighting the British they targeted the Karen. The BIA told the Japanese the Karen were British puppets and we 'had to be pulled up by the roots and killed.' In the cities they killed, burned our homes, and raped our people. In the country we were harder to catch. I realized we must have our own land, otherwise we would be hunted and killed like forest animals. The BIA were fierce and cruel. Even the Japanese insisted they had to stop. Their own leader, Aung San, said his army was undisciplined because of the criminals they had recruited from the jails."

Even if the old warhorse despised his Burman enemies, he still respected Aung San. "He was okay. When he changed the name of the BIA to the Burmese Defence Army, he encouraged Karen to join. There was some understanding between Aung San and us. Maybe it was because Aung San's mother-in-law was Karen. He was always willing to talk peace with us."

Bo Mya began his military career as a policeman, but during the latter part of World War II he joined Force 136. When the Karen revolution started in 1949, he became a Karen soldier, and by the end of the year he was promoted to sergeant in the newly formed Salween Battalion. He quickly rose through the ranks and, by 1966, was general-in-command, and by 1976 president of the KNU. He had also beeen defence minister and supreme commander. (At the time of publishing, ill health had forced him into retirement).

I asked Bo Mya if the Karen people would not have been better off if the KNU had stopped fighting years ago. His reply came with an intense stare that bore through me.

"If we had not fought, there would be no Karen. We're only alive today because we defended ourselves. The Burmese have not achieved what they set out to do after independence. One of their first laws was to ban ethnic languages in schools. Without our language and our culture, the Karen are dead people. The educated Karen were targetted. Those without education were controlled, and those who struggled were killed. I still believe it's better to die fighting than live like a slave . . . what sort of life is that?"

In the long pauses between his words and stares, I felt my question might have sounded flippant to him. His eyes refused to let mine go, and he ignored my attempt at a smile.

"Many ethnic groups have been deceived," he continued. "Signing an unconditional cease-fire is surrender. We don't surrender. We want the right of free people to organize our own destiny."

Various medical NGOs have privately accused Bo Mya of continuing the struggle to the detriment of his people. They say the KNU uses the conflict to generate income for their own ends. The general denied this.

"I'm not against a cease-fire. I want peace. But for us, a cease-fire means no surrender but a mutual discussion to settle for peace with dignity. If it doesn't work out, we go back to our previous positions. Those groups who have signed a cease-fire with the dictators have had all the doors closed on them; there's no way out and their people are worse off."

I put it to Bo Mya that NGOs and Burmese opposition groups have labelled him as undemocratic. His answer was blunt and to the point. "We're criticized by some people, yet we have accommodated them all. No one helped the Karen against the dictators, but in the internal 1988 and 1990 crack-downs we gave the students and opposition groups shelter. We took them in, trained them, fed them, and cared for them when they were sick."

Bo Mya dismissed these critics as politically naïve and self-serving, and predicted there would be an NGO stampede to Burma if sanctions and the conflict ends. "They don't understand politics. They criticize me to further their own careers and ambitions. They are selfish, they don't think about the dignity of our struggle. The KNU is an easy target to tell lies about—the Burmans do this so they can get themselves foreign citizenship. If they wanted to help our struggle, they would stay here and help, but we don't need their kind to defend us. Some are chauvinistic about their own ethnic group; they play political games and call us undemocratic. They depend on us, but keep putting us down. They call us killers, but we have joined or formed every opposition group and held key positions. We have shown our unity, we've kept our dignity—not because we reject peace, but because peace without justice is worthless."

The general did not dodge any questions, so I asked if he was a 'warlord.' The question started a laugh deep inside him that continued until it finally erupted.

"It seems like I was. In the past we [ethnic leaders] may have acted like warlords, but underneath we all wanted to contribute for a genuine federation of Burma. There were no clear laws to guide us. We had to grab our territory and do what we could to protect it. But now we have international laws. I did meet with Khun Sa [the infamous drug warlord], to try to get him to stop trafficking drugs."

I put to Bo Mya the allegations that he was cruel to his troops.

"I'm not cruel. I'm strict. I love my people. I make no apology for commanding my men with strict discipline. If they killed innocent people or raped, I punished them severely. I even killed them. In 1962 some of our KNLA soldiers became like dacoits [bandits]. I fought them and killed them. It is important to have discipline because when you give men guns they can do much wrong. If we do what the Burmans do to villagers, we are no better than them. I don't care if the wrongdoers are Burmans or Karen—they're not with me, they're against me. It also happened in the old 5th Brigade when some of the leaders and soldiers robbed and raped our people. I punished them, I killed those who had raped, looted, and murdered our people. I've been fighting all my life against the Burmans, but I've never considered the Burmans my enemy. My enemies are the dictators and oppressors. I've captured many Burmese soldiers and I've tried to re-educate them. I don't hate them. They've been misled and I release them. I say to them, 'if you go back, don't do anything to hurt our people.' I say to them the Karen and Burmans are no different, it's the leaders who are at fault."

I brought up the grisly rumours of cannibalism on jungle battlefields, and asked Bo Mya if there was any truth to this. It was obvious that the general was becoming tired of my questions about the dark side. He fixed his gaze onto me and said, "War is hell . . . many bad things happen . . . everything is dirty. You cannot have a nice war. It's about hatred. In the past we had some soldiers who did crazy stuff. Some soldiers want revenge for the deaths of their parents killed or tortured by the Burmese, so they might do this. I have heard rumours . . . of Burmese officers cutting off parts off a living soldier and making him eat himself. Human beings commit a lot of crimes during fighting. There's nothing good about war, any war. Do you think America's war in Iraq is clean?"

I could see the old man was getting tired, but I nudged him onto the subject of KNU tax collecting. A variety of sources estimated that, during the 1980s and early 1990s, KNLA/KNU 'tax gates' generated as much as 7 million US dollars a year. Everything that crossed the border—cattle, timber, gems, vehicles—was taxed; the revenue paid for weapons for the KNLA.

"Our tax gates were very important to our resistance. We never needed to ask other countries to pay for the revolution. The gates were useful to everybody. Look at Mae Sot, it was nothing more than huts and dirt roads that turned to mud. Everyone made lots of money off the Karen."

Today, with no control over any fixed territory, the KNLA struggles to compete with the Burmese army and DKBA to tax border trade. At times this throws up scenes straight out of Joseph Heller's *Catch 22*, in which one of the characters sells and buys and re-sells oil, weapons, and food to and from all the warring sides. Thai logging companies have to negotiate with whoever controls the forests and roads. At times they have to pay all three sides to stop fighting while they get the timber out. This has a double-edged effect on the KNLA. It delivers much needed money, but at the same time, roads built to get heavy trucks in and out of the forests provide the Burmese with infrastructure to move artillery, supplies, and troops into once inaccessible areas. The KNLA relies on the dense forests and the monsoon deluge for protection.

Bo Mya accused certain Thai government ministers, ASEAN, and Western businesses of being more interested in making money out of Burma than with protecting human rights.

"These people have no principles. They care only about their pockets. They have democracy in their own countries, but they don't care that we don't. Money is the only thing they love."

The general denied claims that his position had made him rich. "I could have been a wealthy man living in Burma. They promised me big houses, cars. They said, 'you'll have armed guards to look after you and wealth beyond your dreams.' I told them to go and never come to my place again. The reason I'm struggling is not for myself but for my people. I've sacrificed too many years that wealth won't make up for. Our mission is to free the Karen."

The split with the Karen who formed the DKBA still hurt Bo Mya deeply. "The Burmese knew they could not defeat us. They used everything and failed. Then they realized they could win if they divided us. I said to them, 'never join with your enemy. If you do, *you are* the enemy'."

Military strategists blame the destructive split between the Karen, and the inability of their leaders to effectively respond, as the key factors in Manerplaw's fall to the Burmese. Bo Mya said that critics blamed his discrimination against Buddhists for the split.

"I tried to talk with them, but their minds were already made up. They preferred to take what the Burmese offered them."

Finally, I asked the general if he was tired of fighting.

He unfolded a black and white newspaper clipping and showed me a picture of a Karen villager cradling the head of his dead wife.

"This keeps me going. When your people are being killed, you're not afraid anymore. When you lose someone you love, you don't care how much you have to sacrifice."

In the eyes of his people, General Bo Mya was still the most renowned, respected, and strongest symbol of their struggle for freedom. He was in his late seventies and in ill-health at the time of our meeting. His death would leave a void that will be hard to fill. Or maybe, as his detractors said, it would allow a more democratic debate among KNU members.

14 Adventure Travel

It's been a long time since the KNLA has been able to afford to hire mercenaries, but that hasn't stopped a constant trickle of foreign ex-soldiers turning up in Mae Sot looking for action. Over the years, Americans, Canadians, Australians, Brits, Swedes, French, Germans, Israelis, Portuguese, Japanese, and many others have fought with the Karen. It would be hard to find a single motivation why these men fight for the Karen. Some come with a genuine desire to help, some to get their kicks, others are driven by personal demons. But whatever their reasons, it can be guaranteed that it isn't money that attracts them.

James, a young New Zealander in his thirties who I met in one of the KNLA camps, told me his incentive for fighting with the Karen was to get valuable experience learning how to ambush and kill. He intended to enhance his résumé and increase his chances of getting a high-paid contract with an international 'private military' company selling security services in Africa or the Middle East.

But the situation on the border has little in common with the world of private companies hired to protect oil sheikhs or diamond mines in Africa. There are no contracts, no wages, and no special rations.

Many of the self-promoting 'instructors' and adventurers justify their involvement by declaring that the Karen are Christians, the ragged underdogs battling brutal dictators; they are anti-drugs; or against communism. But for all their rationales, it doesn't disguise the fact that these men have come to kill. Sometimes they adjust the Karen's conflict to fit their own out-of-focus perspective.

Against the bravado of the self-announced, another group is almost invisible—professionals who were, or are, still attached to some clandestine military agency. They come to Mae Sot *not to be seen.* They don't brag or walk the walk. They simply say, if asked, 'we're here to give humanitarian aid and train medics.'

In Mae Sot, military adventurers are easy to spot. They come alone or in twos or threes. They look impressively fit. They start out silent, keeping their talk to monosyllabic responses. But it's a game. It usually doesn't take long for them to confide in one or two of the local barflies. Journalists are avoided until they decide they want to talk. Older men may have fought in Vietnam, or, if not, desperately wished they had.

James said he had served with the British army in Northern Ireland. "I wanted a scrap and I heard about the revolution in a bar in Bangkok. I heard that the Karen took foreigners, and they were the good guys. I was a field combat engineer—first in and last out. We were trained to build or blow up bridges, hook up water supplies, lay mines and clear them. But when you stop, you always want to know if you can still do it . . . see what you're made of."

James said the KNLA are fussy whom they let join. "They don't just take anyone. They test you and keep an eye on you. They get a lot of wannabes turning up. They usually fall down, as they can't take the food, land-mines, can't speak the lingo. The boredom is hell, and nobody mentions all the hills. At the other end you get the nutters . . . killers, but they don't last out here—or for that matter in regular armies. War is a bunch of crap."

James told me he came back to the Karen often because he missed the rare flashpoints of action. He got a sense of belonging, and the planned ambushes brought a sense of meaning to his life.

"You need lots of discipline, and those that don't have it leave. Professionals are different. They're looking for something. We've got blokes here who have been with the UN in Kosovo, a couple of Swedes who just wanted a scrap. But coming here was a shock for them, as they were used to good food, clean beds, and strict orders. This last trip, I ate dog. I've eaten monkey, snake, bear, rat, frog, and bugs—I've only missed out on lizard. The Karen are too casual. These guys freaked out when they saw mines lying around the camp in cardboard boxes."

James gave me the impression he didn't really feel the Karen or their struggle was all that interesting. He was unable to offer any insight to what their conflict with the Burmese was about. He was merely there to feel alive, shoot at an enemy, and blow things up. The drama and the re-telling of surviving the battlefield was what he was after.

"The Karen are a real mixture. Some [soldiers] are young and some are very old. We operate as small guerrilla units. We hit and run, fire and move on. I get scared when they're sending down mortar, but half the time you don't think about it. I'm really worried about mines. I was next to a guy who tripped a wire, it was just a blast mine . . . I wasn't too happy about that. I trod on one, but it was old and didn't go off—luckily the detonator had rotted away. The Karen use mines a lot. I just wish they were better made. We have to use them to defend our positions and to divert their soldiers to where we can ambush them. We don't have the money to do anything else. We can only chip away a small piece at a time. Normally we back off. Do the damage and slip away, otherwise it's 400 of them to twenty of us. The Burmese build a road, we blow it up—but the wet season does that anyway. We also use trip-wire claymores. Nobody wants to show they're scared, and that worries me, as they do take stupid risks. The Karen will keep plodding along, hoping America will come along and save them."

James seemed slightly miffed about talking to me, but got some satisfaction at my ignorance about guns as he described the various weapons the Karen use. He used stick drawings in my notebook to explain the differences. I steered the conversation back to try to find out what he knew about the relationship between the KNLA and the DKBA. I'd heard conflicting stories of how some units on both sides still talked to each other, and how, in some instances, the KNLA got warnings about planned Burmese attacks. I wanted to know if James had seen any evidence of this.

"We don't clash very often with the DKBA. They are mainly concerned with their drug business, and unless we're after taking out the drugs, we leave them alone."

James wasn't interested in the political machinations between the KNLA and the DKBA, or the strong family ties that still existed between soldiers in both groups. It was enough to know that the DKBA were the Buddhist bad guys, and therefore justifiable targets. I had the feeling James was lonely. He was without friends, socially awkward, and kept himself comforted by secrets he wasn't about to tell.

"I don't get paid here and I don't have a problem with that. But I will have to find something to make money. My mum keeps saying to me to come home and settle down, but I don't know what I can do after this."

I asked James if he enjoyed killing.

"Killing is easy. If it was my buzz, I wouldn't come to a war zone; it would be easier to do it back home. In New Zealand your enemies don't have guns to shoot back."

The last I heard of James was that he got on the wrong side of a couple of crazed Western adventurers in another KNLA camp. They stuck a gun in his mouth, held him captive overnight, and told him to "fuck off back to your own country" and if he didn't, he was dead. James slipped back to Mae Sot, gathered his gear, and bolted. It was lucky he did, as the two men had second thoughts and went looking for him, armed with pistols, at his guesthouse.

Rob, who I was introduced to at Kung's Bar one evening, was a Vietnam veteran far removed from the tough talking clichés common in Mae Sot. He was in his late fifties, looked fit, and appeared comfortable in his skin. He was quiet, didn't like attention, and said he was determined to help the Karen.

"I don't need to wear a gun to do that," he told me. "I have no problem carrying a gun, but I'm not an aggressor. I'm not combat now, but I go where NGOs can't or won't because of the conflict. Missionaries say they're there to help, but once the shooting starts they leave and start praying. What kind of witness does that make them?"

Rob's words seemed harsh until I realized he was speaking as a devout Christian.

"I see this as an opportunity to prove my faith and my commitment. I'm helping the Karen defend themselves against oppressors. I started doing this work with the blessing of my church, but with the present mood in the US towards armed ethnic groups, they said I was on my own."

I next met up with Rob at a KNLA camp close to an IDP village. He had come to assess what the people needed and to advise on the camp security. As we sat talking and drinking coffee outside his hut, Rob noticed that a ditch he wanted dug around the edge of the camp hadn't been worked. He excused himself, picked up a shovel, and walked towards the trench. He dropped in and started shovelling. Within minutes, Karen soldiers were digging with him.

With the job underway, Rob returned to the table and said the best way to help was to do something useful. But, he added, the complexity of the Karen's struggle was proving hard for him to understand.

"I ask myself should we be here at all. We're not Karen and it's not our fight, but in the short time I've been involved, I've had friends killed by the Burmese. I'm not here because I'm bored with my life. A lot of guys, vets, come here to get prestige that they don't have Stateside. Many are running away from a wife or a life without an edge."

Rob admitted his own Vietnam War experiences were something special. "The excitement and camaraderie were amazing. I never felt anything like that before or since. War produces such a range of emotions—love, fear, empathy, sympathy, and hate. The bond between two men who have fought together is one of the greatest. I believe there's honour in war; it's nasty, but you also see people at their best. People don't hear about the compassion. I saw a lot of people killed, and I killed. We had everything to throw against the Viet Cong—planes, chemicals, and bombs. I had such a lot of respect for them, but I couldn't show it, especially serving in the Marine Corps."

The moon sat fat and bright above the camp. Shafts of light filtered through the jungle canopy. Rob said that he found talking about his war experience was difficult. "Back then, nobody talked about it. Even your best friend wouldn't talk about his fears. We desperately needed to talk, but we couldn't. Back in the sixties, men didn't. I've seen weeping men hiding their tears. I still don't remember the names of friends who died there. I've blocked it out."

The mental anguish was not the only scar Rob carried from the Vietnam War. "I was shot and I had my thyroid removed after I got cancer from constant drenching in Agent Orange."

Later that night, Rob leaned on his bamboo table and read his well-thumbed Bible by candlelight. He got up to pee and left his handgun on the Bible as a bookmark. I took a photograph and noticed the pages were open on the Book of Jeremiah.

Next day we visited the IDP villagers and Rob diligently entered every request for medicine, food, fuel, clothes, and Karen Bibles in a large book. His neat writing listed—alongside photographs and names—details of what was needed: education for a child, medicine for a sick wife, roofing materials, schoolbooks. Each person who stopped him got a hearing. In spite of my impatience to get back to camp, Rob took the time to find an interpreter and listen to a young man tell us that his wife had six-month-old twins but her breast milk had dried up. The woman had fed the twins on rice water for three weeks and was desperate to get milk formula into them but had no money or transport to get to a town or clinic. Rob promised to return with milk, vitamins, and food for both mother and babies.

My time with Rob was in sharp contrast to my first KNLA experience in the major's camp. Rob's focus was on getting equipment to defend villagers or make their lives easier. He brought in medicine, sewing machines, seeds, and built water pipes and tanks.

Rob later went back to the US to raise more funds to help Karen villagers and to tell his family his future was now entwined with the

Karen. He returned to Mae Sot six months later—with his family's blessing—with funds and equipment, including microscopes that could be run from solar panels and would be used to test for malaria and other diseases.

15 Hungry Ghosts And Soul Stealers

As soon as the Asian monsoon ends, photojournalists invade Mae Sot to seek out Karen freedom fighters. The light is right, and there's no more damp mould, mud, or dengue fever. By mid-February the dust and heat is intolerable, and the journalists making promises to tell the world and keep in touch, melt away.

It doesn't help that the Karen are slow to react to news events. Adding to the confusion, NGOs, missionaries, and a whole host of other groups put out their own stories to generate funding for themselves. Some are inaccurate and contradict other versions of the same story.

Tha Ko talked to me about the way the Karen are misrepresented, and accused some journalists and NGOs who ask to be taken illegally across the river of delivering little and understanding even less.

"Unfortunately, we think that everybody is our friend. We are accountable for donated money, but why make us beg. We help researchers, NGOs, and journalists do their work. They say they want to help us, but they often do more harm than good. They see young boys in camps, they take pictures, and write stories saying we recruit child soldiers."

Young boys photographed in uniform often overplay and over-estimate their own level of involvement for the cameras at the urging of Westerners. It is easy to check their stories with a camp commander, but not many journalists bother to do so. Reporters and human rights activists tend to equate the Karen's use of child soldiers with that of the Burmese. But while the Karen may have a couple of hundred volunteer youths in army camps, the regime conscripts and forces as many as 150,000 to fight.

Tha Ko laughed as he told me about international news crews and documentary makers who offer to pay the Karen to use live ammunition and splatter blood plasma around to create fight scenes that never happened. Freelance cameramen have paid for ammunition and offered to 'buy' an ambush for 30,000 baht.

Too often, those who can't find the story are only too willing to fake it. A journalist friend told me of the time he helped an international television crew visit Karen villagers.

"They wanted men with guns, an illegal boat crossing, and jungle backdrops. The whole thing was completely safe, but the reporter wanted drama. He was doing his 'walk-to-camera' surrounded by Karen when the cameraman noticed the villagers had changed into their best clothes. He stopped the camera and said it would be better if they could put their rags back on."

The dog-eat-dog world of freelance journalism attracts the desperate and those willing to get their hands bloodied. They come wired, driven by angst, busting a gut to get started. The adrenalin rush, dead-end contacts, and being outside the local loop, contributes to their anxiety. They're all hurry and have difficulty trying to adjust their already mentally written stories to the complex reality confronting them.

Tha Ko told me many journalists try to coerce him into finding bizarre stories for them. "You journalists are obsessed with what you want. You create an impression you're sympathetic to our cause, but it doesn't go any further than your brief time spent here. I show you victims, starving people, and our soldiers. Does it change anything? Getting involved means sweating with us. We don't want you to become Karen, we want your help."

Tha Ko was talking about me as much as anyone. And he had a point.

A media archive search for stories about the Karen showed that when the media does report the Karen's conflict, it prefers to concentrate on bizarre stories like that of the 'God's Army.'

God's Army was a splinter Karen guerrilla gang led by twelve-year-old twins, Johnny and Luther Htoo. Their 200 followers believed the twins had magical powers. The media latched on to this and, in one article, a journalist managed to describe the twins as "charismatic," "mysterious," "demons," "deities," and "saviours."

The association between God's Army and the KNU was vague, but when they took hostages at Ratchaburi Hospital in Thailand, in January 2000, it caused international outrage and a regional backlash against the Karen. The hostage-taking turned out badly. The twins' Burmese student allies were captured and executed by Thai commandos. The twins were handed over to their mother, Mah Kae, saying that all they wanted was to return to Burma and go to school like other kids.

Aung San Suu Kyi is the main news hook for reporting Burma. She is a more appealing and a more easily digestible story than the Karen struggle. Her beauty, English education, years of house arrest, Nobel Peace Prize, resilience, and non-violent stance against the Burmese generals have created a modern legend. Her story can be simply told—in media shorthand—as Beauty and the Beast.

During the 2002 monsoon, I was hired by a media training agency to teach interview techniques to fieldworkers from the Committee of Internally Displaced Karen People (CIDKP). The workers went deep inside the Karen State organizing aid and medical help for villagers in jungle hide-outs. They also documented eyewitness accounts of killings, rapes, forced labour, relocations, and other abuses. We examined newspapers to see how events were reported. I emphasized how news outlets needed credible sources to quote, and unquestionable proof, before they'd run stories. I stressed that it wasn't enough to just keep repeating the Burmese military was barbaric. A mantra found its way onto the whiteboard: 'Prove it. Use photographs. Interview witnesses and victims. Do it while it is still new.'

As one rainy morning session broke for lunch, one of the older students, Richard, pulled me aside and thrust four or five coloured photographs into my hands. The intensity of the rain increased. Drains, unable to cope, overflowed. Inside, the heat from fourteen of us condensed on two small windows. Mosquitoes hovered around my bare ankles in search of fresh blood. Styrofoam containers of fried rice, cups of coffee, pork buns, open notebooks, and other details of the class blurred into the background as I stood transfixed by the horror caught in the photographs.

The first showed a row of dead children, wrapped from the neck down in Karen sarongs. Each one was crudely tagged and made ready for burial in a shallow dirt trench. The next picture showed a pair of hands trying to lift a shirt over the head and off the bloodied back of a woman lying on mulched leaves and wet stones. I turned to the next: the same woman lay on crumpled green plastic sheeting on a wet jungle floor. The plastic was attached to a thick bamboo pole. A distressed man wearing nothing but loose pink shorts cradled the woman's head with one hand while with the other he tugged at her blood-soaked dress. The last picture showed the man standing over the makeshift stretcher, his body racked and convulsed with grief. He was rain-soaked, bare-chested, and clutched the woman's lifeless hand, unwilling and not wanting to let go. His grief forced his face muscles to lock, drawing his lips back from his teeth in a silent roar of pain.

Richard stood still, waiting for my response to his question, "Is this news, sir?"

I had to double check to see if Richard was making fun, but he was serious. In the Karen State, murder scenes like this were common, but it was rare for fieldworkers to get photographic proof. He thumbed through his crumpled notebook until he found what he was looking for, and started reading.

"At midnight on April 28 and 29, 2002, Burmese troops attacked the Karen village of Hti Law Bler, killing twelve people, seven of them children. The attack was led by Major Win Zaw Oo, who was in command of 120 soldiers belonging to 87/88 Division."

Richard said the man in the picture was Kho Noc, a Karen farmer, who had witnessed the killing of his wife, Naw Dalare, and three of their five children. Naw Dalare was eight months pregnant. She died ten days later, as did her unborn child. Kho

Noc's surviving two children were also injured. His daughter had the bones in her right arm smashed by shrapnel. Richard said the father and the other survivors trekked to Thailand and were now sheltering about five hours south of Mae Sot in Noh Poh camp near Umphang.

During the afternoon session, the photographs dominated the lesson, and it became obvious the CIDKP students expected me to write about the murders and get the story published. If I were to do so, there was an urgent need to interview Kho Noc and the other survivors. Fresh interviews and new information would give the story creedence. The student's expectations were not unreasonable—Richard had supplied what I had been telling them their stories lacked: proof.

The story took on a life of its own, forcing all my other commitments into the background. I made arrangements with Saw Hla Henry, the Mae Sot CIDKP co-ordinator, and Richard, to go to Noh Poh.

Later that evening, Hla Henry phoned and told me to be ready to leave early next morning.

All through the afternoon and night, the rain pounded down. I needed to go into Mae Sot, but by the time I got to the end of the *soi*, I was calf-deep in water. Expensive all-weather hiking clothing failed to live up to its waterproof promise. Instead, I bought a one-piece plastic poncho for seventy baht that did work. The wet season made everything permanently damp. Taking my camera out in the rain was a worry. Leather shoes, belts, bags—all grew a dusty green film of mould. Salt congealed inside containers in moist lumps. Mouldy green shadows crept up internal walls. Bed sheets never dried, and clothes stored in drawers smelled musty. Paper was limp, book covers curled, and pen ink bled on notepaper.

In spite of Hla Henry's reassurances to take nothing with me, I packed mosquito repellent, bottled water, poncho, coffee, and plastic bags to wrap my camera. At 5:00 a.m. I was ready and nursing a strong coffee when the lights of the CIDKP four-wheel-drive moved slowly down the flooded *soi*.

A smartly dressed middle-aged couple sat up front, and the back seat was left for me. After a quick stop on the edge of Mae Sot for petrol and a six-pack of Red Bull caffeine tonic and a bottle of rice whiskey for the driver, we headed off into the darkened curves of Route 1090, 'Death Highway.'

Before the sealed road was completed in 1986, it took fifteen days to travel the 164 kilometres to Umphang; it now takes about four hours in good weather. The jungles of Umphang, back in the 1970s, were home to Thai communists. The road got its nickname when Thai soldiers hunted and fought the communist insurgents with help from General Bo Mya. The killing and fighting on the Thai side of the border may have stopped, but local drivers are still wary of the 1,219 sharp bends they have to avoid dropping into to their deaths in the valleys below. The nickname was still apt.

Making conversation was hard, as both the woman and the driver were rocking away to an Elvis tape. I stared out the window at apple-green rice paddies and misty mountaintops. Conversation was now out of the question, and note taking almost impossible on the twisting road. As I had nothing else to do, I worried. It started with the discreet sips the driver was taking from the whiskey bottle, interspersed by deep swallows of Red Bull. That worry drifted and my anxiety focused outside to the deep valleys and massive trees that rose sixty feet before disappearing into mist. Our driver kept to the middle of the road, often moving to the wrong side of the double yellow lines. We climbed up and around mountains, and I puzzled about rectangular sections of the road marked by four strips of wood. I looked back and saw the earth underneath the tarmac crust had been washed away, leaving only a huge drop. I doubted if the thin veneer in those patches would support the weight of a bicycle let alone a car.

By noon, seven hours later, we reached Umphang and stopped for lunch at a noodle stall before driving on towards Noh Poh. On the last stretch of sealed tarmac before the camp we made parcel drops at several wooden houses on an otherwise deserted road. Finally the driver dropped me off at a wooden shophouse, and the woman said my ride into the camp would be along soon.

Local Karens stared at the rain, chewed and spat streams of betel juice into the mud. I joined them and took up position in the doorway. The rain fell harder and the road to the camp was a mess. Even four-wheel-drive trucks had trouble.

I was stuck where I was for the next couple of hours. My lift wasn't going to show. The men went into a huddle and a decision was made. They would try to get me through. A cannibalized tractor engine attached to four wheels with a wooden flatbed was brought from the village. The roof of the vehicle was a sheet of corrugated tin over the driver's seat. I changed into shorts and the plastic poncho, wrapped everything in plastic bags, and shifted my daypack underneath the poncho. Looking like a green hunchback, I climbed onto the slippery wooden bed and grabbed hold of a beam behind the driver's cab. We set off with a series of bangs, belching black diesel smoke. Even on the flat sealed road I had to hang on. Then I spotted the churned up mud road to the camp. Driving through its waist-deep potholes seemed beyond this vehicle. I almost got decapitated by low hanging branches that whipped by as we negotiated the edge of the jungle. All I could do was hang on as the truck slid around, got bogged down, and churned mud. The sight of a big yellow earth mover abandoned at the side of the road, its huge tyres deep in water, didn't bode well.

Hours later, and in semi-darkness, we slid and chugged our way to the camp gates. My arms ached from the strain of hanging on. I got down and handed my visitor's papers to the Thai officers at the gate, and they noted them in a large logbook. We continued and I was dropped off at a row of bamboo-and-thatch houses. The driver sounded his horn and Richard, who had preceded me, appeared framed by a halo of yellow light from an oil lantern. Water sheeted off the roof. He watched with amusement as I crossed the mud to him. He helped pull my dripping poncho over my backpack and hung it under the awning.

I followed Richard into his dry, candlelit home and was given a hot mug of coffee. He lived in the one-roomed house with his wife, three school-aged sons, two elderly aunts, and his six-month-old baby. The baby was attached to an IV drip fixed to a thin bamboo pole. The aunts took it in turn to either hold the child or the pole. Richard said she had typhoid. Initially I didn't get too close—then, when guilt and my lack of knowledge about the infection had exerted some balance, I made moves to touch the baby and show concern.

Richard had arranged for me to start interviewing people after I had eaten. More candles were lit, and he hung a mosquito net behind a blanket screen, making a separate sleeping space for me from the rest of the house and family. A wooden box was put in front of me, and plates of vegetables, omelette, fried fish, and a heaped bowl of steamed rice were brought out.

After I ate, Richard went to get the Hti Law Bler villagers. One by one, family by family, they came out of the rain to sit on the floor to tell me how their relatives had been murdered.

The soldiers came creeping through the night, their movements silent and precise as they worked their way up the jungle slope. Their target: two bamboo huts hiding a small group of unarmed, defenceless villagers who had disobeyed relocation orders to move to a piece of barren land at Lay Wah Kha.

Inside the huts, women and children lay together. Some had babies at breast. Lack of room had forced the men to sleep outside under trees. It was quiet except for a child coughing as the heavily armed soldiers prepared to storm the huts.

Naw Heh Hser was asleep when the shooting and mortar explosions woke her.

"I panicked and ran. Bullets were flying everywhere. I couldn't think. There was too much noise. I was outside and already running when I remembered my children."

In spite of being eight months pregnant and being hit in the face and side by shrapnel, Naw Heh Hser ran back to the burning hut for her five children, but her eldest daughter, twelve, her second youngest, five, and her mother and father were killed in the first barrage of bullets and shells.

Naw Heh Hser's children were not the only ones to die that night. When the 120 soldiers had left the killing ground, the survivors crept back out of the jungle to search for their missing relatives. The SPDC, using mortars, grenades, and automatic assault weapons, had killed seven children and four adults and wounded another nine people.

Farmer Saw Kho Noc was the man in Richard's photographs who had lost three of his five children and his eight-months-pregnant wife, Naw Dalare, also known as Pele. Tears spilled from his eyes as he told me how he tried to help his wife. As if to anchor him, Kho Noc's hands reached out to touch his two surviving children.

"Pele might have been saved. She was shot in the chest and thigh. I made a stretcher for her and, with help from my neighbours, we set out for the clinic at Mitan."

The day-long trek was the only option he had if he was to save the badly bleeding Pele and their unborn baby. The men had to cross a number of flooded streams and slippery mud tracks.

"We had been walking for nearly six hours when an army patrol stopped us and sent us back to our village. We wasted a day. Pele was in a lot of pain. We had no drugs, nothing we could give her. She was my friend . . . it was terrible to see her suffering."

On hearing that a local medic was going to the nearest town, Kho Noc gave him his life savings—20,000 kyat, about twenty US dollars—to buy medicine. But the medic did not return for four days and by then it was too late.

"Pele died giving birth to our baby. It's crazy. I don't know what their reasons were. We're just poor people."

Kho Noc said his surviving children, Kar Kur, twelve, and Dih Klee, eight, dream about their mother all the time. "They really miss her. I miss her. It was terrible for them to see her die from so much violence. I'm so lonely without her."

Kar Kur was also shot. A bullet smashed her right arm, breaking the bone. She cradled it protectively in its cast made from a bamboo table mat. A fat tear rolled down her dirt-stained face. "We ran away when the shooting started. All the people were crying and screaming. I got knocked over by a big bang and my face filled with dust and stones when I fell."

After he buried Pele, Kho Noc took his two surviving children and joined a large group of people planning to cross into Thailand. From April to June, 2002, 1,273 Karen refugees fled from this small district to Noh Poh camp. They carried what they could, but most had nothing. Kho Noc's main concern was his children.

"I had to stay awake at night to try to keep the children dry. I held large leaves over us, but we still got wet. We were hiding like animals."

But Naw Heh Hser had mixed feelings about leaving. "My memories are back in the jungle. My children and my parents are buried there. Every day I have the same sadness, but I have to be strong for my family and my new baby. This baby is even more important to me now. I will keep my memories of my daughters and parents, but I hope nobody else has to live through what we had to. It was unimaginable."

I awoke to the smell of fried eggs and the hushed voices of curious children trying not to be loud as they examined my sleeping shape. As I rolled up the blanket and net, the eldest of Richards's sons placed a heaped plate of crisp French toast next to me and left a cup of hot coffee.

After breakfast, I asked Richard if it was possible to find Naw Heh Hser, Kho Noc, and his children again, as I wanted to give them some money to buy food. We set out through the rain-soaked camp to find them.

As we walked, I felt an overwhelming sadness. At times like these, I make no pretence of trying to remain remote or hide behind journalistic objectiveness. How can you when you've just listened to a mother describe how her child was murdered? I took how I was feeling as sign to give what I could.

Naw Heh Hser was busy cleaning rice, pounding fish paste, and washing plates. In the daylight it was easier to see the shrapnel wound and bruises on her face. I thanked her for talking to me last night and asked her if she needed anything. She shook her head and then said her children had left everything behind when they fled. I promised I'd send some clothing for her and her children when I got back to Mae Sot.

Walking around Noh Poh in the rain was a comedy of errors for me. Old women watched the show from their homes, smiling every time I slipped. I usually managed to correct my slides just in time to stop falling over, my antics a series of Charlie Chaplin moments for the grinning audience. To emphasize my ineptitude, an amputee slowly and steadily overtook us, making a mockery of my clumsiness.

A queue of men and women gathered for rations outside and under a small window cut in the wall of a large bamboo hut. A woman sat outside the door of a house that blared video action. Inside, hooked up to car batteries, a film played to a packed house. We found Kho Noc staying with friends in their cramped, one-room hut. Kar Kur and Dih Klee played pick-up sticks on the floor. I noticed that Dih Klee had trouble using his left arm. When I asked Kho Noc if the boy had been injured in the attack, he said no, but Dih Klee had almost died four years before when he was badly burned.

"He knocked the rice pot over. He scalded his back. He couldn't sleep on a mat from the pain and we had no medicine, so we boiled banana leaves and wrapped him in them."

I asked Dih Klee to remove the baggy hand-me-down shirt covering his skinny body. His left arm was welded to his side by an ugly patchwork of melted scar tissue that restricted his arm movement. The children were uncomfortable with my examination and began to cry. Dih Klee sobbed, "I don't go near the rice pot now. I don't ever want to cook. I like it here. I don't want to leave. It's dry and we have cake. I never had that before. I want my ma."

Kho Noc comforted his son and I noticed a chicken bone attached to a string around his neck. I asked him what it meant.

"Without Pele, I feel nothing. I haven't given her a burial ceremony. Her soul is still out there in the rain. I have to go back to her. This means my soul, my wife's, and my children's souls have been stolen."

Kho Noc's explanation summed up what I felt the dictators are doing to the people of Burma. They embody the Karen description of *thamus* and *tak-kas*, the ghosts of evil men and vampires who torture and feed off the living.

When I got back to Mae Sot, I began writing the story for the *Bangkok Post*. I had a fever and thought I'd caught a cold getting to and from Noh Poh. I started to shake and my joints ached. I took a couple of painkillers, but couldn't sleep. My temperature reached 41 degrees. I stayed like that for three days, unable to work, before suspecting it might be more than a cold. I was driving myself mad, dipping in and out of a communicable disease handbook. By mid-morning I had yellow fever; by lunch, typhoid; and by the evening something more exotic and deadly. My wife thought I might have dengue fever. If it was dengue, I was worried. I had already had the disease in Ladakh in 1991 and it might now be the more serious strain, dengue haemorrhagic fever. I went to a local doctor for a blood test. The doctor seemed unconcerned, and pointed me towards a young woman, who took my finger and stabbed it with a sharp blade. She collected the blood in a vial and told me to wait. Within fifteen minutes she confirmed I had dengue fever. The doctor told me to drink lots of Coca-Cola and ten packets of electrolyte solution a day. In a daze, I ignored the cola part but drank as much electrolyte solution as the doctor advised.

For days I was wired. I couldn't sleep and couldn't work. In the meantime, my wife contacted Thai friends in Bangkok, who collected four large boxes of clothing and toys for the families at Noh Poh. When I recovered, I finished the story and sent it to the *Post*. I sent photos of Dih Klee's burns to friends in Australia and, within a week, they collected 1,000 dollars for an operation.

Months later, with the help of MSF and Aides Medicale Internationale, we got Dih Klee to Mae Sot for his operation, and Kho Noc came with him. It went smoothly, but Dih Klee was furious with me. He hadn't expected the pain when the doctors shaved layers of skin from his thigh so the surgeons could graft it onto his arm and side. When he saw me after the operation, his face turned into a scowl that made his father and Tha Ko laugh.

To help his recovery, we moved him to a patients' house. One day, I phoned, asking how Dih Klee was, and was confused when, each time, the person on the other end of the phone would hesitate and then crack up laughing. Tha Ko later explained that Dih Klee translated as 'Big Testicles' or 'Big Scrotum.'

When the pain from the graft had passed and he was happier, I took Dih Klee a leather football, grapes, and a couple of large apples. He treasured the apples over the football. I told him to eat them quickly, as they wouldn't keep in the heat.

Kho Noc said that when Dih Klee was better, he would go back to the Karen State to honour his wife and his children with a ceremony to release their souls from the anguish suffered in this life.

Tha Ko explained to me why Kho Noc was willing to risk his life again to perform the ceremony. "Animists believe that their dead go to a world that is upside down to that of the living. When it's night for us, it's day for the dead; but everything the living do, the dead also do. Funeral ceremonies are done to prevent souls from coming back to haunt the living. Kho Noc believes an evil spirit has stolen his soul and he will only get it back by performing a soul calling ceremony. Only then will he get peace."

Tha Ko joked that the Karen needed to perform a lot of ceremonies if they are to rid themselves of all the evil Burman spirits. Kho Noc's determination to return and honour his wife was another brave act of Karen resistance against the hungry ghosts and soul stealers.

16 All Wars Are Dirty

When I ran the journalism-training workshops on the border, I worked with either a Burmese or Karen translator, depending on the group. One of these translators was Aung Naing, the former Burmese student leader I had interviewed about NGOs. He was now a journalist, politically aware and with a sharp sense of humour. I particularly enjoyed working with him, and he had a very interesting history I was curious to find out more about.

Aung Naing had the face of a choirboy, and he dressed like the doctor he should have become: neat blue shirt tucked into charcoal trousers. His English was excellent. He laughed easily as he joked around the edges of the tragedy that was his life. He was a former chairman of the All-Burma Students' Democratic Front (ABSDF) for northern Burma, and had played a central role in one of the biggest scandals to hit at the heart of the Burmese student army.

On February 12, 1992, student soldiers executed fifteen of their comrades accused of spying for the regime. I wanted to interview Aung Naing about it, as he was one of the leaders who ordered the executions. It was a tough place to put him in, although he was surprised that no one had ever interviewed him about the incident before.

He agreed, and we met in Mae Hong Son—where his group's classes were held—at the house of a Burmese doctor, where I was staying. Aung Naing judged it would be a long night as I placed my notebook and tape recorder on the table. He responded by getting a bottle of whiskey and a cooler of ice. He drank heavily as we talked. I let the tape recorder capture his testimony.

"In 1988 I was studying medicine in Mandalay. I was a student leader during the pro-democracy demonstrations. The regime accused me of illegal political activities, so in 1989 I left Mandalay to join the northern ABSDF in the Kachin State, close to the Chinese border.

"It was tough, most of us were city kids with no experience of living in the jungle. We built and lived in basic bamboo huts. The Kachin Independence Organization (KIO) supplied us with food, but it was difficult to survive, and many died. The Kachin didn't completely trust us, as we were Burmans. They gave us a region to make money from jade mining and tax. It was 8,000 feet high, rocky, and difficult to grow rice or crops. We depended on supplies getting through to us.

"In the rainy season the Burmese army attacked our positions, destroying our stores. We went without rice and salt for ten days. We became weak and those who got malaria died. I lost many friends, some only eighteen years old. Each of us got fifty kyat a month to live on. We existed by trapping and eating monkeys, rats, and porcupines . . . anything.

"I was shocked to see people blown up and dead bodies. I had no battle experience, but I did fight. In 1990 we fought for forty days. I took command after our chief-of-staff was injured. We got weapons from the KIO and what we took from dead enemy soldiers.

"At this time I was elected general secretary. I was in charge of our underground network. We used it to recruit students inside Burma. We began to notice we were able to go back and forth through enemy lines without problems, but we found we had recruited students who had family connections with Military Intelligence. Our numbers quickly grew to more than 800. We suspected our network had been infiltrated by MI. Reports from the front line indicated we were losing battles in suspicious circumstances. Our soldiers noticed knife marks had been cut in trees that could have led Burmese soldiers to our positions.

"We started to watch some people. We arrested four or five and, after interrogation, we had a small list. The list included members of our central committee. We found out the National Intelligence Bureau had trained some of these as spies, and others were just used as informers. I think some were motivated by ultra-nationalistic visions of a Burman master race.

"It was very difficult for us to know what to do. I panicked. We knew nothing about human rights, or, more to the point, we didn't understand. We asked the KIO to help us to interrogate. By now we had a list of eighty spies. We made videotapes in case no one believed us. We chained the spies and locked them in the barracks. A Northern ABSDF central committee decided fifteen spies would be given the death penalty. We were at war, in armed struggle with the Burmese regime. Our constitution and law said we could give spies the death penalty. Many of our comrades had been killed because of these spies. Some members called for the death penalty for the entire eighty. We debated, argued, and finally agreed to fifteen. The sentences were determined by what the spies had done and how important they were to the [Burmese] military."

Aung Naing was distressed by his memories and having to replay the events leading up to the executions. I upset him further when I asked him how the death sentences were carried out.

"Some of them were shot and some were beheaded. They were shot at close range by pistol by our officers. We thought the guns caused more suffering, so we thought if we switched to machetes it would be less. But they were not cleanly beheaded, even though the spinal cords were severed. I watched . . . it was done in front of all ABSDF soldiers.

"We would have liked to free all of them—but if we had, it would have sent a message that we welcomed spies. It was a hard decision to make, and before we made it we approached, through the KIO, Amnesty International and the ICRC [International Committee of the Red Cross]. We needed help; we wanted to hand the prisoners over to them. They said they couldn't do anything, as they could not reach us on the Burma-China border.

"It was the hardest thing I've ever done. But we felt we had no choice. It was not uncommon for armed opposition groups in Burma to execute spies. The Burmese army just killed anyone they caught on the spot without a trial."

Aung Naing left the room to throw up. He came back and swallowed hard before he continued.

"When life is peaceful, it's easy to draw moral lines, but in war it's different. In the jungle the only way to conduct politics is with armed struggle. It was said that the killings were politically motivated, but nobody gained any political advantage. We had no internal splits, none of us gained anything. Before the executions we ate fish paste, and after the executions we ate fish paste. It could have been eighty instead of fifteen. It is understandable the families are upset. We asked the parents to come and talk with us. The people who betrayed us were our friends. My friend, Htun Aung Kyaw [ABSDF chairman at the time], was executed. He was like my older brother. We were very close. He didn't admit he was involved, but evidence showed that he was.

"The fighting was hard. War is a different reality. We were isolated and had no connection with human rights groups. We had no opportunity to learn about democracy or human rights. If we had, it may have been different. I believed I needed to take responsibility and resolve the problem. There should be an investigation like South Africa's Truth Commission. People need to know what really happened. The problem will be to get MI to hand over their files. We thought we were emulating our hero Aung San by going to the jungle to fight to free our country. We didn't even know Burma was freed because of the Second World War.

"I was 24. I thought I was old enough, but after this experience I knew I was too young to be a leader. I'm glad I'm out of politics."

During lunch with Aung Naing in Mae Hong Son a few days after the interview, I pointed my spoon at a pungent dish in a wok. Aung Naing laughed and said that it was monkey intestine.

"Have some," he suggested. "It's good. It's mixed with alcohol, lime, vinegar, garlic, and ginger. Mix it into your rice or just use your fingers."

I declined, thankful I had asked instead of diving in. But the dish started us talking about the worst food Aung Naing had eaten while living and fighting in the jungle. He said that at times he was so hungry he ate anything.

"Before, when I lived in the city, I didn't do this, but in my jungle life I ate everything. Rats were especially good. We'd hear the traps go in the night and we got up and cooked them immediately."

I took the opportunity to mention again all the rumours of cannibalism I had heard buzzing around Mae Sot. The stories involved all the warring factions and came from a number of sources, but such talk quickly stopped as soon as I showed interest. If I asked if it was okay to take notes, the speaker usually clammed up and moved away. It was irritating. But my notes eventually added up and confirmed that, at different stages in the conflict, there had been incidents of cannibalism.

Aung Naing replied, matter-of-factly, "No, we never ate people, but when we were with the Kachin, Chinese traders would come down from Yunnan looking to buy human brains. They came after fighting when there were plenty of dead. They told us they put brains in alcohol . . . very strong rice wine. They said it cured mental disorders like epilepsy and improved memory. They also used monkey brains and snakes."

Aung Naing thought some commanders might have practiced cannibalism to make them look brave, while others would do it for revenge.

Other reports I heard came from the most unlikely sources—and when I was least expecting it. An off-duty Thai officer, moonlighting as a driver, once gave me a ride to a refugee camp south of Mae Sot, and out of nowhere said that he hated the Burmese so much, he had to taste one.

"I wanted to know if their hearts tasted bitter or sour," he said. "I was disappointed; it was sweet like deer. I didn't want to eat too much as I was afraid I would get addicted to the taste. Burmese soldiers are cruel and violent to villagers. They are not real men. They pick on people who can't fight back. They even attack pregnant women and cut their stomachs and pull their babies out."

In his booklet, *The Karen Revolution In Burma*, Phu Tah Moo—a Karen elder writing under the pen name, Thuleibo—tells the story of a Karen officer, Bo Hin Tha, notorious for his cruelty.

He had his own laws. Anyone that joined his company must dare eat human flesh, and he did give enemy guts and tripes for his soldiers to eat. He was cruel especially to evildoers. One day he got hold of a notorious big and heavy fellow and punished him in the most severe way. He had him tied to a post, while [with?] a chopping block and a Chinese butcher knife at ready with all the condiments. Looking straight in the eyes of the man, Bo Hin Tha addressed him, "How bad do you think you can be? I'll show you how." Then he cut off one side of his huge hanging breast, minced it with condiments, and everybody enjoyed the tasty treat with liquor to go down, while he wriggled and writhed. Finishing another breast, he ended up by cutting out his heart and liver, etc. having not enough [to eat?]. He had both fleshy thighs and drove his jeep to a Chinese noodle soup shop Zinkyaik. A thigh was carried into the shop to fry. Before finishing that also, one of them said, "Paukpaw, another leg in the jeep." The Chinaman, on taking out the leg, shouted in fright, "tattoos on the leg!" He was frightened out of his wits, poor man, but he had to do it.

I managed to track down Phu Tah Moo at the Karen's Revolution Day celebrations in 2003. He was in his eighties but in very good health, his eyes still bright, his white hair cropped close to his head. We sat on a bench in a bamboo hut and talked as soldiers brought us plates of goat and potato curry, vegetables, and steaming rice. Phu Tah Moo's legs dangled short of the dirt floor. His English was good. I asked him if his tales of cannibalism were true.

"I've seen it many times when soldiers have taken the heart and the liver. It's not strange: even in chickens and pigs, men regard those organs as special. The Wa are not strangers to cannibalism, especially in war. When they fought alongside us they said don't worry about feeding us, we'll fend for ourselves. The

Karen prevented cannibalism by having discipline and a political philosophy to support our revolution. The Karen officer I wrote about was cruel and evil. He forced his men to partake and none, except one, was any good afterwards. The only reason I can think of why men do it is out of hatred. It is not part of our culture. But imagine a thirteen-year-old boy who had both his parents murdered and he's been forced to be a porter or to clear mines. When he's older and he catches a Burman soldier, he doesn't want to waste even a bullet. He wants revenge, the bloodier the better. People objected to my putting the cannibal's name in my book, but I say, 'It happened and I'm just the reporter'."

Phu Tah Moo entertained me with stories of the Japanese occupation, the Karen struggle, and his laughter and good humour was infectious. Soon we had a crowd of curious young Karen soldiers gathered around. Before we said our goodbyes, Phu Tah Moo signed my copy of his book with the following inscription: "Cannibalism is true but not customary, but by hatred."

Saw Lwin, a front-line Karen officer I knew well said he was aware of cannibalism among soldiers, but it was not common.

"It is those who are not educated who do these things. There was also a book by a Burmese army officer, Colonel Thang Wai Oo, who said his sergeant wanted him to join him in eating a captured Lahu rebel. The colonel told him, 'He is a human like us, we don't do this'."

I asked Lwin why he thought soldiers resorted to cannibalism.

"The mentality is hatred. Some soldiers try to show their comrades they have no mercy for the enemy. But it is only a few."

I also spoke with an American soldier-adventurer who claimed he had cut the heart out of a living Burmese and took a bloodied bite from it to scare prisoners and to impress the Karen. His story was the least likely I came across, as I felt it was me he was trying to impress with his bravado.

From speaking with a wide range of military men up and down the border, it seems the urge to eat the enemy can be categorized into reasons of hatred, revenge, superstitious ritual, bravado, and pure crazed bastardry. Hunger or survival was never once mentioned as a motive.

17 Smoke Dreams

The Rangoon generals are not only smart enough to hoodwink the international community with 'democracy talks,' but also succeed in diverting attention from their efficiency as drug traffickers. The regime plays mind games with international law agencies, appearing to respond to their demands to police and destroy the drug trade.

Burma's opium production has increased by 100 percent over a ten-year period, as has land used for growing opium poppies. In 2002, Burma was the world's largest producer of opium and heroin, but lost its position to Afghanistan when production re-started there after the US ousted the Taleban. Still, the US government has estimated that Burma earns up to 1 billion dollars in foreign currency from heroin exports. Burma is the world's largest producer of amphetamines. More than 700 million methamphetamine tablets are smuggled into Thailand each year.

Considering the potential profit, I asked Tha Ko why the KNU didn't run drugs to fund the war, while the DKBA and the Burmese do. His response was preceded by a loud laugh. "It's not our way, but you've come to the right place to find out. Mae Sot is a major distribution point. I'll talk to some friends. It might take time to arrange, but we'll prove to you how the regime uses drugs to fund its war chest."

Tha Ko arranged for one of his contacts to guide me to and through Burma's drug world. The region's mountains and rivers made it impossible for law enforcement agencies to patrol effectively, but ideal country for smugglers. Opium has been a staple crop in the mountain villages of the Golden Triangle for hundreds of years, but few villagers ever get rich from it. Those making money are the Burmese generals, drug warlords, Chinese businessmen, and international criminals.

The arrangements were vague, but I trusted Tha Ko and knew that whoever turned up would not be a flake. As I had no number for my guide, it was left to him to make contact. There was not a lot I could do except wait.

I arrived in Mae Hong Son and paid for a room in one of the guesthouses overlooking the lake. I left my gear in the room and walked around the lake, detouring through the town centre. It was quiet, but in another month tourists looking for treks and cheap accommodation would arrive in hordes. I returned to the guesthouse coffee shop and ordered a mango shake and found a week-old newspaper and an even older *Far Eastern Economic Review*. My mobile phone rang.

A male voice said, "Where are you now?"

I gave the name of the guesthouse and was told to stay there and he would join me.

Over the next ten minutes, a number of men walked past, but none made contact. Then a Honda motorbike pulled up and stopped. The young man took off his helmet, entered the restaurant, and approached my table without hesitation. He asked my name and said his was Sai. He told me he was from the Shan State, part Karen by birth, 28 years old, and was a friend of Tha Ko. We chatted about Mae Sot and various people we both knew, then ordered some food: grilled spicy fish, omelettes filled with minced pork, and rice. We ate in silence except for bursts of broken conversation. The Karen don't talk much while eating.

I asked Sai if he would take me to see an opium den across the border. He said it would be dangerous, as I would attract attention and there were many informers. Even if the villagers didn't inform, they'd endanger themselves if the authorities found out a foreigner had been there. He said he'd try, but wouldn't promise. His word was enough. My experience on the border taught me to expect nothing, but be ready just in case.

Two days later, Sai called to say he'd pick me up at the guest-house in an hour. He arrived on his motorbike and we rode off and crossed the border over a creek in the late afternoon. We continued to a small village and stopped outside a wood and bamboo house. This was the *pang su ya*, the village opium house. Sai spoke to an old woman at the top of the wooden steps as he chained his bike to a big tree. The woman smiled and motioned for us to enter. Sai warned that we couldn't stay long and we would have to leave before someone informed on us. But, as I would discover, his risk assessment came before he had a taste of opium.

Sai pushed me into a large room lit only by flickering candles. The place could accommodate as many as thirty opium smokers, but it was empty now except for ourselves, an old man, and three other smokers hidden in shadows cast by the candles. Cracks in the bamboo flooring allowed the smokers to spit or retch without getting up.

I sat with my back against one of the support beams. The old man spoke quietly to Sai while rubbing his hand gently over the floor covering. Sai lay down facing the old man. The contrast between the two was more than just age. Sai was well muscled and his hair curled from the plastic mat pillowing his head. The old man was bald and looked withered, his gaunt features dominated by a large nose, long ears, and cheekbones that stretched his yellowed skin tight. His ribcage corrugated under his skin before disappearing into his hollow stomach. He lay down and drew his knees into the foetal position, while his fingers balanced a bamboo pipe. Sai lit a small lump of opium for him. The old man sucked at the smoke from the pipe's bulb and his eyes drifted until he was no longer with us or cared about us.

Sai looked at me as if to say 'what the hell' before taking a ball of opium resin about the size of a pea from an untidy pile in a dirty saucer. He pushed it onto a thin metal skewer and lowered it towards a small hole at the bulb end of the pipe. He held it there while moving the bulb towards the flame from a small oil lamp. Sai drew deeply as the resin melted and began to spit.

Sai's opium resin was mixed with dried banana leaf, a mixture he called *kha ku*.

"This is not as strong as black opium. I prefer boiled, oily opium. It's stronger and lasts longer. Opium is like a good dream; everything bad disappears. I relax into a place where no one can reach me. I don't want to do anything practical, just lie here and think. When I smoke, I have no problems, no stress, no pain, no bad feelings, only relief and happiness. It's only when I stop do I feel miserable."

Sai eased onto the floor and let the drug soothe his troubled mind. Thoughts of his lost father, abuse from Burmese officials, the interrogations, violent threats made to his family . . . all his pain was swept away as he inhaled deeper. The rat on the bamboo beam, cockroaches, mosquitoes, the boy retching in the far corner, and me . . . all vanished in a cloud of smoke.

"There are two kinds of people here," he said. "Some hate the Burmans, the others are afraid of them. Mothers scare children by saying, 'stop your crying or the Burmese will come and take you away.' If you fight them, you have to abandon your family, because they will use them to get to you. My mother had to say my father divorced her. MI pressured her, my brothers and sisters, and me about my father."

Sai's activist father left home when he was nineteen, and that's when his opium habit began.

"I had just finished studying. It wasn't easy to get work because of my father's politics. We didn't know if he was dead or alive. But the Burmese kept at us about him. The other villagers looked down on us. They said joining the revolution was bad. People were very scared. Before he left, I was considered a good person and a good student. Friend's got me started on *kha ku*. It wasn't long before I needed more. I started using boiled opium. I smoked everything—*yaa baa*, opium, heroin.

"Heroin is the easiest to use, as you can put it in a cigarette. I'd buy 100 kyats' worth wrapped in a newspaper, about the size of pill. Opium and heroin give you the best hit. I only smoked, but many friends moved on to injecting. Three of them overdosed."

The drug house started to fill. There was no music, no talking, just a steady whispering and long intakes of breath. Some helped each other to light their pipes.

Getting drugs in Sai's town, further northwest inside the Shan State, was easy. He said nothing grew but poppies. "Our town is built on drugs. One *viss* [one kilogram] of opium costs around 200,000 kyat. For about 250 kyat [25 US cents] you can buy ten pieces of black opium, or 600 kyat for thirty balls of *kha ku*. You can buy from almost any house. You can smoke in the *pang su ya* or at home. Sometimes we go to the jungle. It's the easiest business. The police and army are involved, especially when they retire. It is easier to get than noodles. Even school kids use it."

The smoke in the room built up as there was no fan. The light from the candles threw a waxen glow on the shadowed faces. I noticed Sai's face was tear stained, but he was smiling. He saw my concerned look at my watch and whispered, "Don't worry, we'll go. I was thinking of my father . . . he didn't mean to hurt us. I'm proud of him. If they consider me a Karen because of him, then I'm Karen and proud of it."

While I made notes, Sai dozed. I was getting concerned we'd be busted, but darkness dropped me into sleep. It wasn't deep enough to stop me jerking awake every time someone coughed, spat, or moved.

Sometime before dawn, Sai nudged me and said it was time to leave. The village was silent until one dog growled and barked, sending every other dog into a frenzied chorus. Sai started the bike, keeping his lights off until we were out of the village.

Back in Thailand we kept to the sealed roads and were soon back at my guesthouse. It was still early, the restaurant was in darkness, but I could hear sounds coming from the kitchen. The cook said he'd get some coffee and eggs and toast for us, and over breakfast I asked Sai about his involvement in the drug trade.

"If you don't grow it, make it, or sell it, you have no income. There are so many drug traders. I worked for one of the big Chinese bosses. He bought opium and refined it to heroin. We'd take the opium to Khun Sa's militia or to the KDA [Kachin Democratic

Army]. This was in Loimaw, Kutkai, and Mong Si areas. The KDA aren't freedom fighters, they're businessmen. The SPDC lets them do business. Wearing a uniform makes it easier."

The Rangoon generals use a number of con games to dupe the international community. And Sai had seen close-up the sleight of hand used to fool the UN and US Drug Enforcement Agency (DEA).

"Poppy fields are torched, but only after resin is removed. Village fields are confiscated, but the Wa, Kachin, and Chinese Kokang are left untouched.

Sai said he used mules or trucks to transport the drugs bought from the drug armies. "If my boss bought 600 pounds, it took six or seven of us and six mules. We used different uniforms to pass through the different territories. Sometimes we'd wear Shan, KDA, or Wa uniforms."

Getting through Burmese military checkpoints was easy, even when caravans consisted of 200 men and 100 animals. "If Burmese officers weren't with us, we'd pay the checkpoints as we went. Everyone does it. We'd pay them 500 kyats, 1,000 kyats. My boss was best friends with the northeast commander, General Tin Aung Myint Oo. They're partners in a marble and stone cutting factory."

Sai's boss re-invested drug profits into fishing trawlers, mines, and hotels. "He was a Chinese godfather, very rich, very powerful. All the rich people in our town are drug traders. When the opium was turned into heroin, it went to China—that's why drug prices are fixed to their money. We sent our methamphetamine through Thailand and China."

Sai enjoyed the danger, and he especially enjoyed the drugs. "Every trip was like a military operation. I had eight, nine rice bags filled with money to buy opium and pay bribes. We had guns and we ate *yaa baa*. We drove for days in the rainy season on mountain roads, but after taking *yaa baa* we didn't care."

Sai explained the process involved in collecting the poppy resin. "We wait until the flowers fall before we cut the pods. It's best done in the daytime. Cut too deep, and most of the sap will run on the ground. If the cut isn't deep enough, the resin hardens inside the pod. At night the exposed resin hardens to golden gum. Villagers scrape it off the pod and roll it into balls. It's then wrapped in banana leaves or paper. The pods can be cut more than once to get more resin. The resin has to be boiled, otherwise it rots. We boil it three times and filter it until just the oil is left. It's like honey, you can keep it for years.

His description of manufacturing *yaa baa* sounded a lot easier. "Heroin takes about two months. *Yaa baa* can be made anywhere. The pill press is about the size of a sewing machine."

Drug armies in Burma go to great lengths to protect their profits. Sai described the drug factories as if they were army camps. Uniformed, armed soldiers patrolled the bamboo-fenced stockades. To get inside, a special pass was needed. Sai regularly visited a factory controlled by a renegade Shan army and a Chinese warlord.

"They built their own road. The officer in charge lived in a big house with his family and bodyguards. Around the fenced area, six gunposts had three soldiers in each. There was a kitchen, storeroom, and the guestroom where I stayed. My boss stayed at the officer's house. In two large sheds at the back of the camp, they refined heroin and made *yaa baa*. A sign above the gate said '*Tha Ka Sa Pha*'—'People's Militia Against Insurgents.' My boss paid for drugs with cash, uniforms, AK-47s and M-22s. We had seven or eight rice bags filled with money. One of my friends who worked in the factory went crazy. It was strange, as he didn't use drugs. I think he inhaled too much powder. He fired his AK-47 and killed two friends."

As we ate our eggs and toast, Sai flicked through a glossy magazine left behind by backpackers. He calculated that a single designer kitchen chair in one of the adverts cost as much as it did to build a bamboo and wooden house in his village. An article and recipe for Chinese dumplings surprised him. The dumplings, a cheap snack here, were displayed in the magazine as chic, exotic food in expensive surroundings. He shook his head as he tried to understand why a black man waded in a sparkling blue lagoon with a drinks tray and a red hibiscus flower dangling from his fuzzy hair. It was an ad for a Fijian resort.

"This has no meaning for my life," he said. "It's so far above me, I can't reach it. It's a crazy world and everyone's crazy in their own way. Looking at these pictures, I now know even God can't fulfill people's wishes. Sometimes life is nonsense."

Back in Mae Sot, I discussed Burma's drug trade with Professor Desmond Ball. In a café near the official border crossing, Ball drew a rough map to show how drug barons moved their lucrative cargo out of Burma through China, Thailand, Vietnam, Laos, Indonesia, Malaysia, Hong Kong, India, Fiji, and Singapore.

Ball explained that of the estimated 700 million *yaa baa* tablets smuggled into Thailand annually, 60 million were for local sale. The rest are smuggled to other Asian countries, Australia, the US, and Europe.

Ball's research pinpointed militia groups—protected by and aligned to the Burmese military—as the manufacturers of most of the methamphetamines.

"There's no risk of detection by satellite—it goes straight from the pill press to the street. There are fewer people involved, it's easy to make, and traffickers don't have to worry about droughts or insects affecting crops. The profits are also bigger with methamphetamines."

Ball said the drug industry couldn't exist without the Burmese military. "Their army and Intelligence provides security for traffickers, guards for the factories and warehouses, and safe passage for caravans crossing into Thailand. There are more than fifty factories along the northern Thai-Burma border. You can go through each battalion and identify where they're co-located with major factories. It's part of their livelihood. In some areas they're shareholders in the production. They're not only profiting from guarding factories, warehouses, and caravans, but are also active investors."

I asked Ball to show me a drug warehouse he said could be seen from the Thai side of the Moei River. We walked along an unshaded narrow path that twisted and followed the river. Ball stopped and pointed across the murky water. "That building with the green reflective glass was an amphetamine distribution centre for the Wa, and about 350 of their soldiers lived there. A couple of doors away is a Burmese Intelligence compound."

A "Drug Intelligence Brief" put out by the DEA named the United Wa State Army (UWSA) as the "largest drug-producing group in Southeast Asia."

Our visibility made me uneasy, and I was concerned what the soldiers behind the reflective glass thought about the two Westerners pointing and photographing their camp. Behind us, tall buffalo grass blocked our view from the Thai market and the nearest help. If the Wa army were on the other side of the river, we had reason to be worried. They had a well-documented reputation for beheading their enemies.

I took some photographs and we walked back through the heat and grass to Ball's car.

Later that same week, Tha Ko phoned to say he had someone I should talk to. He made me promise to keep the meeting confidential. I also had to agree I would come alone to the interview and take no photographs.

"This guy is scared and has good reason," Tha Ko said. "It's not his real name, but we'll call him 'Moe'."

Tha Ko picked me up early the next morning and we drove southwest away from town, passing hamlets and a number of new factories behind concrete walls studded with broken glass. We stopped at a tin-roofed wooden house that doubled as a tea shop for passing trade. We sat down and a woman poured us glasses from a large aluminium teapot. A man joined us at the table and spoke quietly to Tha Ko, who introduced him as 'Moe.' He was a DKBA driver and guard, but had recently defected back to the KNU. He had inside knowledge and proof of the Burmese military involvement in the trade.

Moe cracked pieces of betel nut against his black-brown teeth. He talked nervously about his past and described his work. It was hard to understand his English as he juggled the betel nut and sucked the mouthfuls of red saliva.

"We'd meet with six Wa to pick up drugs near Myainggalay," he told us. "They'd load six rice sacks onto our truck. Each of the bags contained *yaa baa* pills packed into cigarette cartons. Getting through the Burmese checkpoints was never a problem. Usually an Intelligence officer was there and he spoke with our unit commander. When we arrived at Pa-an, two Burmese officers followed us in their government jeep."

Moe said he was surprised to see the Intelligence officers act so openly, as they usually kept their distance. "I knew we were fifty-fifty partners, but usually they don't get close—they like to pull the strings in the background. One of the Intelligence men got into our truck and two of our men in uniform got in the back with the sacks of drugs."

Moe said the officer wore a pistol and used a two-way radio to warn Myawaddy they were coming. As they approached Myawaddy, the truck dropped off Moe and the other DKBA soldiers at a check-point and took on another four Burmese Intelligence officers.

"One was a major. He didn't wear a uniform, he dressed in jeans. After about an hour, our truck came back empty. Usually the drugs are distributed along the border towns for sending across into Thailand."

If Myawaddy was now a major drug trafficking centre, then Mae Sot, directly opposite on the other side of the river, was definitely a key destination. I called Colonel Ner Dah, General Bo Mya's son, to interview and get permission from his father to visit a KNLA camp acknowledged for its drug busting operations. Ner Dah was helpful and said he'd pick me up in an hour. We drove out of Mae Sot through village hamlets, scattering chickens and children. Ner Dah, one-handed, manoeuvred his vehicle while conducting a series of telephone conversations with a Danish film crew who wanted to film KNLA soldiers, an Australian photographer after the same, and a group of English missionaries who wanted his approval and help to build a church in the Karen State!

We arrived at Bo Mya's large compound, where small groups of battle-hardened men sat playing draughts or polishing heavy pieces of teak furniture. I sat at a table and waited for the general. He arrived, leaning on his stick, and a man brought a tray with cups, teapot, and biscuits.

I asked Bo Mya why the Karen are against drugs while many of the other armed groups make millions.

"The KNLA are against all narcotic drugs," he replied. "Production or trafficking of drugs is strictly prohibited. Those who break this law get the death sentence. The KNLA attacks the Burmese military directly involved in trafficking drugs." He added that the Karen fight drugs because it is in their own interest to do so. "We don't do it to please others. Drugs are harmful to all humanity, not only to the Karen. As long as the international community tolerates the dictatorship in Burma, the more drugs will increase in their countries."

The general laughed before saying that it's common knowledge that drugs go by cargo plane and ship to Western countries, so why can't these powerful nations stop them? "We are prepared to do it, if they're not. But what I don't understand is that when we block drug runners they stay blocked, but when your countries block them they still keep coming? You Westerners are so desperate to believe your talk works. Every year the regime burns what looks like opium, heroin, and *yaa baa*, and the UN and their international guests stand and applaud their circus."

Bo Mya explained exactly how Western diplomats are conned by the annual drug-burning charade. "There might be one or two blocks of real drugs burned, but the rest are carefully made of jaggery [sugar], tamarind paste, and a little opium for smell. They use the real wrapping and even the right type of string to tie the packs."

The old man told me to spend some time with the KNLA to understand how the Karen fight drugs. The brief interview was over. He shook my hand and left. I arranged with Colonel Ner Dah to visit his camp the next day.

Ner Dah picked me up and we went south of Mae Sot passing tractors with trailers filled with farm produce. After leaving the main road we crossed a series of small streams and stopped the car near a couple of wooden houses, where a group of men unloaded sacks of carrots, onions, cabbages, and meat from the back of Ner Dah's truck. We set off in single file down a path that ran along a ridge. The path led to a bamboo bridge with guardhouses straddling a rain-swollen stream. A sign above the bridge said in English, "Welcome to Kawthoolei." KNLA soldiers hurried across and took the heavy bags.

On the other side, there was a large parade ground encircled by bamboo huts and wooden buildings. Ner Dah took me inside a hut, ordered tea, and disappeared for a few minutes. He came back in a black uniform and said he only had time to talk briefly now, as he had to go to the front. As the Karen no longer have fixed territory to defend, the front line shifts depending on where skirmishes or ambushes are fought.

Ner Dah commanded a brigade ordered to ambush Burmese drug traffickers. He said his father's comments may have sounded harsh, but he was deadly serious when he said the KNLA killed drug runners. To prove his point, Ner Dah spread a set of photographs of drug raids on a bench.

"They have more numbers than we do, but we plan our raids to do as much damage as we can to their operations." He pointed at one of the pictures. "Here we killed two and wounded six of their soldiers, and captured six million *yaa baa* tablets. We kept their weapons, radios, and uniforms."

After Ner Dah left with his unit, the camp was almost deserted except for a few men left behind as security. Short bursts of mortar and automatic gunfire in the distance confirmed that their target had been located.

I wandered around, taking photographs, and came across three men chained inside a small wooden jail. The men were opium addicts and their families had asked the KNLA to sort them out. One of the men was smoking a small pipe. In spite of the padlocked chains running from his neck to his ankles, he seemed happy. He told me he was angry with his wife for telling the KNLA about his addiction, but now that he had detoxified he was looking forward to going home. He looked well, unlike the dirty haired, hollow-eyed man shivering in a corner. A medic told me that the man was going cold turkey and doing it tough.

Later, Colonel Ner Dah straggled down from the mountain saying he needed heavier weapons but was confident of forcing the Burmese to retreat. In between mouthfuls of food, radio static, and banter with his troops, he talked to me about drugs.

"I know our struggle doesn't excite the international community, but we are the only people fighting at the source. We are tired of international agencies dismissing claims of involvement by the Burmese military in the drug business. I've seen them. We've attacked them and taken warehouses of drugs off their soldiers. It's ridiculous. In a country like Burma, it's impossible to move the huge caravans around secretly. Their Intelligence knows everything. It's the Chinese and the generals. Look at who owns the mines, and the hotels, factories, shops, and apartment blocks in Rangoon and Mandalay—it's the same people: drug runners and generals."

Ner Dah looked tired. He said he would sleep, as he had to go back up the mountain at midnight. Young men unpacked long bandoliers of ammunition. One of the youngsters tried to wrap a six-foot length of bullets around his shoulders and waist, but ended up in a fit of giggles as its weight knocked him off balance.

After talking to the two addicts at Ner Dah's camp, I was intrigued by a story one of the guards told me about a Karen programme for rehabilitating drug dealers and junkies. I questioned Tha Ko about it later, and he chuckled and said he'd take me to see the "secret KNU jail."

"Journalists love sensation," he joked. "All you want are prisons, brothels, rape victims, drugs, death camps, and corruption. I've heard about your drug experiences over the border…. Be careful, or we might lock you up, too."

181

18 Cold Turkey

Tha Ko came for me in a battered pick-up truck. He was taking me over the river to where the Karen rehabilitated their drug addicts. After about an hour's drive, we swapped the highway for a dirt track that cut through barren fields. All the way to the horizon, blackened tree stumps dotted the dry dirt. The earth lay scorched from the relentless sun and lack of cover. The track threw us around and made conversation impossible. It took longer to negotiate this ten-kilometre track than it did the seventy-kilometre road. The track eventually gave way to flatter, sun-baked mud through fields lush with corn and beans. Tha Ko pointed to squads of farm labourers in hats, towels, and long-sleeved shirts to protect them from the sun.

"The Karen do all the work and the Thais get all the profits."

I had no answer for him. The engine straining against the potholes made talking futile.

We stopped on the crest of a ridge near a battered bamboo hut, and a woman, spooked by our arrival, pulled a sarong over her milk-filled breasts. Leaving the truck in the shade, we stumbled down an embankment to the river. Chickens scurried from under our feet.

Tha Ko said we had a problem. The usual boat had apparently been commandeered by KNLA soldiers to supply the front line. We would have to wade across. "One channel is deep, but this time of the year, it should be okay. It's up to you."

After the dusty trip, the water looked cool, so I let my anxiety drift away with the current. Tha Ko stripped down to his briefs; the driver and I followed. We wrapped our clothes in bundles and I put my camera, notepad, and film in a plastic shopping bag. I kept my sandals on—a better option than stepping on glass or a piece of rusty metal below the surface.

Slowly we crossed, walking diagonally to avoid the deep channel. The deepest part of the river was shoulder high, and the current propelled us quickly to the shallows. On the opposite bank we sat in the sun and talked until we dried out.

I didn't hear the two KNLA soldiers as they appeared on the embankment. Tha Ko looked up, unconcerned, and said they were our security. We struggled up a steep hill, the trail following the river. Sand clung to our wet legs and feet.

Above a bend where the river ran wide, a wooden stockade stood stark against the sun-drained land dotted with stunted mango and banana trees. A large group of men in tattered shirts and shorts hobbled awkwardly towards the building. Clunky steel chains ran from their wrists to their ankles and back to their waists. Their faces were either blank or pinched in pain. The men were recovering drug addicts, some going cold turkey—and it showed. Prevented from treating addicts in the refugee camps, this KNU correctional camp had to be built across the border.

Tha Ko introduced me to Phoo Wa Ko, the camp director. In his office hut he poured us tea with lumps of sugar and told me that drugs caused many problems in the refugee camps. Not only did crime increase as addicts needed money, but drugs sapped the morale of young men needed to fight, and ate away at the camps' fragile social structure.

"They cause havoc at home, but when they arrive here, they're like frightened kids. Their drug is their security and when we take that away they have nothing. Our leaders agreed we had to do something before things got out of hand. So I started this as a pilot programme. We don't have much. We have difficulty supplying food and basic medicine for the 26 inmates.

"Withdrawal is only the beginning. They still want drugs. By the second month they're ready for education, hard work, and meditation. The chains come off. But it depends on the severity of their addiction—they have to be assessed independently. Most are here because their families couldn't cope with their abuse, the shame, or the wasted money."

The prison had a medic supplied by the KNLA to help treat prisoners, but the lack of funds for medicine meant the addicts had to endure at least six weeks of constant diarrhoea, headaches, fever, gastric pain, and bowel cramps.

"They also have mental problems. They can't sleep, crave the drug, hallucinate, and have short-term memory lapses."

Phoo Wa Ko blamed the lack of funds for his treatment being so basic. "I don't feel good doing it this way, but for now it is all I can do. Keep them isolated and deprive them of drugs. Their withdrawal is harsh. I don't want to use chains, but if I've no medicine, I have no choice."

He reasoned that with a little help he could provide better services for his inmates, and found it ironic that the drug-trafficking Burmese regime was likely to get money from the DEA while the anti-drug Karen got nothing. Phoo Wa Ko stood by his tough methods and said he would like just a small percentage of the funding available to Western experts. "Compared to their resources we have nothing. But how successful are they?"

To combat the lack of medicine, the prisoners were given hard labour. "It takes their mind off their pain. We're building a garden, breeding pigs and chickens, and when the rains come we'll get them to build fishponds. We will also try to find fresh water because we can't rely on the river. The addicts didn't want to drink the water after dead Karen were found in it."

Phoo Wa Ko acknowledged that, in the beginning, his programme caught a lot of flack from sceptics, but said the KNU and the families involved were now supportive. "We just released the first set of addicts who were treated here, and they are still not using drugs. Eventually we'd like to treat as many as 100."

He insisted that the inmates were not physically beaten, but they had to be watched 24 hours a day to prevent them escaping or fighting each other. "It looks like a prison, yes. We need more buildings to house inmates according to their condition. But we try to educate them and, as a former monk, I give meditation lessons. Education doesn't mean the end of the problem. It has to go further to get the poison out of their systems."

After two to three weeks, the physical symptoms ease. Sleepless nights continue for longer. The addicts were lucky to get a cup of sweet black tea as they screamed, sweated, shat, and shook their way through withdrawal.

In the communal dining shed, a group of prisoners sat with their guards sipping black tea and chatting.

Moo Day, the son of a Karen leader, had just reached his third month of treatment. He answered my remark about how harsh the chains looked.

"What's the difference between iron chains and mental chains? During withdrawal, the drug chains are worse."

Moo Day's eyes looked clear and clean; he laughed and seemed fit and healthy. "I'm beginning to feel that I can cope and could go home, but I'm not sure if I'm strong enough to resist the drugs. I used them all. My favourite was heroin. It is such a good feeling. Better than sex. I loved smoking it more than anything else."

In spite of being the son of a KNU leader, Moo Day got the same treatment as the other inmates.

"I have no advantage. I came in chains . . . the same chains for all of us."

A new prisoner was making the men laugh with his mood swings.

Ahtoo had been in the prison for less than 36 hours. His dirt-lined face twisted as his stomach cramped. He was too weak to be considered a security risk and was left unchained.

"I'm an opium addict," he told me. "A self-taught injector of raw black opium. I'm hot, cold, have the shits, and I can't eat."

Ahtoo looked bad. His nails were compacted with black dirt, and his tattooed arms and legs were dotted with needle tracks. He had four children and a wife, and his addiction was a cause of shame for the family.

"My wife made me come. She told the camp leaders. I'm not angry with her. I started smoking opium, but then the smoking wasn't enough, so I injected."

The first indication that we were close to a military front line came with the pop-pop of automatic weapons from the mountains behind the camp. None of the men were surprised or concerned.

Ahtoo rolled his sleeve to show clusters of needle dots on his arm. He raised his leg to show more stitched along the inside of his thigh, behind his knees, and around the side of his foot.

"I'm better than a doctor," he boasted. "I've been injecting for three years and I can't stop. My life is well when I use opium."

The boom from a mortar punctuated Ahtoo's talk. Heavy artillery responded. The men were oblivious to the exploding shells.

Ahtoo's head suddenly shook and his body jerked in response to his pangs. He sat upright, balled his fists, and started a frantic but feeble thumping on his legs.

"Spasms are the worst. I have to keep punching my legs, arms, everywhere. It's like having ants in my blood. They say I'll be like this for another three weeks. I hope I can stop. I want to help my family. I shamed them. Many of my addict friends who couldn't stop and couldn't afford opium injected themselves with ice water. It killed them."

But Ahtoo was grateful for the help he got from guards at the camp. He nodded towards a young man in an army shirt and *longyi*.

The man introduced himself as Jeffrey and said he understood how Ahtoo felt because he, too, was a recovering addict. Jeffrey was still serving his sentence, but because his progress was good, he was allowed to help with new prisoners.

"Only a junkie knows what it is like to have your drugs taken off you. I took *yaa baa*, codeine, opium, heroin . . . anything and everything. I was an addict for four years and it's taken four months for me to stop."

He was afraid of being tempted by drugs again and was reluctant to leave the camp. "I want to keep off drugs and the best way is for me to stay here and help other addicts. Drugs ruined my life. I wanted to see if they were as good as people said. They were, but then I couldn't stop. I'd sleep all day and do nothing. I was forced here by the KNU and I was angry, but now I'm glad."

Jeffrey admitted that having drug addicts in the refugee camps was dangerous for his people. He said that addicts could get drugs from the Burmese if they became informants. Tha Ko agreed, saying that drugs were deliberately being sold cheaply in the camps by the DKBA and Burmese military to destroy the Karen resistance.

"Drugs are an effective weapon. We have nothing to fight it except this. The Burmese know that one *yaa baa* tablet is more effective than a bullet."

The only way into the wooden cell that held the 26 detainees was a small trapdoor just above the concrete floor. The door was about two-feet square and required the inmates to either squat awkwardly or crawl in and out. Inside, the prisoners sat staring at nothing. Some of them gathered fistfuls of heavy chains as they arranged themselves into more comfortable positions. A few floor mats covered small areas of the grey concrete.

The KNLA also kept two young deserters from the Burmese army, Cho Win and Salai, under guard at the camp. Cho Win was just a teenager, and had been press-ganged into the army. "I was eleven when they took me. I had to march with the older soldiers and if I didn't keep up, they would beat me. After training in Rangoon and Pa-O, I didn't want to fight, so I decided to escape."

Salai was arrested on his way to school. He was posted to Regiment 210 at Moulmein and then to the front line, where he met Cho Win.

"Many [Burmese] soldiers run away. We were afraid to escape. They told us the Karen would torture, kill us, and eat us."

Both the boys' eyes filled with tears as they described the beatings, poor food, and insults they were subjected to by their officers because they were not Burman but from the ethnic States.

Salai said, "Our food was rotten. The rice had sand, stones, and old husks in it. Here the food is better. The officers insulted us all the time because we were not like them."

The not-so-distant battle intensified as mortar and grenade explosions became more frequent. Occasionally the heavy blast of an exploding land-mine pushed through. Tha Ko said it was time we left.

I asked him, while trying to sound calm, if we were leaving because the fighting was getting too close.

"No," he replied. "It's because the Thais will be coming to see what's happening and we don't want to run into them on the way back. How are we going to explain you? They might think you're our military adviser."

We both laughed, but it wouldn't be the first time on the borderline that I'd been asked if I was military.

Months later I was due to return to the drug prison with photo-journalist Jack Picone, but we cancelled the trip at the last minute. It was a fortuitous decision. On the day we were supposed to be there, it was reported in the *Bangkok Post* (July 9, 2002) that at least six SPDC troops from a 100-strong force were killed when they attacked the camp. Tha Ko told me the reason none of the Karen were killed was because they got a tip-off from sympathetic DKBA soldiers about the attack. It seemed that some of the DKBA could not stomach attacking their own people in spite of their allegiance to and pay-off from the Burmese army.

Tha Ko told me that Phoo Wa Ko was working to convince the KNU leadership to invest in his programme. He had found another site free of land-mines and was trying to raise funds. He needed just 60,000 baht—two days' salary for a UN consultant—to get started again. It was highly unlikely that any Western NGO would fund him—addicts in chains don't look good in glossy fund-raising brochures or annual reports, even if such methods have merit.

Tha Ko looked at me as if I was stupid when I suggested the Karen should start to publicize how the KNLA attack drug runners.

"How can we? If our people, who are funded from international aid groups, even suggest they have the slightest links to the Karen army, they risk their funding. You people have trouble understanding that we have to defend our people, and to do that we have to fight. We know your help is only given if we do what you want. We Karen are slow learners. Even after the British betrayed us, you'd think we'd learn."

19 The Cease-fire Is Killing Us

As 2004 began, there were signs that Burma's civil war with the Karen—the world's longest—might soon be over. Rumours swept along the border causing fear in refugee camps, anger in KNLA units, and confusion among NGOs. It was hard to get reliable information. Everybody had an opinion but nobody seemed to know. Those who should, didn't, and could only shrug with embarrassment when asked.

The whispers of a cease-fire came about following secret talks in December 2003 between a small group of Karen officers, under General Bo Mya, and staff of Burma's then prime minister, General Khin Nyunt. It seemed the wily old general had initiated the talks without first consulting his KNU colleagues. If this was true, it was a dangerous game he was playing. The Burmese military had the rest of the country in its iron fist, and nobody could see it giving in to Karen demands for autonomy. Many of the Karen leaders in exile in Thailand knew—and the regime knew—that Thai politicians with Burmese business interests could be relied on to exert pressure on the KNU.

An agitated Tha Ko came to see me. He confirmed that lurking beneath the Karen's optimism were concerns that the ailing Bo Mya was up to the task of negotiating a peace that would not sell out their 55-year-old revolution.

In May, 2003, eyewitnesses had fled to Mae Sot with horrific stories of how government-sponsored thugs attacked Aung San Suu Kyi's entourage as she toured Depayin in northern Burma. Spooked by huge crowds jamming the streets, the regime ordered her convoy attacked. Suu Kyi was injured and arrested and as many as seventy of her supporters killed. Hundreds were seriously hurt. The US, the EU, and Japan criticized the regime's brutality. In response the generals launched a clumsy campaign—a democracy "Road Map"—to divert attention.

The catchphrase sounded all too familiar. It wasn't the first time the junta had tried to tidy up its image. By 1998, Burma's appalling record was good business for American public relations and lobbying companies. The *Washington Post* (February 24, 1998) reported that "several firms have been conducting a campaign on Burma's behalf in classic Washington style—producing upbeat newsletters, arranging seminars and interviews, and funding all-expense-paid trips—partly to persuade the Clinton administration to lift trade sanctions...." The regime was prepared to pay 500,000 dollars a year to hire a former assistant secretary of state for narcotics control, Ann Wrobleski, and her lobbying firm, Jefferson Waterman International. The lobbyists were hired through a Rangoon-based company, Myanmar Resource Development Ltd., to influence US politicians and change perceptions about the regime. According to the *Washington Post* article, "internal State Department cables have identified Jefferson Waterman as the 'US-based lobbying firm' for the junta itself."

In May 2002, the Burmese generals hired DCI Associates for 450,000 dollars a year to help improve relations with the United States. DCI was set up by Thomas J. Synhorst, and his firm's clients included President Bush when he was governor of Texas, as well as the tobacco industry and the National Rifle Association. At a time when the US had trade sanctions against Burma and a ban on their officials, DCI set up two meetings for the SPDC with White House National Security Council, Southeast Asia director, Karen Brooks, to discuss Burma. The *Washington Post* (May 31, 2002) said documents filed with the US Justice Department showed that "DCI's contract was made directly with the State Peace and Development Council." DCI was hired to "brief members of the Bush administration and Congress that Burma was now committed to democracy and human rights" (source: *Washington Post*, reporter Al Kamen/www.prwatch.org).

While Burma's pro-democracy opposition groups were being battered or jailed, the international media put the generals' "Road Map" on the agenda. The coverage gave the regime ill-deserved legitimacy. Journalists and editors should have known better.

Cease-fire negotiations with the Karen were beginning to look like a ploy to create division and confusion among Burmese opposition groups. It wasn't long before television crews and newspapers were asking Karen leaders why they had split with and dumped Aung San Suu Kyi and the opposition alliance. The generals had managed to re-direct the media spotlight away from their ongoing atrocities.

Cease-fire talks and rumours that the US was taking refugees caused a stampede at the Mae Sot office of the UNHCR. Many Karen secretly applied, to avoid being seen as deserting the cause. It was hard to walk through Mae Sot's gem market or back lanes without getting stopped by someone wanting help with their application letter.

Getting Bo Mya to the negotiating table was a massive symbolic victory for the regime. It legitimized the dictators' claim they were genuine about political reform. But Tha Ko remained sceptical.

He asked if I was interested in going to the anniversary of the 55th Karen Revolution Day, as it might be the last. I thanked him for his offer, but as Padho Mahn Sha had already invited me, I assumed I would be well looked after.

Padho Mahn Sha's son picked me up at 4:00 a.m. on January 31. It was dark, cold, and too early for chat, so we drove in silence past the camps as our headlights beamed across the foggy road and caught refugees in ghostly silhouettes carrying cane panniers, lighting fires, and collecting firewood.

We left the sealed road and bounced down a rutted dirt track until we stopped above the riverbank. Pockets of mist stretched across the dark Moei River. Shards of light brought colour to the shadows. Groups of Karen soldiers eased mobs of excited villagers, journalists, and KNU officials along the rocky riverbank to a line of waiting longtail boats. Diesel fumes hung in dirty black clouds as we chugged across the river to KNLA 202 headquarters—one of the scattered, permanently-held outposts in the Karen State.

The steep path up from the river was lined with Karen soldiers and medics decked out in neat uniforms kept for such occasions. Photographers, cameramen, and journalists jostled with each other for better positions. Their backdrop was dramatic: guns, jungle, and lots of battle-scarred and tattooed Karen veterans. Tempers frayed as it became more difficult to keep the amateur photographers or video-toting sightseers out of their frame. Muttered threats and shoving amongst the media mob amused the Karen villagers.

Spectators found shady spots to watch the dances and military parades, and to listen to the speeches. Thai security agents took notes and used their digital cameras to record the attendance of NGOs and Western journalists. The parade ground turned to dust as activities peaked. A couple of European photographers amused Karen villagers as they tied Arab headscarfs around their heads and faces, masking everything except their designer sunglasses. Kitted out with backpacks, pocket vests, and up to four cameras hanging from straps, they looked like Dennis Hopper in *Apocalypse Now*.

As the parades and speeches finished, I asked Padho Mahn Sha if he would join General Bo Mya for a joint interview. The morning had left Bo Mya tired. He relied on his walking stick and the arm of his son, Colonel Ner Dah. Our group attracted the attention of a gaggle of journalists and curious onlookers. Before the two leaders sat down, photographers battled for position. I watched from the back while a series of rapid questions in Thai and Burmese were translated for General Bo Mya to answer. Padho Mahn Sha kept silent. I waited until the local media had got what they wanted, and put my first question to Bo Mya.

"Are any or all of Saw Ba U Gyi's four principles on the bargaining table with the Burmese dictators?"

Bo Mya slowly looked me over. Padho Mahn Sha tried unsuccessfully to hide a smile as journalists thrust their microphones forward.

"We will not surrender, we will always keep our arms, we want a free Karen State. The four principles of our revolution are still the same. We will decide our own political destiny."

There was a collective sigh of relief from Karen soldiers and villagers. Their fears that their hero had sold them out had just been exorcised.

"Your critics have said the cease-fire talks have caused a split between the KNLA and the KNU and you acted in your own interests. Are the Karen a united front, or is there a split?"

Padho Mahn Sha's smile stretched to a grin as General Bo Mya answered.

"We are united. Both the KNU and the KNLA are one."

Padho Mahn Sha nodded his agreement. News that Bo Mya was talking about the cease-fire had spread and the crowd grew.

"How confident are you that this isn't just a Burmese public relations stunt to appease the international community and get [trade] sanctions lifted?"

"Our negotiations should not stop the international pressure on the SPDC. They should continue until we achieve our victory, self-determination, and our freedom. They have to apply more pressure so the dialogue will be successful. They have to stop their military and political abuse of not only Karen people, but all people in Burma. It doesn't matter who the regime talks with—us or the NLD—the important issues common to both groups are the same. The KNU will work together with other opposition and ethnic groups for a genuine federated union and democracy."

I asked a few more questions about the future role of the DKBA.

Making policy on the run, Bo Mya said that if the DKBA rejoined the KNU, they would be welcomed back and given an amnesty.

International news crews wanted their own interviews and tried to entice Bo Mya away, but the old general preferred to eat. He invited me to join him. I accepted, but first I wanted to ask Padho Mahn Sha about the cease-fire. Interviewing Padho Mahn Sha was always good value. He was tough, intelligent, straight talking, with a sense of humour. I followed him under the trees overlooking the river. He spoke English slowly but didn't need a translator.

"The Karen want a third party to mediate," he said. "We'd ask the UN, but the Burmese won't accept that. They fear outside involvement. But the international community has to be involved because Burma is an international problem."

Padho Mahn Sha said Burma should be a concern to both the UN and ASEAN. "Burma is the second biggest producer of heroin and the biggest supplier of methamphetamines. Refugees continue to pour over the borders of our neighbours; illegal migrant workers do the same. The generals took power illegally. Human rights abuses, child soldiers, systematic rape, forced labour, and the environment are all a disaster. If we have assistance, we can fix our problems, but if we don't, we will continue our resistance."

Padho Mahn Sha declined lunch and I went into the house where Bo Mya had retreated. Without looking up, the general pointed to a chair opposite him and waved for me to sit. Soldiers handed me a plate of rice and set out bowls of fried pork, soup, chicken curry, vegetables, and omelette. An English missionary tried to engage the general in small talk, not realizing that Karen people prefer to eat in silence. The missionary poked the food around his plate as if he was unsure of what to do with it. After eating, Bo Mya rose from the table with the help of one of his orderlies and left the room without speaking.

As I was leaving the house, one of the general's officers, an acquaintance of mine and a member of the delegation to Rangoon, pulled me aside and gave me a box of CDs that he said contained footage of the whole trip to Burma—including the talks with Khin Nyunt.

Right away I was eager to get back to Mae Sot to look at the film. I knew Tha Ko would want to read between the lines of Bo Mya's performance. I went in search of a lift back to Mae Sot.

Tha Ko was excited I had the CDs and came to my house the next morning. The film quality was good. Khin Nyunt had swapped his army uniform for a designer suit. Bo Mya and the other Karens had dressed for the meeting in traditional Karen shirts. Chuckling, Tha Ko said it looked like the old man had dyed his hair, but his good humour turned to dismay as he watched Bo Mya lean on Khin Nyunt's arm as he led his party into the building. Tha Ko groaned, dropped his head, and pointed at the screen. "It looks bad. Bo Mya leaning on Khin Nyunt sends a message that the Karen need Burmese support."

After introductions were made, both Khin Nyunt and Bo Mya played polite, but both sparred to gain an edge.

Khin Nyunt looked for an opening. "I still have one responsibility left. All the ethnic groups have signed a cease-fire—only the Karen have not. I still have this to do for the country. We should not allow others to interfere in our internal affairs. If we keep talking about the past, it will never end."

Bo Mya sidestepped and hit back. "The Burmese are not our enemy. Our enemy is the military dictatorship."

Khin Nyunt responded with a lie. "We're not a dictatorship anymore. Soon we will develop our road map [to democracy]."

Bo Mya shrugged it off. "We must solve our problems based on sincerity and trust. If we don't have that, we can't solve any problem."

Khin Nyunt said, "Uncle, you've made a lot of sacrifices fighting in the jungle. How long can you keep doing that? Why not come and live peacefully here and enjoy the rest of your life."

Bo Mya threw an uppercut and connected. "It's true I spent a lot of years in the jungle. I cleared a space and built an ordinary house so I could live peacefully, but you came along and burned it down."

Tha Ko said Khin Nyunt called Bo Mya 'uncle' to avoid acknowledging him as the general of a legitimate resistance army.

Tha Ko was relieved at Bo Mya's resilience and proud of his strength. "He's honest, blunt, and that's good. He loves his people. But we will need more if we are to withstand Khin Nyunt's trickery?"

But Tha Ko's good mood turned black as he acknowledged how difficult this would be. "Our history shows we have been tricked time and time again. These talks are just the first step. Bo Mya is too old to keep going. We now need experienced, expert legal help. Without it we will lose."

Tha Ko's concerns soon became a reality. Just weeks after the meeting in Rangoon, reports from the Karen State confirmed that Burmese troops took advantage of the cease-fire to build roads, camps, and move heavy weapons to areas formerly under Karen control. Karen people were fearful. Secure jungle hide-outs were found and mapped by the Burmese.

Tha Ko's visits to my house became more frequent. He felt and believed that because I was a Westerner and a journalist, somehow I would have connections to the outside world. He had no idea of the lack of media interest about the Karen.

One morning, a car dropped Tha Ko at my house, and as he came up the path I could see he was agitated. I led him inside. He was so caught up in what was bothering him, he couldn't keep still.

"I told you they couldn't be trusted. These Burmans are snakes. They twist and turn and their words of peace are written on oil."

He went back outside to his car and brought in a white-haired, middle-aged Karen man. "This is Eitha. He's just got back from inside the Karen State. Talk to him, he knows what's going on."

Eitha said he recorded human rights abuses, and I asked him what changes there had been since the cease-fire talks. He smiled and said, "The [Burmese] army have moved thousands of soldiers into the Karen State. In February they beat to death ten villagers, and 10,000 more have lost everything: their homes, schools, temples, churches, clinics, crops, animals, and even the graves of their ancestors. This has happened because our soldiers can't fight back while cease-fire talks are on."

I put it to Eitha that he was making the Karen sound like saints. Surely the KNLA would also take advantage of the cease-fire.

"To do what?" he replied. "Our struggle is about defending our people. We don't have enough ammunition to attack. If the cease-fire is genuine, we want it. Our children need it. We don't live like this from choice."

I asked Eitha how Karen soldiers felt having their hands tied by the cease-fire. He looked across at Tha Ko before replying.

"I'm a major in the KNLA. I speak as a soldier. We will obey our orders, but it's difficult to watch soldiers abusing our people. If we don't have to kill each other, that's good. If we don't keep our weapons, we will be defeated. If the talks fail, it will be very hard to reclaim the territory we're losing now. But no matter, I will fight if I'm the last man standing."

The US offer to take refugees had created an air of excitement in Mae Sot. If accepted, successful applicants were quickly whisked to Bangkok and onto resettlement homes in Austin, Seattle, and Houston. The numbers of Karen leaving began to worry Tha Ko.

"They're taking the most qualified from our community—teachers, medics, leaders, and skilled workers. All those years and thousands of dollars invested in training and education. It's as if they created an educated elite so they could export them. What will happen if we are ever repatriated? Where will we get our teachers, our medics? Why is it happening now when there's all the talk about going back to Burma?"

Dr. Cynthia had similar worries, as many skilled medics had already left for America, leaving her with a difficult vacuum to fill. Medics doing essential work at the clinic were now cleaning or washing dishes in Texan restaurants. It had become a brain drain for the Karen.

Unfortunately for Sein, his dream of getting to the US and setting up a gem exporting business had to be put on hold. I was cycling past the gem market when I heard my name shouted. I stopped and Sein hustled towards me. He was unsteady on his feet, wearing a bright-pink nylon ski jacket, several sizes too small for him. Unable to zip it up, he had tied rope across the gap where his belly poked. To complete his bizarre look, he wore purple sunglasses with matching lens.

I parked the bike and we went to a café. Sein's US application had been rejected without explanation. He shook his head and said he couldn't understand why. I asked him what he had put in his application.

"I tell the truth, always. Many people tell lies. Make up a story for the UN. These bad people got taken, but not me. Why, Mr. Phil?"

Aware of his underground background, I asked him again what he had told them.

"I tell the truth, only."

I began to suspect that Sein's honesty had cost him his place in America.

"I'm not a bomb maker now. That was a long, long time ago . . . 1989."

"But you told them you were a bomb maker?"

"Always tell the truth. No lies."

"Sein, what religion did you put on your application?"

"Muslim."

"Sein, remember September 11?"

The penny dropped and Sein's sudden enlightenment was signalled by a crackly laugh. He continued gurgling and laughing until he wiped tears from his eyes.

Sein's story was a bad joke, but it captured the madness of Mae Sot and the Burmese conflict. It was tragic, sad, ironic, pathetic, insane, and funny all at the same time.

The wet season was coming to an end, and this was an annual concern for Karen soldiers, who knew that the Burmese military, with access to dry roads, would increase their efforts to wipe them out. I was curious to see if the cease-fire was working, and to verify the alleged violations. One afternoon when I was at the CIDKP offices, a couple of Karen men in their mid-twenties turned up, just back from inside the Karen State. The men spoke of being ambushed in June when taking medicine to an IDP village. In July, they said, a village had to be evacuated when the DKBA attacked with mortar and rifle grenades. The men showed me radio transcripts of Burmese officers ordering the DKBA to attack KNLA camps. The men said the cease-fire worked better the closer you were to the border. The men had come to the CIDKP for money to buy medicine and supplies. I asked if Blacktown, one of my journalist students, and I could go with them?

I had planned to go to Chiang Mai at the end of that week and had already bought a return air ticket. It was a Monday, and if we left on the Tuesday I could be back in time to catch my plane on the Friday.

Saw Hla Henry quickly arranged for me and Blacktown to accompany the medics to a clinic at Hti Per, supposedly a short walk from the border. Saw Hla Henry told me to be ready at 6:00 a.m. next morning.

At home I packed my usual supplies, decided on sandals over boots, as it would still be wet, and got a good night's sleep. I was picked up on time and we drove north from Mae Sot, passing sleeping villages, jagged limestone cliffs, rivers, and rice paddies. We pulled into a roadhouse for breakfast. A cluster of shops and food stalls sold traditional Karen clothing, army hammocks, fishing hooks, soups, curries, snacks, noodles, cheroots, soft drinks, and beer.

We ordered food just in time: clouds turned the sky black, lightening cracked, and thunder crashed overhead. Rain sheeted down, turning the car park to a muddy lake. It was impossible to move. We sat staring at the deluge as it forced vehicles to stop.

Saw Hla Henry made use of the time to buy us tightly rolled nylon hammocks, packs of instant noodles, and bottles of water.

The clouds shifted to reveal shafts of sunlight, increasing the humidity and sweat. Saw Hla Henry said it was time we left, as the medics had a lot to do.

We crossed a 200-metre-wide, rain-swollen river, turned coffee colour by washed-away earth. The boatman expertly navigated against the fast current until he was in position to let it take him downstream to a landing spot. Getting out of the boat and negotiating the embankment was difficult, and I was glad I wore sandals as I sloshed through mud in search of an easier place to climb. Our camp—Battalion 22—was at the base of a mountain but sat high on a sandstone cliff above the river. KNLA soldiers rushed down to help carry our supplies and bags.

At the top of the track, men sat in bamboo huts talking, strumming guitars, playing chess, or cleaning weapons. On a piece of flat ground, two groups played volleyball and *takraw*. We were taken to a small but solid wooden hut with a covered deck overlooking the river and mountains. It belonged to Colonel Gringo, who welcomed us and told us we would be sleeping there tonight. We put our bags inside and sat around a table laid with cups and water bottles.

Saw Hla Henry and the colonel scrawled village names and distances on a small whiteboard and marked how long each leg of the trip would take: section 1, two hours; section 2, one day; and section 3, seven hours. I realized my overnight trip had suddenly become a five- to six-day trek. I would miss my Chiang Mai flight. I asked Saw Hla Henry to tell my wife, when he returned to Mae Sot that evening, to cancel my ticket.

The other realization to creep over me was my unfitness. I had recently returned from Australia, where my exercise regime consisted of coughing fits to get rid of the flu, mall shopping, and tapping my computer keyboard. I knew the scribbles on the whiteboard were no indication to hill gradients or the pain of climbing. Dark rain clouds matched my mood. The square of sunlight framing the volleyball patch shrunk. A cool wall of air preceded a torrential downpour.

As quick as it arrived, the rain stopped, and a soldier tiptoed through puddles with heaped plates of rice, uncooked herbs, boiled pumpkin, and soup. As we ate, an animated discussion broke out among the men about my ability to do the trip. They worried I wouldn't be able to drink village water and I'd get dehydrated. Could I sleep in a hammock? What about malaria? And did I have a change of clothes? I was more worried about being unfit.

Their talk switched from me back to the medical needs of the mobile clinic. A list of drugs and medicines were read out and ticked off. The medic, Shwe Htee, said medicine would be taken to the village clinic, but expected he would have to treat people and hand out tablets along the way. He had worked as a medic for about ten years and said the problems were always the same: never enough medicine, hungry people, and malaria. He said he also collected malaria samples for an NGO researching the disease.

Shwe Htee supervised the filling of bamboo panniers with medicines and waterproofing them with plastic shopping bags. A wall of sound erupted from the riverbank and trees as birds and nocturnal animals greeted the night. Radio static crackled in the background. Candles were lit, instantly attracting hordes of insects. Blacktown tied his hammock under the roof of our hut. He lit a green cheroot and slid into the nylon sheet. He blew out smoke and said, "Karen mosquito repellent."

I sat and made notes until the candle died. I lit another, said goodnight, and worried about the trek, rainstorms, land-mines, DKBA patrols, Burmese soldiers, and all the things I could have brought with me but didn't. I began to wonder what I was doing, thousands of miles from my favourite beach and café, with armed soldiers, a young student translator, and impoverished villagers, while government forces roamed the hills trying to hunt us down. Surprisingly, and in spite of these thoughts, I slipped into a warm and peaceful sleep, and it wasn't much after nine o' clock.

It was still dark when hushed words woke me. I struggled from the warmth under my borrowed blanket. It wasn't my ideal way to wake up. I like to get there slowly, moving between dream and sleepy thought. The idea of taking my slumbering body down the muddy track to the creek at the back of the camp was chilling, but not as cold as the water. I cleaned my teeth and threw icy water against my face. What remained of sleep disappeared. When I got back to the hut, a tin mug of hot coffee steamed, as did plates of rice, thin watery curry, and vegetables.

Men made last-minute adjustments to their panniers. Soldiers and porters leaned against huts smoking or chewing betel nut. Some wore *longyis*, others wore shorts or full uniforms with black boots. An assortment of kit bags littered the ground. By 6:30 a.m. we were ready to move. A heavily armed soldier led, and was followed by quick-moving porters, their panniers strapped to their foreheads by sarongs. Behind came relief porters, Blacktown and me, more soldiers, and, fifty metres further back, the rearguard. In single file we took a narrow path through head-high grass. The track was slippery, the mountainside a sheer wall of mud held by bamboo and small trees covered with nail-like thorns. The humidity had already soaked my clothes.

The path wriggled almost vertically up the mountain. There was no relief. It just got steeper and steeper. The KNLA captain stopped the column and inched his way back to me and said, "We're going through a mined area. Keep to the path. Don't walk off it for any reason, don't throw anything away, and don't piss . . . keep up."

Some of the mines, he said, were booby traps, triggered by trip wires and possibly wired to others, like claymores. The captain took up position between Blacktown and me. He signalled the group to continue. We had walked only a short distance further when he pointed to a spot inches from the track and asked if I could see the mine?

All I could see was mud, rotting leaves, and fallen sticks. He pointed again, and this time I saw the edges of a small disc.

"The rain has washed the dirt off," he said as he bent to replace leaves over the explosive. This happened about four or five times. The mines were almost impossible to see, but their effect was easy to imagine. Any step off the path could be fatal.

The effort of climbing and a lack of oxygen getting to my brain made my legs feel independent of me. Hours passed and we were still climbing. The map showing one hour to our first village began to look like a sick joke. We reached the top and the view was blocked by thick mist. We rested on wet rocks and fallen trees. The Karen looked fresh and clean in comparison to me. My clothes were coated in mud and soaked from sweat. The men lit cheroots; I passed around my bottled water and it was soon finished. I picked up one of the half empty bottles and kept it. I noticed a leech arching its way across a leaf, and this motivated me to rub insect repellent over my bare legs, arms, neck, and face. I passed the tube to Blacktown, who did the same, and he passed it on to the next man. I experienced an intense moment of selfishness as each man squirted and rubbed cream on. That feeling was soon replaced by shame when Blacktown took off his new (fake) Adidas running shoes and swapped them with the medic for a torn and string-tied pair of rubber galoshes. I asked Blacktown why.

"Because his need is greater than mine. He'll be out here for a long time. I can buy more back in Mae Sot."

Blacktown wasn't quite telling the truth. He didn't get paid, and to buy another pair of shoes would be tough. My concern at seeing my water supply and insect repellent disappear paled when compared to his decency. My generosity came with conditions: 'sure you can have my shoes, when the trip's over.' Time and time again I had seen the Karen make genuine acts of kindness: money, clothes, shelter, medicine, and years of commitment and service given without question to help their people survive.

The Karen walked fast and for good reason. All around us, DKBA and Burmese patrols were out there hunting. If the Karen listened to radio intercepts, I assumed their enemies did the same. Each side often knew the whereabouts of the other, and I prayed we were not walking towards an ambush. It explained why the

Karen didn't tack across mountains but went vertically. The enemy would have to be extremely motivated to chase up mountain tracks to catch them.

I asked the captain how long before we reached the first village. He said it shouldn't be long, and I had to settle for that. I worried about drinking water, and the more I thought of it, the more I wanted it.

We walked across the ridge until it disappeared into thick foliage and we started our descent. Giant trees, some as high as eighty feet, stood all around as we climbed down. In other circumstances I would have stopped in awe at these majestic specimens. The path twisted above enormous drops into raging rivers, and my fear shifted to not falling. The strain on my knees was excruciating. Bone grated on bone. I often lost balance and grabbed at thin trees, just missing their inch-long thorns. Blacktown tried to keep my mind off my aches and pains by pointing out waterfalls, deer, bear, wild boars, and elephant tracks. The landscape was awesome, but with my mind on avoiding tree roots, biting red ants, and keeping on the path in mined areas, the flora and fauna took a back seat. As we descended, the path followed a fast-flowing, twisting river. Water roared over and around hut-sized boulders, foam bubbled against fallen trees. We were either crossing different rivers or re-crossing the same one again and again. I was relieved again that I hadn't worn boots. My sandals were perfect. The cold water soothed my tired muscles. While crossing, I tried to submerge my legs as much as I could. I refilled my water bottle, and any worries I had about parasites were swept away by my thirst.

Seven hours after we left camp, signs of village life appeared. Buffalo tracks dotted the riverbanks. Goat droppings lay scattered in grass-chewed patches. Wood smoke filled the air. Rice, corn, and other crops grew in small enclosures. The prospect of sitting down and resting couldn't come quick enough.

By the time Blacktown and I got to the village, the porters and soldiers had already shed their loads and were cooking lunch. Shwe Htee led us to a house. The village was suffering from the monsoon. Mould covered bamboo walls, clothes hung damp under houses, black pigs thrashed walkways to mud, and children wiped at snotty noses. We entered the house, where a group of women sat smoking pipes, breast-feeding babies, and chatting. We put our bags on a bamboo platform that ran around the inner walled room.

The women shuffled across the floor to make room for us. I sat down, stretched my aching legs, and felt muscles cramp. Suddenly, a woman appeared at the doorway and spoke briefly to Blacktown. He told me the woman had terrible fever and wanted medicine, and she laid down on the floor while he went to get Shwe Htee. I thought her problem must be serious, as it is unusual for Karen to ask so openly for help.

Blacktown returned with Shwe Htee and a porter who carried bowls of instant noodle soup, boiled rice, and crisp-fried tinned sardines. Shwe Htee opened a small bag containing pills and his stethoscope as the woman lay coughing. He asked how old she was, and she said forty. She looked fifteen years younger. In spite of her good looks, Shwe Htee said she was worn out from sickness and harsh living. She had given birth to nine babies, but only four had survived. He said she was anaemic, lacked vitamins, and was recovering from malaria. He gave her a fistful of paracetamol and iron tablets.

Outside, Blacktown was sharing betel nut with a couple of porters. He had made coffee, and we shared a lump of two-day-old coconut bread I had brought from Mae Sot. The combination of sugar and starchy fat washed down with the hot coffee was immensely satisfying. Between slurps of coffee, I talked with the porters, and they answered accusations made by international NGOs that by using villagers as unpaid porters, the KNU were no better than the Burmese army.

Kwla, one of the men, said that it was taken for granted that he would help another Karen. He referred to the KNLA as "green scarves" and to the DKBA as "yellow scarves." While the Burmese and yellow scarves forced villagers to carry munitions, Kwla said that the green scarves only asked villagers to carry medicine, clothes, or equipment to help them.

Our rest break came to an end and we prepared to leave the village. We had to move on as our presence, especially mine, would be reported to both the DKBA and the Burmese. I felt betrayed when I heard that these villagers we ate with and gave medicine and clothes to would inform on us. But the captain made clear that the villagers would give us time to get away. He wasn't worried about this, and said they had to inform, as punishment would be vicious if they didn't. He said it was nothing to get upset about, as our radio chatter would have been picked up and our column was not a secret.

We left the village and started to climb. The captain told me we had two more ridges to cross and the next one was the hardest. There were fewer trees, less mud, but more rocks. It was hotter now, and rivulets of sweat rolled down my back and legs. The captain told me to go slow if I needed to. The dislodgment of small stones from above announced the arrival of a buffalo led by a Karen villager. It seemed impossible the huge beast could squeeze between the small cuts and twists in the rock-face. The captain pulled me off the path into a thicket so we wouldn't spook the animal. Blacktown joined us. When the captain whispered we'd wait until the whole herd passed, I was relieved and delighted at the prospect of a rest, but soon I was cursing the beasts for churning the path to mush and for fouling the rivers.

By mid-afternoon I could just about put one foot in front of the next. It wasn't too hot, but the climbing had drained me. I had nothing left. Soon it would be night and we would either reach a village or make camp, as it would be too dangerous to keep going. I didn't fancy sleeping in a hammock without protection from the rain, but I was one of the lucky ones, as most of the porters and soldiers would have to lie on the wet ground.

It started to rain and thunder as we moved off the ridge. I asked Blacktown how long to the next village. He said about an hour, but when I quizzed him three hours later, we were still walking. My ankles and calves were ripped and striped with dried blood, slashed by branches. As the ground flattened out, banana trees and cultivated patches appeared, and colour filtered through the trees from the sky. I could just make out bamboo planks suspended across a fast-flowing river. The single-span bridge was about seven feet above the water, very rickety, with a vine guide-rope stretched from one bank to the other. A notched bamboo pole acted as a ladder and led up to the walkway. I made my way up and braced myself for the step-by-step crossing. I decided to shuffle sideways. I grabbed the vine and tried to steady myself, but it swayed down and out and I almost fell. I inched my way across.

My relief soon faded when I spied another wider river and higher bridge on the other side. I slowly crossed this one, then forded a fast-flowing shallow creek and hiked fifty metres through dense scrub to the village. My feet were bruised from the sandal straps and I knew that if I sat down I'd find it hard to get up, so ignoring my pains I dropped my bag and went back to the river with Blacktown to wash. The walk was agony and the water cold. Naked, I lay on the submerged rocks and let the water rush over me. I drank and washed and massaged my calf and thigh muscles. The cuts on my legs and arms stung. When I was clean, I smeared mosquito cream all over.

We were housed at the headman's home, a large bamboo hut. The central room was closed-in and surrounded by a wide platform, where Blacktown and I would sleep. The headman spread a blue plastic sheet for us to sleep on. I felt happy and content. I had dry clothes, I was washed, and had finally stopped walking.

A steaming, blackened aluminium rice pot was brought from the inner room. Blacktown rinsed plates and spoons and helped the headman's daughter, Naw Chit Chee, to serve dinner: noodle soup, fried sardines, rice, and pumpkin. The family didn't know anything about me, but their hospitality was generous. The mother even apologized for not being able to speak English. The Karen villagers shared everything they had and expected nothing in return.

After dinner, the family retired to the inner room, and for the next couple of hours they giggled and laughed their way to sleep. Blacktown shared his packet of cheroots with soldiers on our platform and swapped his good hammock for a ripped one. Rain hammered the village, adding to my sense of well-being. I was dry, warm, and relaxed.

The soldiers and a fresh group of porters from the village were up before first light, making noise as they checked panniers, ate rice, and crouched over fires. The soldiers wrapped cotton tubes filled with rice diagonally across their chests. My legs felt fine. The cuts were deeper than I'd first thought, but had started to crust.

The radio operator put his hand up for us to be silent. He leaned over his radio, listened to the static, and handed over to the captain. The captain said that Hti Per, our next destination, had been attacked by the DKBA. Villagers had been seriously wounded and needed urgent help. They would have to be stretchered out to the border. I asked him what his plans were. He said we had to keep going, and if we met up with the stretcher party we'd give them what help we could. I asked when we would be heading back to the border, and he said in about a month.

I froze. I hadn't planned on being away that long.

I looked at Blacktown, in his swapped shoes, two sizes too small. I knew my wife would panic if she didn't hear from me for a month. I also realized that Blacktown and I had an opportunity to get out if we accompanied the stretcher party back to the border. The captain said four soldiers had finished their tour of duty today and were expected here later, on their way back to their own village. The stretchers would also probably arrive here just before dark, and the four soldiers had been ordered to wait for them. I asked the captain if Blacktown and I could wait here and return to the border with them. He was not pleased, and I thought he might think we were quitting on him. I found out later that our bravado, or lack of it, had nothing to do with his concern. I convinced him that if I waited for the injured mother and son from Hti Per, I could write up their story and get photographic proof the cease-fire was being violated.

The stretcher party would take about ten hours to arrive at the village and we could not leave until the next day, as it would be impossible to travel with stretchers in the dark. The captain worried that we would be alone in the village without armed security. By staying here, I was at risk—and I put the villagers at risk, too. The captain had been given the responsibility of making sure I got in and out of the Karen State safely, and I had just dismissed him and his men without realizing the consequences of my actions. If I were caught here, the villagers would be punished for sheltering a foreign spy. I had been selfish, but I was also relieved that I could rest up, interview villagers and porters, swim in the river, and prepare for the return hike to the border.

The captain waved goodbye and led his party single file into the mist. We lost sight of them as they followed the path down to the river. But in minutes they reappeared on the other side. Their pace was astonishing up the steep slope. I lost sight of them as they disappeared into dense jungle.

I spent the morning talking with the villagers. My fatigue had almost gone and I had time now to look around and appreciate how beautiful the Karen State is. Forested mountains, fertile valleys, deep clean rivers, and tall hardwood trees are all left unspoiled by the lack of roads or business interests. But when roads are built and the greedy Thai and Burmese consortiums arrive, the destruction of the forests will be devastating.

Blacktown and I went for a swim, avoiding a surly bull tethered to a stake by a long lead. The water was cold, about head high in the shallows but much deeper in the middle. After an hour or so swimming, we returned to the headman's house to eat. Blacktown prepared instant noodles and Naw Chit Chee gave us hot rice. The rice had been recently harvested and she said it was almost glutinous and tasted best if eaten when new. Red, brown, black, and off-white grains blended together to create a nutty tasting dish. Naw Chit Chee brought out a plate with small pieces of cooked dark meat on it, and urged me to try some. I hesitated. It looked unappetizing, but after my praise about Karen food I could hardly say no, even if I did suspect it was monkey or some other exotic animal. I scanned the plate looking for the smallest and least greasy lump. I popped it into my mouth, hoping to get rid of it when no one was looking. The meat was sweet, salty, and tasty. I quickly chewed it, swallowed, and went back for more. Blacktown said it was barking deer, an endangered species in Thailand, but still abundant in the Karen State. He said the villagers here were lucky: they had fish in the river and wild animals in the mountains to hunt. The headman said there were many animals including tiger, bear, deer, monkey, elephants, and lots of birds. It was hard not to stare at the headman, as a huge scar split his face diagonally. I assumed his injury had been caused by a mine, but he said he had been attacked by a black bear when harvesting corn.

The four soldiers turned up. They had been ordered to be our security. The leader, Sergeant Klaw Kler, was a short, muscular man. A series of facial scars and tight jaw muscles made him look tough and battle hardened. He said he would stay with us until we got to his village, but if there were no other soldiers to take us on to the border, he and his men would go with us. He looked tired. They had been out on patrol for a month and were looking forward to spending time with their families. Yet he was prepared to put in a fourteen-hour walk to get us back to the border. He asked to be excused as he and his men needed to wash, eat, and rest before the rescue party turned up.

Heavy rain fell, and when it stopped, the sun appeared and drew moisture out of the ground. By late afternoon the ground had dried to sticky mud. I took my camera and Blacktown and I wandered down to the river. A whistle split the air and we looked up to see the stretcher party coming out of the mist like ghosts, a thin single file, sliding and slipping down the mountain, soldiers and porters trying to keep two stretchers from falling.

We ran to meet them. Inside one of the green plastic sheets tied to a bamboo pole, a mother whimpered from fear and the piece of shrapnel lodged in her gut. Following close behind, held high in another stretcher, was her son, aged eleven, also bleeding. His foot was a bloodied, shattered stump; a piece of mortar was buried in his forearm, and he was hot from fever.

The tired men pushed through to the village and lay their bleeding charges on the ground. The woman struggled to sit up and villagers rushed to help her. The boy was helped out of his stretcher, his shirt stained with blood.

The woman was thirsty and hungry but afraid to eat or drink in case her insides had been perforated. No one in our group was qualified to advise. We had no medic. Blacktown looked at me and asked if I thought it was okay for her to eat. I shrugged, unable to say. She took my smile as a yes and started to swallow rice and soup. The boy wolfed down his rice.

Outside, the sky dumped more rain, making the mountain pass a mudslide. The stretcher bearers said tomorrow's walk to the border would be hard. The nearest medical assistance was still sixteen hours away. The tension in the hut was high, the woman and child a grim reminder that armed thugs were only hours away. We tried to settle down. I gave the mother and son paracetamol and they slept.

Throughout the night the woman cried with pain. At 3:50 a.m. a loud gunshot woke everyone and caused panic among the villagers. People crashed into each other, and Blacktown mumbled, "DKBA." Another explosion and I grabbed my bag and got ready to run.

The sergeant told us not to move for the moment while he and his men went into the darkness to check on the situation. When he returned, he was smiling. One of the villagers was celebrating the birth of a son by firing off his home-made musket. The gunpowder accounted for the volume of the blasts.

I drifted in and out of an uneasy sleep until Blacktown pushed a cup of coffee at me and urged me to get up. Sergeant Klaw Kler spoke to our group and signalled for us to get ready to move out. Mist peeled off the mountains and thunder rumbled as the mother and child were placed in the stretchers and we left for the border. Porters and soldiers took turns to carry the injured, stopping only to rest when fallen trees, boulders, and backbreaking hills had been beaten. The pace was more suited to my level of fitness. Being able to walk in the large footprints left behind by a wild elephant also helped for a while. The animal had squashed the mud hard, leaving easy-to-walk-in pads for us to follow. I was disappointed when its tracks disappeared and hoped it had managed to avoid land-mines.

After another six hours of slog through mud, water, and rocks, a health worker, soldiers, and relief porters met up with us. The stretchers were laid on a patch of shaded ground and an IV drip was attached to the woman. It would take another five hours crossing the jungle-shrouded Dawna Range before the mother and son could escape the confines of their hot plastic stretchers.

The last stretch of the rescue mission was the most hazardous, as we passed through DKBA positions and minefields. The latter was terrifying, as the IV bottle and tubing kept catching on overhead branches, requiring someone to step off the narrow path to cut them free. Adding to our anxiety, radio static confirmed that some of the KNLA's border camps had been attacked and a large contingent of DKBA and Burmese soldiers were moving through the area with orders to wipe out all KNLA positions. We topped the last ridge, but going downhill brought its own problems. The welcome sound of a longtail boat's engine cut through the jungle, but keeping the stretcher bearers from falling on the greasy path to the river was proving difficult. I constantly snatched at branches to stop myself falling. The porters struggled in the thick mud, the last obstacle before the mother and son could be placed in the boat and taken to safety.

At the riverbank, the relieved sergeant looked at the grateful faces of his charges and said, "They're safe now, but our people have no security. This cease-fire has no rules."

Back at 22 Battalion, Colonel Gringo was relieved to see us. We climbed the steps to his hut and got ready to wash before eating. I felt elated and I promised Blacktown a meal of his choice in any restaurant when we got back to Mae Sot. I had driven him crazy in the jungle with my talk about food.

The colonel translated his radio intercepts into English, and if they were reliable, the border situation was going to get worse. He confirmed our earlier intercepts. "[Burmese] Strategy Commander 773 ordered 'all battalions to attack KNLA positions along the Moei River and clean them out'."

A patrolling Karen soldier had been killed, and Saw Hla Henry had been worried when he found out we had left our security. He had heard from KNU intelligence sources that we were walking towards enemy soldiers. In our case, ignorance was bliss.

When I got back to Mae Sot, talk of repatriation of refugees back to Burma was sending shockwaves through the camps and local NGOs. The UNHCR held meetings with the KNU and a workshop in Bangkok on the issue. The reports of what was discussed were quickly leaked and circulated among Mae Sot activists. I had been sent as many as seven copies of each. Whispers grew louder, but little or no open and honest debate was held.

Repatriation threatened refugees, but resettlement in a third country offered them an opportunity of a new life. The cease-fire had made Karen soldiers insecure. Rivalry between NGOs intensified. Talk of engaging with Burma's regime dominated conversations. The people of Burma did need help. Arguments for and against bounced around. Those pushing to give aid to the regime argued that it could bring about political change and move the junta towards democracy. When I put this viewpoint to Tha Ko, he looked at me as if I was stupid.

"Who has created the humanitarian crisis in Burma? Who abuses the people? Who locks up their opponents? Who sends their army to attack ethnic people? If you want political change, tell your governments, China, ASEAN, to stop trading with and making money out of Burma. The military is incapable of taking its foot off the throat of the Karen people."

Later, while in Bangkok researching a separate story, a number of senior people working with international aid agencies wanted to tell me why the UNHCR's plans for repatriation were doomed. As usual, they were not prepared to go on the record. But their accusations against the UN hit hard. They claimed it was a political move by the UNHCR to appease the Thai government, which wanted rid of refugees.

Meanwhile, the UNHCR's Mae Sot director and her staff battled away trying to do the best they could. In spite of criticisms levelled at the UNHCR, the director and her assistants were good people. Refugees insisted they were always available to all those who asked to see them. This placed an enormous strain on them. Local staff had done much to gain the respect of Karen and Burmese people.

I received a phone call from the head of a large international aid agency who said she wanted to "update" me about the "big political picture." I usually avoided 'big-picture' scenarios pushed by politicians and the like. I was more interested in the cracks between their words where I'd find the so-called ordinary people. The politics of aid had pushed this particular woman into a dark hole of cynicism and to the edge of burn out. I felt sorry for her as she tried to cling to some part of her past that used to be fuelled by anger, passion, and justice. I recorded her words in my notebook after giving her my reassurance I wouldn't name her or her organization.

"They [the UNHCR] will just push them [refugees] across the border, as they did in Bangladesh. There will be no international outcry. It's an easier option for the UNHCR, as refugees have no legal status in Thailand. The UN is looking for a quick solution to appease Thailand. Burma's cease-fires are nothing more than imaginary castles. The biggest tragedy is that Burma's minorities are fighting a lost cause and they don't know it. The international community wants Burma to be one country. They will never agree to smaller states. It would be a bureaucratic nightmare for them."

It all made political sense, but why not speak out, especially as any decision to relocate refugees back to Burma came without retribution for her.

Tha Ko read my leaked copy of the UNHCR report on repatriation of Karen refugees back to Burma and exploded. "They [the UNHCR] want to establish reception centres across the border. These places are the same as the ones being promoted as special economic zones by the Thai government! What a coincidence!"

Tha Ko got angrier as he read on. "They say the local DKBA leader would welcome Karen refugees . . . he can accommodate 1,500 farming families . . . he has a large shelter near the river that could be used as a reception centre. Don't they know that many of our refugees were forced from their homes by DKBA guns? Don't they realize Karen refugee camps have been attacked and burned by the DKBA? This will go ahead, I know it. They [the UN] have already worked it out, listen to this…. They need a 'total of fifty ten-wheel trucks making two trips a day. It will take seventy days to transfer all Mae La refugees….' I don't want to read any more."

Disgusted, he threw the paper on the table.

A series of workshops and meetings to deal with the fallout over repatriation were planned. Journalists were banned from attending. Reports were deemed too sensitive for circulation. I wasn't too worried about being kept informed—confidentiality was a joke among Mae Sot NGOs. After all, what's the point of knowing a secret if you don't share it.

Epilogue

By July 2004, the regime had put its plans for a National Convention on hold. In September, East Timorese foreign minister, Jose Ramos-Horta, was quoted as saying there was no sign of political progress taking place in Burma, and systematic human rights abuses continued. By early October, the generals had scored some international success. ASEAN had, against much opposition, promoted and backed Burma's inclusion and admission into an Asia-Europe Meeting (ASEM) in Hanoi. This was an important win for the regime. It looked like Burma had lobbied its way into the international political arena without having to release Aung San Suu Kyi or do anything about its atrocities or drug trafficking.

Before he had time to bask in his Hanoi success, General Khin Nyunt was arrested by the Burmese military on October 19, 2004 and held on corruption charges. Khin Nyunt had again swapped his uniform for a designer suit as he tried to promote himself as reformer. It worked, and the international media obliged him. Khin Nyunt was now cast as the "moderate" good guy, and Burma's head of state (since 1992), General Than Shwe, as the bad guy "hardliner." In reality both men were brutal thugs. There was nothing remotely moderate about Khin Nyunt. An independent report by the Karen Human Rights Group (KHRG), "Death Squads And Replacement" (1999), showed how vicious Khin Nyunt was. The report took an in-depth look at the activities of a secret group hand-picked by MI with a "clearly stated purpose to execute without question anyone suspected of any present or past connection to the KNU or KNLA." The death squads took orders from the chief of the Directorate of Defence Services Intelligence (DDSI)—General Khin Nyunt.

Karen fears about Khin Nyunt's replacement were realized when General Maung Aye was appointed. Maung Aye had demonstrated a personal hatred of the Karen when he walked over the Karen flag and wiped his boots on it.

Khin Nyunt's arrest had thrown the international community into turmoil. They had placed their bets on the "moderate" delivering reforms. It also threw a huge scare into Thailand's government, as they had approved a massive loan to the regime via Khin Nyunt.

Karen New Year 2005 was held on the January full moon. The villagers of K' Law Gaw prepared a huge welcome with food and drink for guests coming from scattered locations to celebrate. Football and volleyball games had been arranged, and traditional dances and singing competitions organized. Burmese soldiers from Light Infantry Brigade 356, under the command of a Captain Taung Taung Aung, had other plans. Colonel Ner Dah had negotiated with the Burmese to keep the cease-fire during the celebrations. Ner Dah had sent presents and invited the captain to visit unarmed. The captain declined and instead attacked the village. About 500 villagers fled to the Thai border.

Karen Revolution Day celebrations had an empty feel to them. The number of foreign journalists could be counted on one hand. There were fewer soldiers on parade. I walked over to General Bo Mya's house to see if the old man had turned up. I was surprised to see him dressed in full uniform, but in a wheelchair. Rumours of his ill health were confirmed: he looked all of his 78 years. But his eyes shone bright and locked on mine with intensity and challenge. He stayed silent and, with a dismissive shrug, prepared himself to be lifted down the stairs by his orderlies and his son. The old man was pushed and half carried across the grass and dirt to the podium, where people waited to hear his speech. He didn't disappoint. He spoke without notes and told the Karen to be strong and to fight for their freedom. He spoke of the survival of the Karen people, their culture, and their struggle for justice, freedom, equality, and peace.

Padho Mahn Sha, dressed in Karen national shirt, followed Bo Mya to the microphone. Padho Mahn Sha spoke of an age of democracy when the world no longer accepts military dictatorship as a form of government. He talked of the 56 years the Karen had fought their resistance. He invoked the name and words of the father of the Karen revolution, Saw Ba U Gyi. "If they fight, we will fight back against them. If they say tomorrow they want peace talks, we are also ready for that."

Unlike previous years, the festivities wound up quickly. I ate a meal with the author, Phu Tah Moo, and the old man was again good company. I listened intently as he analysed the long years of Karen struggle. He said with some feeling that the Karen may not have a lot of soldiers, but their strength lay in their people. "All of us will fight for freedom. Some of us are teachers, politicians, soldiers, medics, or farmers, but we all know the survival of our culture and our race depends on us never ever giving up."

By mid-2005, rumours began to circulate that the cease-fire was not high on the regime's agenda. I met with my KNLA acquaintance who had gone with General Bo Mya's party to Rangoon. He told me the cease-fire was initiated by Karen field commanders sick of fighting. They persuaded Bo Mya to be involved, but his bad health changed everything. "After Khin Nyunt was jailed, second-level Burmese officers told Than Shwe there was no need for a cease-fire as they could easily wipe out the Karen. We have to be careful that some self-serving Karen officers and politicians might cut a sub-standard deal. They won't be hard to identify: they'll be the ones with luxury cars and houses."

Bo Mya's replacement, General Mutu Saepoe, was blunt and realistic when I met him in August 2005 at the CIDKP offices in

Mae Sot. "The Karen cannot expect to stop their struggle just yet," he told me. "It might take generations. If the regime wants to fight, we are ready. If they want to find a compromise, we will compromise. All dictators are crooked men, but men can change, even dictators. But we want them to know that no matter how big they are, we can kill them."

In late September 2005, Tha Ko called on me and I related to him a story I had read about Burma's foreign minister, Nyan Win, speaking at the UN General Assembly earlier the same month, in New York. Nyan Win had said Burma would quickly achieve democracy if the international community stopped its interference. He also used the UN forum to brag about Rangoon's efforts to stop drug manufacturing, terrorism, money laundering, and people trafficking.

Tha Ko was outraged. "This is a nonsense. Their words are cheap. Don't be tricked. When they boast about 'development programmes' it sounds as if they are a benefit to our people. But for every road, school, hospital, bridge, and hotel built, atrocities are committed. Development in Burma equals forced labour, land confiscation, and money extortion. They rule by the gun. Political dialogue with them is impossible. Our cease-fire talks have fizzled out because they don't take seriously the Karen position. It's all window dressing."

Also in late September 2005, former Czech president Vaclav Havel and Nobel laureate Archbishop Desmond Tutu of South Africa echoed Tha Ko's words when they jointly demanded the UN Security Council take immediate action against Burma's regime. They said that after fifteen years of disregard for UN recommendations, the situation in Burma was getting worse. Tha Ko said it would continue to deteriorate unless the Security Council forced the regime to involve all the people of Burma—a member of the UN—in a real democracy process.

Glossary

ABSDF All-Burma Students' Democratic Front
ASEAN Association of South East Asian Nations
BIA Burmese Independent Army
carry illegal 'job agent'
CIDKP Committee for Internally Displaced Karen People
DEA (US) Drug Enforcement Agency
DKBA Democratic Karen Buddhist Army
EU European Union
gawlawah Caucasian
IDP Internally Displaced People
jaggery palm sugar
khao tom rice soup
KHRG Karen Human Rights Group
KIO Kachin Independence Organization
KNLA Karen National Liberation Army
KNU Karen National Union
KRC Karen Refugee Committee
KWO Karen Women's Organization
longyi Burmese sarong

MI (Burmese) Military Intelligence
MSF Médicins Sans Frontières (Doctors Without Borders)
NGO Non-Government Organization
NLD National League for Democracy
SLORC State Law And Order Restoration Council
SPDC State Peace and Development Council
Songkran Thai, Burmese, and Lao 'New Year' festival in April
songtaew pick-up truck bus (literally 'two benches')
UNHCR United Nations High Commission for Refugees
UNICEF United Nations Children's Emergency Fund
yaa baa amphetamine (literally 'crazy drug')

About The Author

Phil Thornton is a journalist who likes to document the lives of ordinary people. He has an MA in journalism from the University of Technology, Sydney, and has written features and news reports for numerous international magazines and newspapers.

Phil is also the author of *It's Only A Job* and *I Protest!* Since leaving school at fifteen he has dug graves, built houses, worked in factories, dee-jayed in nightclubs, coached and played soccer, taught at universities, and written speeches for politicians. He currently lives in Mae Sot.

More Southeast Asia Insight
from Asia Books . . .

"Like a gonzo rant from Hunter S. Thompson."
Time.

Phnom Penh is a city of beauty and degradation, tranquility and violence, and tradition and transformation. For some, it is an anarchic celebration of insanity and indulgence. Amit Gilboa provides a fascinating, disturbing, and often hilarious picture of the city and the bizarre collection of expats who make it their home. An unparalleled firsthand account that leads straight into the dark heart of Cambodia's tragic history, its violent politics and rampant corruption, and its guns, girls, ganja, and more.

. . . Laos

"Begins like a spy novel and ends by raising the hair on your head."

Here is the incredible inside story of the world's most extraordinary covert operation—Air America, a secret airline run by the CIA, which at its height had the biggest commercial airfleet in the world.

This updated edition of Air America now includes a new prologue, looking back over the years at the reaction to the book—from the pilots, the CIA, the US government, and the general media; plus a new chapter which provides a stinging critique, and the real story behind the making of the widely criticized motion picture of the same name.

. . . Laos

"Makes Vientiane jump off the printed page."
Joe Cummings, author of Lonely Planet Laos.

Two decades after the war in Indochina and the communist
takeover, Laos re-opened its doors to the world and Brett Dakin
was hired as a consultant to the country's fledgling tourist
industry: a sudden leap from his Princeton classroom to
Laos' corridors of power and living rooms of the poor.
This is a firsthand account of a desperately poor country
struggling with economic crisis, political change, and the legacy
of war. Above all, it is the story of a young American coming
to terms with his country's role in the world in a new century.

. . . Burma

A spine-tingling tale of murder and conspiracy.

English detective John Jessel is on a downhill slide as booze claims
his lonely life. His latest case is out of control. Postcards signed
"The Paw" have taken credit for the murders of several children,
and the perpetrator has threatened John's family. Dr. Shirley Heigh
is a Karen intern working on the Burmese border, but her intentions
are not wholly ethical. There is a great wrong from her past that
she intends to right. Heading in the same direction, hunting
and being hunted by the same prey, it's only a matter of
time before the paths of Dr. Shirley and John Jessel cross.

. . . Thailand

"From the hi-so to the lo-so and everything in between."

From boxers, business tycoons, bargirls, and bodysnatchers, to street vendors, slum-dwellers, socialites, and singers, Bangkok People takes the reader into the daily lives of city denizens—both Thai and expat, and from the filthy rich to the just plain filthy. Penned by one of Thailand's best-known writers, this fascinating, funny, sometimes serious, and occasionally odd collection plunges right into the heartof the myriad masses who make this mad metropolis tick.

. . . Laos

"A funny, moving tale of how a pool-ball factory changed the course of lives and loves in war-time Laos."

The year is 1970. Waldo Monk is 65 and two months from retirement at Roundly's pool-ball factory in Mattfield, Indiana. Enter Saifon, a twenty-something Lao-American girl with an attitude. Saifon has come to the US under mysterious circumstances. She's just arrived at Roundly's, and it's Waldo's task to train her for his job as pool-ball quality controller. Saifon hates everyone, and even though Waldo is tempted to strangle her at first, a friendship grows between them. Two disasters in Waldo's life lead to him 'adopting' Saifon instead. But Saifon's mission at the factory is to make enough money, by hook or by crook, to get back to Laos—for she has sworn to discover the truth about her past.